PEOPLE
AND
CHANGE

PEOPLE
AND
CHANGE

An Introduction to Counseling
and Stress Management

CATHERINE M. FLANAGAN
Center for Cognitive Therapy
University of Pennsylvania

LAWRENCE ERLBAUM ASSOCIATES, PUBLISHERS
1990   Hillsdale, New Jersey   Hove and London

Table 4.1, Fear Survey Schedule, reprinted with permission. Geer, J. (1965). *Behavioral Research and Therapy, 3,* 45–53.

Table IV.1, Daily Activity Schedule, © 1980, David D. Burns, M.D.

Lawrence Erlbaum Associates, Inc., Publishers
365 Broadway
Hillsdale, New Jersey 07642

Library of Congress Cataloging-in-Publication Data

Flanagan, Catherine M.
    People and change : an introduction to counseling and stress management / Catherine M. Flanagan.
        p.   cm.
    Includes bibliographical references.
    ISBN 0-8058-0450-1. — ISBN 0-8058-0451-X (pbk.)
    1. Counseling.   2. Stress management.   I. Title.
BF637.C6F42   1990
158′.3—dc20   90-3074
                                                               CIP

Printed in the United States of America
10 9 8 7 6 5 4 3 2 1

Contents

Preface

Change is the key feature of modern living. Everyday experiences lead to constant, small changes—in people's behavior, in their outlook, in their feelings, and in their health. Independent changes take place in people's environment and in the people with whom they share their world. This book is about how and why such changes come about. It is about how people develop their personal habits of behaving and thinking and how these habits can consolidate or hinder their efforts to cope on a day-to-day basis, as well as over time.

Multifarious factors interact in the complex stress process: Bad habits are exacerbated, and areas of vulnerability are exposed, sometimes leading to psychopathology. How clinical levels of psychological difficulty are reached is outlined, as well as how problems such as phobias, depression, obsessive-compulsive disorders, shyness, marital and sexual difficulties, and overindulgences are treated. Contemporary cognitive and behavioral therapies, which reflect advances in theory over the last 30 years, are described and explained. The pervasiveness of change and the necessity of equipping people to handle it through self-knowledge and personal coping skills are emphasized throughout.

If your career engages you with other people and their problems, an understanding of the dynamics of behavior change and stress management is essential. This book will provide you with such knowledge and information. Students of psychology, future counselors, social workers, psychiatrists, general medical practitioners, nurses, management consultants, nutritionists, and physiotherapists—in fact, anyone involved in the promotion of health and, in particular, mental health—will benefit from studying this book. The reader will glean a contemporary understanding of complex learning processes, as well as how psychological problems arise and are treated.

Catherine M. Flanagan

Acknowledgments

I dedicate this book to the many people who have shared and shaped my life. My parents, Bonnie and Des, and my sister Ann, who have always been there for me in their different ways—my mother deserves a very special thanks; Tom Adachi, Doctors Michael Smurfit and Tony O'Reilly, and St. Patrick's Hospital (Dublin) for giving me the time and resources to put pen to paper; Aileen Keeley, for typing the manuscript, but even more, for being such a true friend. In this category also are Buck Rogers, for his generosity of spirit and his continued support and guidance; Professor Stanley Rachman for his invaluable observations and suggestions for modifications to the manuscript; the staff at Lawrence Erlbaum Associates for their encouragement throughout; and Brian Nason and Gerry Simon, for their practical advice and assistance on more than one occasion. Without all of these people, the book might never have been completed.

I must also include a number of my wonderful friends: Mary Keating, Patsy and Declan, Kate and Ronnie, Cathy and Des Sharkey, Paul Dubsky, Therese Brady, Bob and Linda, Gail, John Ludgate, Phillip Sheppard, Mary Mahon, Finola and Don, Bill Maher, Anne Vinnicombe, and Leonard Bernstein. These are the people who have kept my inner fire burning through the years, with their belief in me and their love. Thanks are also due to Professor Richard Lazarus, Professor Michael Mahoney, Professor Aaron Beck, and Professor Marvin Goldfried for their precious time and for helping me expand my horizons, both professionally and personally.

Finally, and by no means least, thanks to my clients—one and all—who, over the years, have taught me so much about living and learning, sharing, and caring.

Introduction

Talking to someone whose life has spanned over 80 years is always a rare and enriching experience. I had the privilege of sharing an afternoon with such a gentleman recently. In that time, he traced nearly a century of changes, large and small. Familiar names came and went; places and times appeared and disappeared. But his parting words have stayed with me. "You know," he said gently, "you psychologists go on about stress as if it were something new . . . as if *we* had life real easy. You just put the fancy name on it. Things have always been the same. There have always been the good guys and the bad guys, the guys on the make and the ones who get left behind, the ones who are content with what little they have and the ones who have everything and still want more. The only difference is that now, with all the new learning, *everyone has more of a chance*." I would like to think so, and I hope this book will increase the odds.

People experience stress when they feel unable to cope with the demands of their environment, with other people, or with their own self-imposed pressures, or unrealistic expectations. For some people, things are never happening quickly enough; for others, they are always moving too fast. In both cases, there is a feeling of not having things under control. Effective coping comes with the development of a set of personal coping skills, which allow people to maintain a healthy lifestyle both physically and psychologically. If they are not acquired, bad habits, and eventually problems arise. The odd late night at the office somehow turns into a habit of working every evening. An argument every so often—about money or sex—develops into constant bickering matches. Occasional "down" days become a nightmare of depressing thoughts. Periodic, unattended backache results in chronic pain . . . and so on. Coping skills come with self-knowledge.

The term *problems of living* refers to such things as anxiety, fears and phobias, depression, obsessions and compulsions, difficulties in relating to other people socially or sexually, overindulgence in food or drugs (including nicotine and alcohol), and psychosomatic complaints, such as tension head-aches and stomach upsets. Many people think that these problems are experienced by only a relatively small percentage of people. The facts are: In any one year, between 10% and 15% of the population consult their medical doctors with a complaint that is largely, if not entirely, psychological in nature. About 1 in 15 persons spends time in a psychiatric hospital at some stage in his or her life. One study predicted that 43% of men and 73% of women can be expected to suffer from a psychological disorder over a lifetime of 60 years. Largescale surveys carried out in the United States and Canada suggest that, at any time, over half of the population is suffering from emotional problems of some kind. It is estimated that 15% of the populations of the United States and Great Britain take tranquilizing drugs on a regular basis. Malcolm Lader (1975), of The University of London, estimated that "about a third of the adult population suffer constantly from nervous complaints, especially anxiety" (p. 22). Because most of the difficulties that make up these figures are "problems of living" of the type outlined previously, what they clearly indicate is that many people have troubled emotional lives, and, furthermore, that a surprising number of people do not know how to cope.

Before proceeding, another important point needs to be made. I have termed the type of difficulties to be discussed *problems of living*. Psychological and behavioral difficulties of this kind are not the same thing as "mental illness." This is a distinction of which many people are unaware. Problems of living are exaggerations of normal behaviors and experiences. Everyone knows what it is to feel frightened, nervous, rejected, low, worried, unde-cided, or self-conscious. Everyone experiences times when they do not perform very well—physically, socially, professionally, or emotionally. Some-times, such difficulties can build up to a point where professional help is necessary. But even so, these problems generally make sense in terms of the individual's particular circumstances or pressures, experiences or character-istics. Depression, for example, might result from an inability to cope with a bereavement or redundancy, or even from a shyness problem, which, over time, has led to isolation, frustration, and loneliness. Likewise, excessive checking or self-doubting might be traced to a long-standing lack of security or fear of failure, which is suddenly exacerbated by even such a seemingly positive occurrence as a promotion, or a decision to marry or move house.

Mental illness is very different. Generally speaking, the mentally ill person behaves in a very uncharacteristic or unpredictable fashion. He is obviously "not himself." He may behave strangely or suspiciously, see or hear things that are not physically there, or swing from very high to low spirits for no apparent reason. Unlike dealing with *problems of living,* it can be very difficult or impossible to make sense of such behavior changes in terms of current pressures or past events. The principal mental illnesses are endogenous depression, manic depression, and schizophrenia. The successful businessman who suddenly, and for no apparent reason, feels that life is not worth living, loses interest in food, sex, or his appearance, has difficulty sleeping, and cannot explain his change of outlook is depressed. The person who suddenly finds that he or she has boundless energy, a racing stream of ideas and projects, superconfidence, and little apparent need for rest or sleep exemplifies elation—the "up" side of a manic-depressive episode. The normally gregarious woman who unreasonably and unprecipitatedly begins to suspect that people are talking about her and plotting against her may signal a paranoid psychosis.

The causes of mental illness are very complex and not fully understood. In some cases, hereditary factors are involved. In others, the causality is less clear; but, it is likely that it is a physical change, or imbalance, in the brain or body's biochemistry that makes people behave in such unpredicted and unpredictable ways. Because the underlying problem is a physical one, these disorders need to be tackled with medicines and other forms of physical treatment, which are usually prescribed or administered by a psychiatrist. The methods described in this book are not appropriate for treating mental illness. They are psychological techniques for helping people cope with *problems of living.*

So, what are these techniques? There have been profound changes in psychology in the last 30 years. The behaviorism of the 1960s focused exclusively on external influences on behavior. People's actions were shaped by and explained in terms of reinforcement contingencies; that is, rewards and punishments. Treatment techniques, to counter faulty learning in the shape of psychological problems, were developed to mirror these advances in theory. The "cognitive revolution" of the 1970s revalidated the importance of central processes, that is, of mental things, such as thoughts and attitudes, in explaining human behavior and change. Psychology rediscovered its mind; and, with this broadened perspective, came a number of cognitive techniques for changing maladaptive thoughts and erroneous beliefs.

The 1980s see the continued growth of the cognitive movement and the emergence of numerous different "cognitive therapies." The emphasis remains on the importance of central versus peripheral processes. However, within this area of consensus, there has been a parting of ways between those who continue to focus on what are now regarded by some as "surface" interventions, as described earlier, and those who feel that an exploration of the dynamics of "deep," structural change is also necessary. The latter group endeavours to understand the complex interface between thinking, feeling, behavior, and emotion and to identify the subtle factors—sometimes not consciously registered—that trigger and facilitate the profound changes that can take place in the course of psychotherapy. The emphasis is on the active, generative, and intentional dimensions of clients' knowing and development—a far cry from the passive recipients of impinging external stimuli who were the clients of the 1960s.

It is an exciting time. Although many questions remain unanswered, new techniques are constantly being developed to match the body of increasingly complex theory. It is important to point out, however, that although the limitations of purely behavioral explanations and therapies have been defined, the ongoing value and effectiveness of these techniques is not questioned. The nature of the problem largely determines the most appropriate type of intervention. For example, systematic desensitization, a behavioral technique, is still the treatment of choice for phobias. The older therapies are by no means obsolete. The process is one of continually building on, and from, what is already known. This will be apparent throughout the book.

Part I (Chapters 1–3) deals with how people learn, how habits develop, and how problems arise. Chapter 1 explains how people develop their characteristic ways of behaving and thinking, and why much of this learning becomes "overlearned" or habitual. People rely heavily on habits of thinking, as well as behaving, and, consequently, are bad observers of both themselves and others. Current gaps in our knowledge—for example of unconscious influences on behavior—are also discussed. Chapter 2 examines sources of stress. External sources of pressure come in the shape of life events and daily *hassles*. How and why events and circumstances can lead to both physical and psychological disorder is described, as well as the factors that render some people more vulnerable than others. Internal sources of pressure are an ill-maintained or unhealthy body, maladaptive behavior patterns or bad habits, and problematic or distorted thinking. Chapter 3 looks at how people respond to stress. Bodily, cognitive, and behavioral reactions are outlined, as well as the reciprocal interaction between these three main areas of functioning. Individual differences in styles of response are also explained.

In Part II (Chapters 4–11), the main areas of psychological difficulty are identified and discussed. Each chapter deals with a particular problem area and provides up-to-date facts and statistics, as well as information on the signs, symptoms, and theoretical explanations of how these problems arise and are treated. The areas covered are: fears and phobias, including agoraphobia (Chapter 4), depression (Chapter 5), obsessive-compulsive problems (Chapter 6), social difficulties (Chapter 7), marital difficulties (Chapter 8), sexual problems (Chapter 9), and problems of overindulgence (Chapter 10). In the final chapter of Part II (Chapter 11), the problems of attrition, adherence, and relapse are addressed. The questions of why people drop out of treatment, fail to follow prescribed guidelines, and relapse are discussed in the context of significant sex differences both in "paths into care" and in attitudes to and behavior during treatment.

Part II is followed by a series of six appendices that detail the major techniques used to treat this range of psychological problems. In Appendix I, the essential steps in preparing clients for therapy are outlined. These involve identifying where the problem (or problems) lie, establishing whether or not the client really wants to change, and what exactly needs to be changed. Appendix II deals with ways of helping clients get in control of their environment. Problems can sometimes be alleviated by simply getting people to acquaint themselves with their environment and its resources. Pertinent behavioral techniques, based on the theoretical concept of self-control through advance preparation, are also detailed. Appendix III addresses body maintenance in three main problem areas: eating, exercising, and relaxing. Sensible eating involves both the quality and quantity of food intake as well as eating patterns, which often relate to lifestyle. Exercise and its importance for health of mind and body are outlined. Relaxation—both 'formal' and informal—is also essential. Finally, the ingredients of adequate and regular sleep and the common problem of insomnia are discussed.

In Appendix IV, a number of recognized methods of behavior change are described. These include techniques such as systematic desensitization for overcoming fears and phobias, behavioral rehearsal for acquiring skills, and response prevention for eliminating compulsive rituals. Getting started can also be a problem due to depression, procrastination, or bad time-management; these specific problems necessitate different therapeutic approaches. The treatment of compulsive behaviors such as excessive checking and cleaning, as well as overcompulsiveness on a more general level, is also covered. Appendix V describes the major cognitive techniques that have been developed in the last 20 years and that cater to diverse problems. These include ways of changing maladaptive thinking and beliefs; developing and utilising visual imagery, both as a general coping tool and in the treatment of specific fears; and attention-focusing strategies for overcoming indecision, obsessional ruminating, and excessive daydreaming. Finally, because an ability to communicate is such an essential part of coping, it is discussed in the final Appendix VI. The complex range of communication skills is outlined, and the related guidelines for making conversation, problem solving, communicating emotions and feelings, and assertion are then explained.

PART I

HOW PROBLEMS DEVELOP

1

Learning

Why do you spend lots of time doing some things and avoid doing others? Why do you feel at home with certain kinds of people and uncomfortable with others? Why do you do the things you do? How did you become the person you are? To an extent, what we all are can be accounted for in terms of our genetic inheritance; but far more important is learning. Living is learning. Even infants have a capacity to interact with and learn from their environment from the very first days of their lives.

Largely unknown to ourselves, we are learning new things and picking up little pieces of information all the time. We are constantly changing. However, as well as learning new things, we are also gradually becoming more practiced and efficient at the things we do repeatedly. These things, then, become habits. Learning applies to thinking as well as to behaving. We develop habits of thinking and, over time, a unique set of attitudes, beliefs, and values—a personal view of the world, or outlook on life.

BUILDING BLOCKS

For centuries, psychologists have been studying the multifarious aspects of how we learn. Learning is infinitely complex. However, familiarity with a small number of basic principles will explain how problems come about and the rationale of the therapy techniques that are described in later chapters.

There is a large body of rather sterile-sounding terminology relating to the processes involved in learning. This is a pity, because learning is essentially such a dynamic and vital activity and such an integral part of our existence. A minimum of jargon, and two terms in particular, are essential. These are *stimulus* and *response,* often referred to as *S* and *R,* respectively. A stimulus is anything (sound, sight, touch, thought) that triggers a response (action, behavior, feeling thought, image). The smell or sight of food (S) might make a hungry person salivate (R), and maybe say "Mmmmm" (R). A broken date (S) might make a lonely or depressed person feel even more despondent (R). A slightly soiled tablecloth in a restaurant might make an obsessionally clean person highly anxious about contamination (R) and maybe also trigger a compulsion to wash (R). It is the *meaning* of the particular stimulus to the particular person at the particular point in time that determines the response. To someone else, a broken date might trigger a mental note not to rely too much on that person again; the soiled tablecloth might spark an assertive request to simply have it replaced. Likewise, food will do little to tickle the salivary glands just after a large meal.

All sorts of things can serve as stimuli, from the most obvious and concrete (e.g., loud noise) to the most subtle and transitory (e.g., a fleeting expression on another's face). The same can be said of responses. In sum, we are both taking in and responding to our environment all the time and on many different levels. Sometimes, we are very aware of what is affecting our behavior, and we are conscious of our response. For example, you might be aware of a very bright light in a room (S) and conscious of turning away from it (R). In the same way, some people are "louder" and more noticeable than others, and our reactions to such persons also occur on a more conscious level.

At other times, we are much less aware of what is influencing us, or how. In fact, sometimes we only realize in retrospect that we took in details of a situation or a person. Although the information did not consciously register at the time, it was nonetheless processed. In the same way, we are not always aware of our responses, until we realize them—or someone else points them out to us—at a later stage: "Every time you go shopping, you come back in a bad mood." Really? "Yeah, and now, if I ask you how much you spent you'll go all quiet." This decreased level of self-awareness in relation to both stimuli and responses can be due to a number of things: being in a situation where too much is going on, being in a bland situation where nothing really stands out, being very tired or inebriated, or simply having other things on your mind at the time. In other words, stimuli and responses are processed on many different levels under different conditions.

DEVELOPING PATTERNS OF BEHAVIOR

Simple explanations of human behavior are impossible. Nonetheless, a look at how we acquire patterns of behavior over time will fill in the picture a little bit more. Learning takes place in three ways: by association, by consequence, and by observation.

Learning by Association

The first experiments on what is also called *classical conditioning* were carried out by a Russian psychologist, Pavlov, early in this century (Pavlov, 1927). He found that if he repeatedly paired the sound of a buzzer with the presentation of food to a hungry dog, the dog eventually salivated to the sound of the buzzer alone. In other words, learning by association refers to the fact that when two unrelated things are repeatedly paired together, or consistently occur together, we come to associate the automatic response to one with the other.

A friend's cat jumps up and meows loudly in anticipation of food whenever a newspaper is rattled, because her food tray is placed on a newspaper at eating times. If you have ever felt anxious in a particular place on a number of occasions, you might find that seeing the people who were there on those occasions makes you feel uncomfortable again, even though there is no longer reason to be.

Learning by Consequence

Learning by consequence, also called *operant conditioning,* is particularly important in understanding how problem behaviors develop. In the 1960s, B. F. Skinner, the father of modern behaviorism, highlighted the subtle ways in which behavior is determined and maintained by what he called *reinforcement contingencies* (Skinner, 1969). Simply, if the consequences of doing something are pleasant, or "reinforcing", people tend to do more of it. If not, they do less. If you were never rewarded, in any way, for your efforts, never paid for your work or praised for your commitment, you would be unlikely to continue with the same enthusiasm. If you were punished, you would certainly think twice about the stakes.

Learning by consequence also helps explain why people avoid certain situations or persons they find upsetting or anxiety-provoking. Avoidance temporarily removes the threat of unpleasantness; and the immediate relief that this brings makes the person more likely to avoid the same and similar situations again. Shy people avoid social situations that trigger anxiety; but this only adds to their isolation, as the response *generalizes* to more and more situations. Likewise, people who experience "panic attacks" often find themselves going out less and less, and many eventually become housebound. In the same way, people can develop exaggerated fears and phobias—of animals, heights, thunder, flying—that, over time, curtail more and more of their activities. Obsessional people often check or clean excessively to avoid the (irrational) feared consequences of *not* carrying out their ritual—for example, illness or contamination. The ritual provides temporary relief from anxiety, a feeling of having things under control, but also perpetuates the problem.

Learning by consequence also has a role to play in problems of overindulgence. For example, many people find eating so gratifying that this activity increases out of proportion—along with their figure. The same is true of alcohol consumption, smoking, drug taking, gambling, and spending too much. These problems involve a conflict: whether to succumb to the temptation of immediate enjoyment and pay later, or to exercise restraint and enjoy more significant positive consequences in the long term: "Will I give in and have a cigarette, or enjoy healthier lungs and finances 6 months from now?" Unfortunately, immediate enjoyment is often more compelling.

Learning by Observation

Learning by observation, also called *vicarious conditioning* or *modeling* was first systematically studied by another well-known psychologist, Albert Bandura, and his colleagues (Bandura, 1969). In essence, people learn about things and how to do things by watching other people. It is easy to forget or to simply not realize that, without the luxury of language to communicate and ask questions, children spend large amounts of their early years learning by looking. Young children learn by watching and then imitating the people around them—switching on the television, doing household chores, washing, showing affection. They also observe and learn the "feeling tone" with which these activities are carried out—the smiles, the frowns, the sighs, the groans. This is why young children are often, unwittingly, so revealing when they repeat an observed activity *along with* all the attendant grimaces and moans with which it is usually done by familiar figures. These are simply part of the child's understanding of *how* it is done.

By observing others in everyday situations, over many years, children pick up innumerable gems of information and knowledge, which they then practice and perfect. Learning how to "read" and handle the complexities of social interaction clearly illustrates this. Other major sources of vicarious learning are movies, videos, and television. People model themselves on the behavior of those they admire; thus, the power of advertising and the media in general.

Observational learning has a large *emotional*, as well as informational, impact. Keeping in mind the large amounts of learning that take place before children can even talk, one can only speculate as to the effect of, for example, seeing familiar people in active disagreement or open argument. The child may *learn* how to handle or avoid such situations, but he may also *feel* confused, upset, afraid, or even guilty that it was in some way his fault. After all, everyone was frowning at him. Do they not love him any more? Are they going to go away and leave him? Not, as yet, able to understand the dynamics of the disagreement, or perhaps even what was being said, the memory of the unpleasant *feelings* will remain ingrained long after the incident itself has passed (see Guidano & Liotti, 1983).

In the same way, adults watching television news or, perhaps, a war documentary learn new facts, but also can be left *feeling* emotionally upset or disturbed. This can be because the program was genuinely sad *or* possibly because it struck some deeper, personal chord from a long time back—an experience they might not even be able to remember. Similiarly, we sometimes do not know, and cannot explain, why a relatively innocuous event upsets or moves us so much; and this, in itself, can be disturbing. On a day-to-day basis, horror movies generate a lot of adrenalin, whereas "tear jerkers" use up a lot of tissues. Observational learning plays an important role in how we develop our unique emotional reactions, as well as our general outlook on life, our personal beliefs, attitudes, and values.

DEVELOPING PATTERNS OF THINKING

Like learning behaviors and developing habits, our attitudes, beliefs, and values are also built up over a number of years. One of the major vehicles for this developing identity and outlook is language. Language is one of the most significant acquisitions of early childhood. It greatly increases the child's capacity to learn, as well as the range and depth of potential experiences. Words allow people to think abstractly in concepts, to relate disparate events, to link past and present, and to objectify themselves and their experiences. Words allow us to communicate in a meaningful, reciprocal way with other people.

However, this does not all happen overnight. All through childhood, thinking remains very much tied to the concrete and the visible, to objects and people that are physically present. The child cannot yet think hypothetically, cannot philosophize or ponder altruistically on the human condition or the existential dilemma of modern man and the future of mankind. Nonetheless, his psychological world becomes progressively richer and more complex. New experiences, faces, places, and feelings are gradually incorporated and assimilated into a flexible and accommodating structure. It is not until adolescence that the young person first begins to think in a truly scientific and moral way (Piaget, 1970). Understandably, the onset of these capabilities is frequently accompanied by a search for answers and a search for self— the adolescent "identity crisis." Language provides a vehicle for such searching and thinking. It is both the tool and the material with which we construct our personal view of the world and self.

Another essential aspect of language and thinking is its *relationship to behavior*. We constantly regulate our behavior by what we say to ourselves, by our silent evaluations: "I don't like the look of her." "I just know I'm going to make a mess of this." *Private speech*—also called *self-talk, internal dialogue,* and *automatic self-statements*— has been a focus of research by Russian psychologists for many years (see Copeland, 1983). They discovered that, with increasing use of language, the ability to regulate one's own behavior develops in three stages. In the first stage, the speech of *others* controls and directs the behavior of the very young child; he has to be told what to do, he cannot tell himself. In the next stage, the child comes to regulate and control his own behavior; but he has to tell himself what to do, to instruct himself, *out loud.* You may have noticed toddlers talking their way through a task, or mumbling happily as they play. Indeed, adults, when confronted with a problem situation or when learning something new, often revert to this more primitive level of self-regulation. They talk out loud: "If I put this little nut in here . . . and turn it around . . . slowly . . . then . . . the other piece . . . should . . . slide in too . . . Aha!"

When learning any skill—for example, driving— people frequently start off by going through such a mental routine out loud: "Adjust seat and mirror. Fasten seat belt. Start engine . . ." With practice, however, things become more automatic, and the audible mumbling gradually disappears. Likewise, in the normal course of development, self-talk is gradually "internalized." It goes inside and becomes silent. This is the *third* phase of self-regulation, when silent or covert speech takes over. The child can now tell himself what to do silently, like adults (Luria, 1961). In other words, he no longer needs to guide his actions out loud. Self-talk still goes on all the time, and in every situation, but inside, silently. This is what thinking is.

It is through such self-talk that, gradually, in the course of development, we acquire our habits of thinking and our characteristic ways of interpreting and evaluating situations. It is through constant repetition of habitual mental routines that our attitudes and beliefs come into being. We go over and over things in our heads all the time. We talk to ourselves constantly, silently telling ourselves things about ourselves and about the world. In other words, as well as learning to *behave* in characteristic ways, we also come to *think* and interpret the world in certain patterns and styles. These patterns of thinking eventually form our personal worldview, or outlook on life. Furthermore, thoughts and behavior are in constant interaction. Thinking regulates behavior, the outcome of which provides more "food for thought."

OVERLEARNING

Most tasks and skills are learned gradually. People gradually become more proficient, efficient and practiced at things. They gradually become better drivers, better cooks, better at dealing with other people, or better at pleasing partners. In the early stages of learning something new, we are very conscious of the process. In learning to drive, for example, people are initially very aware of their movements. However, as they become more skilled, they also become less conscious of their behavior. People who have been driving for years hardly notice themselves looking in the mirror, changing gears, braking, or indicating turns—although they do all of these things. Driving has become automatic. Generally speaking, the more skilled we become, the less aware we are of our behavior. Many things become so well learned that we hardly notice ourselves doing them. Everyday behaviors, like dressing, eating, and chatting, become *overlearned*. They enter the world of habits.

The same goes for thinking. We gradually acquire certain attitudes and beliefs—initially by consciously thinking things through, and sometimes by arguing points and opinions with others. We pay attention to details and particulars of situations, and this information guides our behavior. As we become more clear and definite in our ideas and beliefs, however, we do not need to stop and examine ourselves so often. Once our ideas are clarified, they become incorporated into an overall personal view of the world. This, in turn, acts as a filter system, making us more sensitive to some stimuli than others, and influencing what we take in and perceive in various situations.

What we perceive then influences how we respond. With repeated experience of the same events or type of events, there is a diminished need for such conscious attention. The perceptions and responses are repeated and rehearsed until they become automatic. Both are then enacted with a minimum, if any, conscious awareness. Consequently, in familiar situations, people respond on the basis of minimal cues, and then switch on what I call a "tape," or "script," that effectively takes over. They define situations by virtue of their similiarity to other situations, and then fire ahead relatively mindlessly. So, although "thinking" occurs in every situation, it is often a brief similarity evaluation, followed by a selective integration and admission of information that tallies with this initial perception.

In new or problem situations, we *are* initially more conscious of how we feel and of our ongoing evaluations. "This is really unusual—what am I meant to do?" Once we feel even a little more familiar and have some grasp of the situation, we find ourselves entering into the spirit of things *or* deciding that we do not like the scene and effectively switching off. In *either* case, there is a decrease in conscious attention and in self-consciousness. The situation has been labelled (e.g., "great party" or "waste of time"), after which we go into automatic. We switch on a tape that is appropriate to the evaluation, and we proceed mindlessly.

WHY SUCH CREATURES OF HABIT?

Developing such habits of thinking and behaving has many advantages. Habits allow us to get more accomplished, more quickly and efficiently than if we had to consciously register and monitor our every movement or thought—even if this were possible. It is therefore both beneficial and necessary to develop habits—for economy of mental and physical energy. Habits leave us with time and space to take in novel aspects of situations and to learn new ways of behaving. There is, however, a much more basic reason why we rely so very much on habits. We do not have a choice.

At any point in time, the available attention capacity of the human brain is surprisingly limited. Over 30 years ago, a psychologist, George Miller, examined a variety of experimental results about judgment and memory (Miller, 1956). His experiments dealt with such things as the maximum number of dots that could be taken in at a glance and how many words or telephone digits could be retained in short-term memory. Analysis of his results lead Miller to conclude that all such measures showed a tendency to cluster around the number seven—which has become known as the "Magical Number Seven." Out of the millions of colors, shapes, sounds, textures, movements, and smells that theoretically constitute any situation, we can only take in, on average, seven of these at any time. So, in order for it to perform as well as it does, the brain must develop strategies for focusing and putting order into what it processes.

Psychologist Jerome Bruner has suggested that the mind employs two basic rules in its attempts to put order and meaning into the confusion of everyday existence. Both strategies aim at economizing on the amount of processing. The first rule is "minimization of surprise;" people expect things to stay the same. In a series of experiments, he showed the alarming degree to which people perceive what they expect, *despite* evidence to the contrary. The second rule is "maximization of attention." At different times and in different circumstances, the mind can deploy its resources differently, depending on the purpose of the moment. A hungry motorist will be aware of little along the highway but restaurant signs (Bruner, Goodnow, & Austin, 1956).

Another famous example of the mind's ability to cope with confusion and to focus purposefully and effectively on a particular portion of the incoming information is the "cocktail party effect" (Cherry, 1953). People, at noisy parties, somehow manage to hear the person with whom they are chatting or on whom they are eavesdropping (i.e., to hear one voice in the babble). They can use snatches of speech to reconstruct the message in their head and, during the process, to continually reevaluate their construction. Neisser (1967) has summed up the whole situation as follows: "seeing, hearing and remembering are all facets of *construction,* which may make more or less use of stimulus information, depending on circumstances" (p. 10).

THE PRICE OF CONVENIENCE

In sum, we are necessarily "creatures of habit" and these habits carry many advantages. There are also, however, a number of major disadvantages. Two are of particular significance. Firstly, because our attention capacity is so limited, we cannot take in every detail of every situation, so our perceptions are highly selective. We perceive the most obvious or salient details and features of a situation, or some aspect we consciously focus on. These are what we remember. Much more goes unnoticed and unprocessed. Consequently, we are bad observers of the outside world. This point is illustrated by incredibly different eye-witness reports of the same incident. Quite simply, people report what *they* processed, what *they* saw. Two people might remember the same party, stroll through the park, or train journey very differently, depending on what they focused on, what caught their eye, what interested them, or what happened to be on their mind at the time.

As well as having a very limited perception of external events, for much the same reasons, we are also bad observers of *ourselves* and our *own* behavior. Have you ever noticed, in retrospect, that you have made the same mistakes again and again in personal or professional affairs? The same people constantly get taken for granted, overtired, overcommitted, or let down by others. People tend to eat and drink things that repeatedly disagree with them or to get involved with the same wrong kind of person. Again and again, we all say "never again." If, right now, you were asked to describe first yourself and then a friend, in five sentences, you would find it much easier to describe your friend. Why? Because we can be objective about others, and they can be objective about us; but it is not so easy when it comes to ourselves. This is why photos, videos, or tapes of ourselves often seem strange and unfamiliar. We do not have an "outside eye" on ourselves. This is why we are all so good at giving advice to other people, and vice versa. Indeed, others can often point out our weak spots or personal habits to us in a way that we cannot do for ourselves.

Unfortunately, the fact that we are such bad observers of the world and of ourselves has some further negative consequences. The main one is that we do not notice ourselves getting into *bad* habits. We do not notice that we are eating, drinking, smoking, working, complaining, or criticizing too much. We do not notice that we are beginning to take partners and friends for granted, to neglect our responsibilities, to let work pile up, or to avoid situations that we find unpleasant. The same can be said of our habits of thinking. Keeping in mind that automatic self-talk is both silent and very rapid, we sum up situations very quickly, and we are generally unaware of what has gone through our minds, of what we have said to ourselves about the situation or person. People can get into the habit of interpreting most situations through a "Monday morning" set, seeing everything in shades of grey, or thinking that they are not as good as everyone else. They can all too easily get into the habit of consistently interpreting and responding to situations in biased and maladaptive ways. The potential consequences of developing faulty patterns of *thinking* are particularly detrimental, because thinking goes on to influence behavior. We behave according to our evaluations.

Consequently, if and when we wrongly evaluate a situation, we fire ahead without even realizing.

WHEN DO PEOPLE STOP AND THINK?

Have you ever summed up a person after exchanging just a few words, only to discover later that you were very wrong in your evaluation? Thinking back, you wonder how you could possibly have been so far off the mark. We do not realize the degree to which we label situations and people, and then go on to filter our perceptions and tailor our behavior accordingly. We do not realize the degree to which our perceptions are self-limited, the degree of our own mindlessness, unless circumstances point it out to us.

When do we stop and think? We consciously stop and think when something unexpected happens—the key gets stuck in the lock, the toilet will not flush, a zip breaks, someone sharply disagrees with an opinion, we suddenly feel ill, or we are very wrong in our evaluation of a person or situation, for example. We also think when we are learning something new or when we find ourselves in a totally novel situation for which we have no "script." Perhaps you are stopping to think about all of this right now, because it is new, unexpected information, because you disagree with it, or because it is something you have never thought about before.

When we do stop and think, how efficient and accurate are we? About 100 years ago, William James, one of the earliest psychologists, put forward a view that people could stop at any time and accurately examine their reasons for doing things and their feelings about them (James, 1890). In other words, he thought that people had direct introspective access. A number of years later, he and his colleagues had to revise their thinking. The situation is very complex, but what seems to happen is this: When people are asked why they did certain things, they *can* usually, and quickly, come up with all sorts of plausible explanations. Providing explanations is not the problem. In fact, people are quite fluent when asked why they behaved as they did in a situation, or why they liked or disliked something. However, they are often caught when asked for *details* of the situation—their memory of a place, person, or their own behavior. Memories are more likely to be accurate and vivid when the important stimuli were very *salient,* or when the cause of a behavior was very obvious; but, in many cases, people are unaware of the existence of a stimulus that influenced their behavior, unaware of a response, and unaware that the stimulus affected the response (Nisbett & Wilson, 1977).

So, if there is no direct introspective access to memory, what is the source

RESEARCH

The idea that we are not consciously churning out new ideas, not logically and objectively processing everything that is happening around us, may come as a bit of a surprise, even a letdown. Are we all going around like zombies in some kind of automated haze, assuming retrospectively that we were thinking, when, in fact, we were only assuming? Not quite; but, the fact is that a very large part of everyday behavior and thinking occurs on an automatic level. Contrary to what we might like to think, we do not operate with computer-like efficiency. We do not weigh up the pros and cons accurately and consciously in every situation.

An American psychologist, Ellen Langer, has studied the whole phenomenon in depth. Her ingenious experiments show convincingly that we do not indulge in much thoughtful action or conscious thought and that many of our everyday behaviors and reactions are habitual responses to habitual situations. She has suggested that there is a continuum of awareness, along the thought dimension that accompanies actions, that ranges from awareness to nonconsciousness. In between these two extremes lies what she has called the category of "mindlessness of ostensibly thoughtful action" ... "the instances where people believe they had been thinking, but where, in fact, they were behaving according to well-learned and general scripts, rather than on the basis of new incoming information" (Langer, 1978; p. 38, 39). Two of her experiments will illustrate. Both are taken from everyday life: coin tossing and burglary.

Coin tossing is a purely chance-determined task. Yet, when people who were engaged in predicting coin tosses were presented with a sequence of outcomes in which there were several "wins" early in the series, they saw themselves as "good" (as opposed to "lucky") at the task, and they were confident of further success. In addition, about 25% of these people felt that their performance would be hampered by distractions, and 40% felt that it would improve with practice. Had they been *thinking* about what they were doing when engaging in the task, they could not have insisted that anyone could be either "good" or "bad" at coin tossing or that skill-relevant factors, such as distractions or practice, would matter (see Langer & Roth, 1975).

Secondly, a study that compared attributions of responsibility for crime prevention provides more evidence that people simply do not spend much time in thoughtful action. Both people who had been burglarized and people who had not were interviewed. Past victimization did *not* result in taking greater precautionary measures, such as more locks on doors and windows, or availing of a police department free security service. Both burglarized and nonburglarized were equally likely to take preventive measures against burglary, although when asked to *think* about it, both groups attributed responsibility to nonchance (see Miransky & Langer, 1977).

of the confident verbal reports? It seems that self-reports are based on personal theories or judgments about the extent to which a particular stimulus is a *plausible* cause of a given response. In other words, people supply reasons why they *assume* they must have behaved in the fashion they did, and they suggest the most obvious stimulus to account for this behavior. Consequently, when we do stop and think about our motives for doing something, unless there was a very obvious cause or sequence, our explanations are not always accurate. In fact, what we unknowingly rely on to explain our own behavior is our knowledge of ourselves and of our characteristic patterns of behavior and thinking.

Furthermore, it is becoming increasingly clear that people can perceive and be influenced by information that is not well represented in consciousness (i.e., noticed); and that, even when information *is* noticed, it can effect people's thoughts and behavior in a manner that is not fully understood (Bowers, 1987). It is a very complex area, and efforts to explain these phenomena have sparked a renewed interest in unconscious processes, subliminal perception, and the limits of introspective access (e.g., Bowers & Meichenbaum, 1984; Erdelyi, 1985; Mandler, 1984). After focusing on behavior in the 1960s and on cognitions in the 1970s, psychologists are now exploring feelings, emotions, and motivation, and their interface with thinking and behavior (Greenberg & Safran, 1987). They are endeavouring to understand the whys and wherefores of the small personal changes that are so integral to the fabric of everyday living and coping, as well as the more profound, or "deep", changes that occur in the course of psychotherapy and personal growth (Mahoney & Gabriel, 1987). Answers to these questions will, in turn, be translated into more effective assessment and therapy techniques over the coming years.

FURTHER SUGGESTED READING

Theory and Research

Anisfield, M. (1984). *Language development from birth to three*. Hillsdale, NJ: Lawrence Erlbaum Associates.

Bowlby, J. (1985). The role of childhood experience in cognitive disturbance. In M. J. Mahoney & A. Freeman (Eds.), *Cognition and psychotherapy* (pp. 181–200). NY: Plenum Press.

Brewer, W. F. (1974). There is no convincing evidence for operant or classical conditioning in adult humans. In E. B. Weiner & S. Palermo (Eds.), *Cognition and the symbolic processes* (pp. 1–42). Hillsdale, NJ: Lawrence Erlbaum Associates.

Craighead, W. E., Kazdin, A. E., & Mahoney, M. J. (1976). *Behavior modification: Principles, issues and applications*. (Chapter 7: Principles Of Operant Conditioning; Chapter 8: Cognitive Influences In Behavior Modification) Boston, MA: Houghton Mifflin.

Hebb, D. O., & Donderi, D. C. (1987). *Textbook of psychology* (4th Edition). Hillsdale, NJ: Lawrence Erlbaum Associates.

Kahneman, D. (1973). *Attention and effort*. Englewood Cliffs, NJ: Prentice-Hall.

Kesser, F. S. (1987). *The development of language and language researchers (Essays in honor of Roger Brown)*. Hillsdale, NJ: Lawrence Erlbaum Associates.

Leva, L. M. (1984). Cognitive behavioral therapy in the light of Piagetian theory. In M. A. Reda & M. J. Mahoney (Eds.), *Cognitive psychotherapies: Recent developments in theory, research and practice* (pp. 223–250). Cambridge, MA: Ballinger.

Meichenbaum, D. (1977). *Cognitive behavior modification*. NY: Plenum Press.

Mahoney, M. J. (1974). *Cognition and behavior modification*. Cambridge, MA: Ballinger.

Overton, W. F. (Ed.). (1983). *The relationship between social and cognitive development (The Jean Piaget symposia)*. Hillsdale, NJ: Lawrence Erlbaum Associates.

Rubin, K. H., & Mills, R. S. L. (1988). The many faces of social isolation in childhood. *Journal of Consulting and Clinical Psychology, 56*, 916–924.

Shiffrin, R. M. & Schneider, W. (1977). Controlled and automatic human information processing: II. Perceptual learning and automatic attending. *Psychological Review, 8*, 127–190.

Singer, J. L. & Singer, D. G. (1981). *Television, imagination and aggression: A study of preschoolers*. Hillsdale, NJ: Lawrence Erlbaum Associates.

2

Sources of Stress

Pressure and stress come from two main sources: from the outside world and from within oneself. Stress from the environment comes in the shape of unexpected life events, the strain of ongoing, unsatisfactory circumstances, and from daily hassles. Equally important are internal sources of stress, many of which are, unwittingly, self-imposed. Internal pressure can come from an ill-maintained, sensitive, or ailing body, from faulty learning, which results in problem behaviors and habits, and finally, from maladaptive patterns of thinking and erroneous beliefs about oneself or one's world. Furthermore, what starts off as an external pressure (e.g., low-paying job) can take its toll on health or lifestyle or affect one's outlook on life. Equally, ill health, problem behaviors, or faulty thinking can exacerbate the impact of external events, ongoing life circumstances, or daily mishaps. Sometimes, everything becomes a problem.

EXTERNAL SOURCES OF STRESS: LIFE EVENTS, ONGOING CIRCUMSTANCES, AND DAILY HASSLES

Life Events

Life events have been established as antecedents, and at least partial determinants, of a wide range of physical and psychological problems. They have been associated with heart disease, tuberculosis, diabetes, and many other disorders. A small number of studies have also shown a relationship between life events and minor physical complaints, on a day-to-day basis (Henry & Stephens, 1977). Life events can also cause or exacerbate psychological problems, ranging from anxiety-related difficulties—such as tension, panic attacks, and interpersonal difficulties—to depression.

The formal study of life events was initiated by Holmes and Rahe, at the University of Washington, in the late 1960s. Their aims were to identify the life events that were, in and of themselves, extreme in their psychological impact; to pinpoint what it was that made these events so particularly damaging; and to rate them according to the degree of trauma likely to be experienced. They listed many such events and concluded that the crucial factor was the degree of *change* or *social adjustment* associated with them. They then developed a scale (Table 2.1), by which people could measure the cumulated degree of stress they had experienced in the previous 6 months, by totaling the number of such life events they had experienced (Holmes & Rahe, 1967).

Life Events . . . And More

Later research validated the work of Holmes and Rahe, to the extent that some events *are* unconditionally stressful. However, valuable as their attempts to rate life events in this way have been, recent findings have highlighted the fact that the stress process is more complex than was initially realized. Holmes and Rahe had effectively ignored the importance of the *relationships between events,* including event accumulation and underlying causes. Things simply do not happen in isolation. For example, loss of employment might lead to financial problems, which might lead to a change in living conditions, which might lead to a further change in social activities and outlets, and so on. These would all have been regarded as separate, autonomous events in the original rating scale.

Furthermore, *ongoing* life strains and circumstances, chronic microstressors—such as ill-health, a bad marriage, a frustrating work environment, or financial pressures—can gradually wear people down. Over time, people can become more vulnerable and less able to handle even relatively small problems or changes. *Underlying causes* are also important. Certain life events are of such magnitude that they can affect a person's whole psychosocial world. A natural disaster, like a flood or an earthquake, can wipe out a large part of a family, or even a community, as well as create multifarious changes (e.g., job loss, house move, death of loved ones, change in financial status, personal injury, or disability) that touch every sphere of one's existence.

As well as event interrelationships, research is now also focusing on the *meaning* of the event for the person. It seems that a critical factor in determining the impact of an event is how it is perceived and evaluated by the

Are you under stress? You can measure the amount of stress in your life, using Dr. Richard Rahe's stress scale. He has calculated the amount of stress that is caused by major life-events, and given each a numerical value. Have any of these events happened in your life in the last six months? If so, score for each that occured, then check your total to see if your life is overstressful.

Table
2.1: Rahe Stress Questionnaire

1.	Death of spouse	100
2.	Divorce	73
3.	Marital separation	65
4.	Jail Term	63
5.	Death of close family	63
6.	Personal injury or illness	53
7.	Marriage	50
8.	Fired at work	47
9.	Marital reconciliation	45
10.	Retirement	45
11.	Change in health of family member	44
12.	Pregnancy	40
13.	Sex Difficulties	39
14.	Gain of new family member	39
15.	Business readjustment	39
16.	Change in financial state	38
17.	Death of close friend	37
18.	Change to different line of work	36
19.	Change in number of arguments with spouse	35
20.	A large mortgage or loan	31
21.	Foreclosure of mortgage or loan	30
22.	Change in responsibilities at work	29
23.	Son or daughter leaving home	29
24.	Trouble with in-laws	29
25.	Outstanding personal achievement	28
26.	Spouse begins or stops work	26
27.	Begin or end school or college	26
28.	Changing in living conditions	25
29.	Change in personal habits	24
30.	Trouble with the boss	23
31.	Change in work hours or conditions	20
32.	Change in residence	20
33.	Change in school or college	20
34.	Change in recreation	19
35.	Change in church activities	19
36.	Change in social activities	18
37.	A moderate mortgage or loan	17
38.	Change in sleeping habits	16
39.	Change in number of family get-togethers	15
40.	Change in eating habits	15
41.	Holiday	13
42.	Christmas	12
43.	Minor violations of the law	11

HOW TO SCORE

Below 60: your life has been unusually free from stress lately. *60 to 80:* you have had a normal amount of stress recently. This score is average for the ordinary wear and tear of life. *80–100:* the stress in your life is a little high, probably because of one recent event. *100 upwards:* pressures are piling up, either at home or work, or both. You are under serious stress, and the higher you score above 100 the worse the strain.

individual. If the stressor (e.g., loss of employment) threatens a person's sense of mastery and self-confidence, its impact will be particularly significant (Pearlin, Lieberman, Menaghan, & Mullan, 1981). Furthermore, the less control people feel they have over events, the less they feel able to cope, and the greater the threat to self-esteem. Scheduled events, such as retirement, can be stressful, but they can be planned and prepared for. Redundancy and, likewise, accidents and sudden deaths are unpredictable, and, therefore, their impact is likely to be more extreme.

In sum, while life events remain an integral component of the stress process, "they are being conceptualized increasingly as part of a larger process leading eventually to disorder" (Monroe, 1982, p. 450). The trend is away from the notion of relatively discrete, circumscribed life events and towards an emerging appreciation of the more complex relationships between events, as well as the nature and meaning of the event for the individual.

Daily Hassles

Over the last 15 years, Richard Lazarus and his colleagues at the University of California at Berkeley have produced a significant body of information on the dynamics of stress management and coping. Central to their research also is an emphasis on the individual's interpretation, or personal appraisal, in determining the impact of a stressor. They define stress as "a particular relationship between the person and the environment that is appraised by the person as taxing or exceeding his or her resources and endangering his or her well-being" (Lazarus & Folkman, 1984, p. 19). In a series of studies, it has been shown that the accumulated effects of daily hassles (e.g., getting stuck in traffic, losing a wallet or keys, rising prices) are *more* significant in relation to morale and to physical and psychological well-being than more major life events (De Longis, Coyne, Dahof, Folkman, & Lazarus, 1982; Kanner, Coyne, Schaefer, & Lazarus, 1981). In other words, it is not the "acts of God," but the *little* things, that really get to people and gradually erode health and self-confidence.

Several *developmental* and *sociodemographic* hassle patterns have also been identified. Different things are more likely to constitute hassles for different sections of the population and at different times of life (Lazarus, 1984a). Middle-aged people are particularly concerned about their weight and the health of family members, as well as the rising price of common goods, taxes, and property investments. The concerns and potential hassles of college students are primarily academic and social; the pressures of meeting high academic expectations, relationships, and the problem of loneliness. Finally, the hassles of a sample of health professionals were clear: too many things to do, not enough time to do the things they needed and wanted to do, too much responsibility, and trouble relaxing—a fact to keep in mind for the future.

Because hassles are such an integral, but potentially lethal, part of everyday existence, people most learn how to cope with them. Coping requires accurate appraisal, followed by the application of either *problem-focused* or *emotion-focused* coping skills, or both. Problem-focused coping involves attempts to modify or eliminate the source of stress through one's own behavior; that is, by *doing* something. Emotion-focused coping relates to behavioral and cognitive responses whose primary function is to manage the emotional consequences of stress and help maintain emotional equilibrium. Both are essential. Allowing oneself to *feel* upset about a friend borrowing and carelessly damaging one's car will not repair the car. On the other hand, *repairing* the car and arranging for reimbursement, while *denying* that one is in any way upset or annoyed, could lead to internal "wear and tear."

There are also significant sex-related and situation-related patterns in *styles* of coping. Men are more likely to tackle stressors and problems by using problem-focused strategies, whereas women are more emotion-focused. The nature and dynamics of the *situation* also play a role in determining the style of coping; job-related stressors elicit problem-focused coping, whereas health-realted stressors trigger emotion-focused coping (Folkman & Lazarus, 1980). One can only speculate as to the reasons for these patterns; possible explanations are discussed in chapter 11.

Finally, a word about "uplifts." A downward spiral can sometimes be neutralized by the occurrence of something good; a hassle can be offset by an uplift. Not catching one's usual train, for example, might result in meeting an old friend on the next one and reestablishing contact—a fortuitous event that would not otherwise have come about. Likewise, even life events can sometimes have beneficial psychological consequences. For example, loss of employment might lead to a change of address, which might lead to making new friends who prove to be more genuine and supportive in every way than previous neighbors; which compensates for losses in other areas and provides a potential source of support for the future.

In fact, social supports can serve as major mediating factors in times of stress; but they are *not* simply coextensive with social networks. In other words, it is not the quantity but the *quality* of relationships that counts. Again and again, research has indicated the importance of having at least "one close confiding relationship, based on intimacy and trust." One such relationship is much more important than a large number of casual acquaintances. Usually, and ideally, this is a partner, but a best friend of either sex, a parent, a priest, *or* a caring professional often fills the same role.

Self-Efficacy

Coping skills are of many kinds, and all sorts of strategies for surviving and thriving are learned in the course of growing up. But, there are gaps in our knowledge and expertise; no one is perfect. The important thing is that, once people know their weak spots, with planning and perseverance they can acquire the necessary skills to make them feel more in control of their lives. In this context, Albert Bandura has proposed a theory of what he has termed *self-efficacy*. He has shown that the degree to which people feel able to cope in a situation (i.e., their degree of perceived self-efficacy) will determine three things: whether they will approach *or* avoid the situation entirely, how much energy they will expend in the face of difficulties and obstacles, and how long they will persist before giving up. In other words, when people do not feel confident about their ability to handle a situation, they will be less likely

RESEARCH: SOCIAL SUPPORTS

A revealing project (Brown, Bhrolchain, & Harris, 1975) investigated the effects of life circumstances on vulnerability to depression among women living in South London. What they found was that women suffering from depression had, on average, experienced two-and-a-half times more stressful life events in the 9 months preceding the onset of their depression than did others. However, results also indicated large class differences in the prevalence of depression, with the higher rate among working-class women. These differences were not attributable to the greater frequency of events among the working class but to a higher likelihood of breakdown occurring once the events struck.

Vulnerability was related to both social and environmental factors. Four factors were identified. First and most important was the *quality of interpersonal relationships*. Women who had a close, confiding relationship with another person (e.g., husband or boyfriend) were much less likely to experience depression in response to unpleasant environmental events. The existence of such a relationship, in fact, gave almost complete protection: Only 4% of those who experienced major stressful events, and who had such an intimate tie with another, became depressed, compared with 38% of those without ties. The other three factors found to interact similarly with environmental stressors were: loss of mother by death or separation before the age of 11, having three or more children under the age of 14 at home, and being unemployed. *All* of these factors could be seen as potential curtailments of supportive interpersonal relationships.

Further research to investigate why working class women, in particular, were so vulnerable explored the relationships between marital status, socioeconomic status, and mental disorders in females (Meile, Johnson, & Peters, 1976). Defining socioeconomic status in terms of educational attainment, they found that, among the lower socioeconomic status women, married women had more disorder than those who had never been married, irrespective of age or employment status. These differences were not found among women of higher educational attainment, suggesting that education provides people with both real and perceived coping ability (i.e., information), as well as behavioral and cognitive coping skills. Furthermore, having a sense of confidence in one's ability to cope greatly determines how people actually *do* respond to stress.

In sum, studies of predisposing factors in the social milieu suggest the importance of one, or a network of, close and supportive interpersonal relationships. They also suggest that a sense of control—of competence or coping ability—which may correlate with greater educational exposure, is equally important. These factors can modify the potentially detrimental effects of stress, and render an individual less vulnerable.

to try at all; and, if they do, they will not persevere for very long, if the going gets tough (Bandura, 1977). On the other hand, knowing that one is equipped to meet the demands of life's myriad problems and mini-crises provides an invaluable feeling of being in control. It reinforces a perception of being in charge of one's life.

Effective coping, therefore, will be determined by a number of factors. Firstly, there are the multifarious *behavioral* coping skills, including social skills, problem-solving and decision-making skills, and expertise of various kinds. *Cognitive* coping skills include an ability to deal with emotional arousal by being aware of and utilizing one's self-talk and feelings in a constructive and healthy way. Being reasonable and flexible enough in one's beliefs and outlook to be able to accept the unpredictables of life and of other people's behavior is also essential. *Social supports* are a vital security cushion. So also are *material resources*. Finally, good coping and good living will also be affected by *health status* and contingent energy level.

It is also important to remember, however, that a certain amount of stress and pressure is inevitable in life, and even serves to keep one on one's toes. In other words, although clinical research has concentrated on the adverse effects of life's pressures and problems, it is also likely that people benefit (e.g., in terms of acquired skills, lowered tension, and increased confidence) from coping with a range of life events and experiences that are, for the most part, inevitable at some stage or other. The challenge is to help people develop adequate coping skills—not only to survive such experiences, but to grow from them.

INTERNAL SOURCES OF STRESS: THE BODY

The effects of the body's well-being on the mind have long been recognized. The major psychiatric illnesses—schizophrenia, endogenous depression, and manic depression—are acknowledged as being related to changes in the body's biochemistry. It is understood that premenstrual syndrome, menopause, and pregnancy can also influence psychological status and mood. People sometimes get depressed after the flu. In a world where feelings of anxiety or depression are quickly attributed to external pressures and stress, it is important not to ignore the body as a source of psychological problems.

Data accumulating from a wide variety of psychological and psychiatric health care delivery services indicate that a significant proportion of their clients are actually suffering from physical problems (Hall, Popkin, DeVaul, Faillace, & Stickney, 1978). This is not surprising, because almost all of the major life-threatening illnesses can be accompanied by feelings of anxiety or depression. Cardiovascular and endocrine disorders are the most frequent physical causes of psychological symptoms, followed by infection, pulmonary disease, gastrointestinal disorders, blood disease, disorders of the central nervous system, and malignancy. Depression, anxiety, sleep disturbance, appetite disorders, and diminished concentration are among the characteristic psychological symptoms.

These findings remind us again of the intricate interplay of the physical and the psychological. Physical disorders can be accompanied by psychological symptoms, and vice versa. Furthermore, these relationships can change over time. As well as the major life-threatening illnesses, other physical conditions that are frequently masked by psychological symptoms fall into four groups:

1. Endocrine disorders
2. Nutritional disorders
3. Reactions to drugs, toxins, and pollutants
4. Allergic reactions

Endocrine Disorders.   An imbalance, or a shift in the body's production and distribution of hormones, can produce symptoms that mimic those of psychiatric and psychological disorders. Perhaps the best known of the endocrine disorders is diabetes mellitus. As well as the physical symptoms of excessive hunger, thirst, and urgency of urination, there is often depression or generalized weakness and lassitude. In severe cases, amnesia and states similar to drunkenness can occur. Mood swings can also accompany changing blood sugar levels; so people can feel depressed and irritable yet not know why. Diabetes insipidus, although basically unrelated, presents some of the same symptoms. Similarly, a lazy pituitary gland can result in depression, apathy, and drowsiness. People with an underactive thyroid can also experience depression, whereas an overactive thyroid can lead to unpredictable changes of mood. Premenstrual symptoms of depression can also be related to endocrine malfunctioning.

Nutritional Disorders.   The body must receive a proper balance of vitamins, minerals, and other nutrients. Having said this, however, people vary widely in their chemical make-up and in their dietary needs, and, consequently, individuals can be suffering from nutritional deficiencies even though they are, in theory, eating appropriately. Severe deficiency diseases, such as pellegra, scurvy, beriberi, and rickets are now relatively rare in the Western world, but it is likely that milder levels of deficiency are quite common. To complicate matters, early symptoms of nutritional disorders are difficult to recognize and are often psychological in nature—depression, tiredness, dizziness, apathy, irritability, and reduced alertness or concentration. A lack of B vitamins and iron, for example, can result in anemia, which, in turn, can lead to feelings of listlessness and depression. Nutritional disorders are particularly common among chronic alcoholics and people on fad diets. See Table 2.2.

Drugs, Toxins, and Pollutants.   Psychological symptoms can also occur in response to drugs, environmental chemicals, and industrial pollutants. For example, cocaine is the most potent of the widely used anxiety-producing drugs, and it can cause panic attacks. Once cocaine panic attacks start, they can continue indefinitely and can lead to agoraphobic avoidance symptoms. Both people who are sensitive to anxiety-producing drugs and those with a genetic predisposition to anxiety can be particularly vulnerable. Likewise, over-the-counter diet pills, as well as amphetamines and other forms of "speed," can also contribute to anxiety. These drugs mimic the physical, emotional, and cognitive symptoms of true anxiety.

Furthermore, laxatives, some drugs used to treat arthritis and gout, anti-convulsants, and drugs to counter cholesterol can interfere with vitamin, fat, and mineral absorption and can thereby indirectly have psychological effects. Similarly, some drugs remove minerals from the body, and others can cause an increase in vitamin needs (see Table 2.3). Oral contraceptives, for example, deplete vitamins B and C if the person's diet is already deficient in these nutrients or if they are suffering from problems of malabsorption. With age, people need fewer calories; but nutrient needs do not change. Elderly people are, therefore, particularly prone to vitamin deficiencies; antidepressants, antitubercular drugs, antibiotics, and alcohol all deplete vitamin B12.

Environmental toxins can also alter vitamin needs. For example, being exposed to cigarette smoke increases the need for Vitamin C. Likewise, exposure to some plastics can deplete Vitamin A and niacin. In addition to increased vitamin needs, toxins from heavy metals, such as lead, mercury, and selenium, can have direct psychological effects, as outlined in Table 2.4.

Allergic Reactions.   There are many kinds of allergies to food and drugs, as well as to substances in the environment. Some people are much more allergic than most; but, people in general can be allergic to almost anything or can develop an allergy to something they have been using or consuming for years. Classic allergic reactions include physical symptoms such as skin complaints (e.g., swelling, nettle rash, eczema), respiratory tract problems (e.g., intrinsic asthma, rhinitis or runny nose, bronchitis), digestive problems (e.g., stomach pains, constipation, diarrhea), swelling of part of the face or tongue, and migraine. However, some experience *psychological* reactions, such as dizziness, restlessness, hyperactivity, difficulty concentrating, depression, fatigue, confusion, irritability, and anxiety.

Allergies to food are very common. The most common are to milk and

TABLE 2.2
Some Symptoms of Selected Vitamin and Mineral Deficiencies

Vitamin	Symptoms	Rich Natural Resources
Thiamine (B1)	Apathy, confusion, fatigue, insomnia, headaches, indigestion, diarrhea, numbness, anemia, heart palpitations.	Wheat germ, rice polish, brewer's yeast, bran.
Riboflavin (B2)	Cracks in lips or corners of mouth, trembling, dizziness, insomnia, sluggishness, oily or scaly skin.	Milk, liver, organ meats, brewer's yeast.
Niacin (Niacinamide)	Fear, apprehension, depression, headaches, insomnia, burning sensations, fatigue.	Lean meats, poultry, fish, peanuts, brewer's yeast, wheat germ, desiccated liver.
Pyridoxine (B6)	Depression, anemia, low blood sugar, dandruff, numbness and cramps, cracks on mouth, nausea, insomnia.	Meat, organ meat, fish, whole wheat bread, soybeans, avocados, peanuts, walnuts, fresh fruits, bananas.
Pantothenic Acid (Calcium Pantothenate)	Fatigue, insomnia, depression, pain in small of back, loss of appetite, low blood pressure, burning feet, irritability.	Brewer's yeast, organ meat, bran, peanuts, peas. Present in all foods.
Cobalamin (B12)	Pernicious Anemia, numbness, apathy, mood changes, poor memory, poor concentration, confusion.	Meat, poultry, fish, eggs, brewer's yeast, dairy products.
Folic Acid (Folicin, Folate)	Anemia, poor memory, apathy, withdrawal, irritability, peeling lips.	Leafy green vegetables.
Ascorbic Acid (C)	Fatigue, listlessness, confusion, depression, breathlessness, loss of appetite, anaemia, fleeting pain in limbs, bruising.	Citrus fruits, green vegetables, tomatoes, berries, peppers, cauliflower, parsley.
Vitamin A	Insomnia, fatigue, depression, pains in extremities, acne, burning eyes, headaches, night blindness.	Green leafy vegetables, yellow tubers, fruits, cod liver oil, beef and chicken liver.
Vitamin D	Exhaustion, rheumatic pains, soft bones.	Cod liver oil, sunlight.
Vitamin E	Restlessness, fatigue, insomnia, destruction of blood cells, need for oxygen.	Wheat germ oil, safflower and cottonseed oil, cabbage, broccoli.

Mineral

Calcium	Irritability, tension, depression, insomnia, cramping in legs, anxiety, poor memory.	Milk, dairy products, molasses, vegetables, hard water, bone meal.
Magnesium	Tremors, dizziness, rapid heart beat, fatigue, depression, insomnia, irritability, anxiety, restlessness.	Whole grains, green vegetables, nuts, seafood.

(continued)

Sodium	Lassitude, low blood pressure, anorexia, flatulence. *Excessive symptoms:* dizziness, swelling, tension, irritability, premenstrual dysphoria, high blood pressure.	Table salt, ham, processed cheese, bacon, sausage, dried fish, nuts, butter, pickles.
Zinc	Lethargy, delayed wound healing, loss of taste and smell, poor appetite, stretch marks on skin, irregular menses, white spots on nails, frequent infections, hair loss, poor circulation.	Meat, fish, seeds, wheat germ, maple syrup, yeast, milk, whole grains, nuts, peas, vegetables, liver, herring, oysters, onions.
Iron	Anemia, poor concentration, poor memory, depression, flattened nails, swollen ankles, hair loss, exhaustion.	Meat, liver, eggs, leafy green vegetables.

Adapted from Tables 1, 2, 3, 4, and 5 in *Nutrition and Vitamin Therapy* by M. Lesser (1980). New York: Grove Press.

milk products, grains such as wheat, and fruits such as strawberries. Other fool allergens include eggs, nuts, chicken, tomatoes, peas, potatoes, onions, berries, fish, yeast, and pork. Furthermore, many people respond to allergens *in* foods (e.g., EDTA, the stabilizer in mayonnaise and salad dressings) rather than to the foods themselves. In vulnerable individuals, psychological symptoms can also result from exposure to chemicals, synthetics, exhaust fumes, and cosmetics, as well as to airborne agents, such as pollens and animal dander.

INTERNAL SOURCES OF STRESS: BEHAVIOR AND FAULTY LEARNING

In the course of growing up, people gradually develop a range or repertoire of skills, or patterns of behavior that allow them to get on with everyday living. People learn—by association, by consequences, and by observation—how to deal with other people, how to cook, drive, study, have fun, show affection, and how to express their feelings, for example. In chapter 1, I explained the ease with which people develop such habits, as well as the necessity for them. Problems arise when people either fail to acquire these necessary skills *or* when learning takes place but is in some way excessive or inappropriate (See Blackman, 1974).

Not Learning The Necessary

Problems can arise when people, for a variety of reasons (e.g., lack of opportunity, laziness, anxiety) do not learn how to handle particular everyday situations. In behavioral jargon, the necessary *skills* are not acquired. Areas where this frequently occurs are social skills (including self-assertion),

TABLE 2.3
Major Drug Effects on Vitamins and Minerals

Therapeutic Class	Major Drug	Depletion
Hypotensives	Hedralzine	Vitamin B6
Antitubercular drugs	Isoniazid	Vitamin B6, niacin
Alcohol		Vitamin B1, and B6, folacin, magnesium, zinc
Antacids	Aluminum Hydroxide Magnesium Hydroxide	Phosphorous, phosphate
Antibacterial Agents	Neomycin, Kanamycin, Paraaminosalicylic Acid	Fat, nitrogen, calcium, iron, sodium, potassium, vitamin B12
Anticholesterol Agents	Cholestyramine	Folacin, vitamins A, D, E, K
Anticonvulsants	Diphenylhydantoin Phenobarbital Glutethimide	Calcium, folacin, vitamins D, K, B6
Anti-inflammatory Agents	Aspirin Indomathacin Phenylbutazone Colchicine Sulfasalazine Mefanamic Acid	Fat, nitrogen, sodium, potassium, folacin, vitamin B12
Cardiac Gycosides		Calcium, magnesium
Diuretics	Chlorthiazide Spironolactone	Calcium, magnesium, potassium, zinc
Hormones (Steroids)	Cortisone Prednisone	Calcium, potassium, zinc, vitamins B6 & C
Laxatives	Mineral Oil Phenolphthalcin Bisacodyl	Potassium, vitamins A, D, and K
Oral Contraceptives	Mestranol Ethinyl Estradiol Conjugated Estrogens	Folacin, riboflavin, zinc, vitamins A & C (increases iron, copper, calcium)

Note: Adapted from Clinical Nutrition for the Health Scientist by D. A. Roe (1979). Boca Raton, FL: CRC Press.

problem-solving and decision-making skills, study and work habits, and effective management of time and financial resources.

For example, failure to acquire the basic building blocks of social inter-course—making conversation and small talk—can make even simple every-day situations (let alone interviews and dates) problematic and unrewarding. People who do not know how to approach or talk to other people can come

TABLE 2.4
Increased Vitamin Need as a Consequence of Drugs
and/or Environmental Chemicals.

Nutrient	Exposure Resulting in Increased Vitamin Needs or Reduced Blood Levels.
Vitamin A	Polychlorobiphenlys, benzopyrene, spironolactone, DDT, bile salt sequestrants used to tread hypercholesterolemia, neomycin, mineral oil.
Folacin	Oral contraceptives, anticonvulsants, methotrexate, pyrimethamine, alcohol.
Vitamin B12	Biquanides, anticonvulsants, oral contraceptives, antibiotics, antituberculous agents, alcohol, hypoglycemic agents.
Vitamin B6	Isonicotinic hydrazide, thiosemicarbazide, penicillamine, L-Dopa, hydralazine, oral contraceptives, alcohol.
Thiamine	Alcohol
Niacin	Polychlorobiphenlys, isonicotinic hydrazide, phenylbutazone.
Riboflavin	Boric acid
Vitamin D	Anticonvulsants
Vitamin K	Anticonvulsants, antibiotics
Vitamin C	Smoking, aspirin, oral contraceptives, *nitrosamines*
Vitamin E	Oxygen, ozone

Note: Adapted from "Drugs and Environmental Chemicals in Relation to Vitamin Needs" by M. Brin. In *Nutrition and Drug Interrelations* (1978). New York: Academic Press.

across as anything from unfriendly to insensitive, disinterested, bored, or stupid. By and large, they are not sought out or asked back. Such people are often acutely aware of their own shortcomings, and this adds to their upset and frustration. Likewise, an inability to assert oneself can give rise to constant frustrations, both social and professional. Unassertive people are often exploited because of their inability to say "no"; at the same time, opportunities for self-advancement or promotion can be lost because of their inability to speak out.

People who lack basic problem-solving and decision-making skills live in constant dread of the unexpected. They panic in even minor crises, because they know that they do *not* know how to cope. "What will I do if . . . ?" Ineffective management of time or resources can lead to the same kind of anticipatory anxieties and self-fulfilling prophecies. Despite their best efforts, such people often hop from one job, assignment, or project to another, finish none, and end up exhausted, frustrated, and with little accomplished. Unfortunately, for such people, the worst frequently *does* happen: Exams are failed, and opportunities, as well as time and small fortunes, are wasted. It is almost unnecessary to add that others also find these people disorganized, ineffective, unreliable, and irritating. No one is left feeling good.

Finally, *all* of these learning deficits can lead to inconsistencies and, ironically, excesses. The unassertive person might let himself be walked on most of the time, but occasionally, in a frustrated effort to change his situation, will overreact in an aggressive fashion. Likewise, people who have difficulty in expressing their emotions can come across as unpredictable and inconsistent—sometimes cold and insensitive, and other times overly effusive or familiar. People whose work habits are ineffective can see-saw from relative inertia to bouts of frenetic activity, which exhaust everyone and accomplish little.

Learning The Unnecessary

Sometimes, learning *does* take place but is maladaptive, due to faulty associations, problematic reinforcements, or unrepresentative observations.

Traumatic experiences involve high levels of anxiety and generally lead to avoidance behavior. Being attacked by a dog can result in fear and avoidance of dogs. Likewise, experiencing cramps and panicking while swimming, being involved in a car accident or a fire, being in an airplane that experiences difficulties in flight, or being sexually assaulted, for example, can all have profound and long-lasting effects. People, furthermore, can continue to experience high levels of emotional arousal in situations that even vaguely resemble those in which the original trauma occurred. This is especially true if the event is followed by a period of conscious avoidance, during which the fear is allowed to *incubate* and grow. Interestingly, many people also respond to the physical arousal that they experience when anxious or excited with *physical* self-indulgence. An argument or disagreement—or even good news—can lead to a raid on the cookie jar, liquor cabinet, or cigarette pack. Furthermore, these kinds of associations and reactions often become so automatic that the cookie, can of beer, or cigarette has disappeared before the person even becomes aware of his or her behavior, or how it was triggered.

If the consequences of doing something are pleasant, people do more of it; if the consequences are unpleasant, they do less. This is why people who experience panic attacks in crowded or enclosed places, like supermarkets, churches, and elevators, often come to avoid these places. Many agoraphobics avoid traveling on planes and even buses and trains, which greatly curtails their lifestyle in terms of holidays, trips, and ordinary activities, such as visiting friends or going shopping. Some stop going out altogether. Not quite so dramatic in their consequences, but nonetheless significant, are incidents such as unpleasant or embarrassing social encounters, after which people protect their shattered confidence by avoiding the person or persons concerned. They do not go to places where these people are likely to be, or they avoid the place where the upsetting incident itself took place.

If there is not enough reward or there is a *decrease* in the reward value of an activity or a situation (e.g., no promotion or wage increase on a job, no praise or recognition for effort, little social support, or deteriorating conditions), there will be a contingent decrease in the behavior that the situation used to elicit. This is why people can lose interest in jobs, learning courses, and hobbies, and also in friendships and relationships. Quite simply, these things are no longer rewarding in the way they were before. There is no pay-off. Even if nothing objectively changes in a situation, just repetition or a lack of novelty (which is very rewarding and motivating for many people) can result in loss of interest. This is not as simple as it may sound. People are generally unaware of the reinforcement contingencies that maintain their behavior; they frequently just find that they have lost interest in certain activities or people, for no apparent reason.

Reinforcements are very complex. As well as material, they can be social, intellectual, and emotional. For example, you might sometimes wonder what exactly is keeping people psychologically locked in a situation that they are free to leave, and that is, by any standards, totally unrewarding or even punishing. The answer is that they are getting *something* out of it. It serves some function, however elusive, even if only in that it provides an uneasy haven from facing other, even greater, fears and uncertainties. Reinforcements can be very obscure, and people frequently cannot identify them for themselves. As explained in chapter 1, people do not always know the reasons for their feelings and their behavior.

On the other hand, even when outcomes are *positive* and lead to an increase in behavior, the behavior so increased is not always adaptive. The immediate enjoyment, or reinforcement, of a cigarette, beer, or ice cream can quickly grow into a bad habit of overindulgence. Likewise, because the results of working hard—money or intrinsic job satisfaction—are so gratifying for some, it is easy for them to get into the habit of working too much. If staying on late in the office becomes an everyday occurrence, time is being borrowed from other areas of one's life—family, friends, recreation, body maintenance, or sleep. In the same way, people who enjoy the satisfaction of things being well done can become overly fussy and perfectionistic. Excessive amounts of time can be spent improving or ruminating over minor details of a project—at the expense of not completing the job on time, or at all.

Problems can also arise when a person has not learned to discriminate the *situations* in which a behavior or skill, which has been perfected and rewarded, is simply not appropriate. An extreme example would be the person who has a particular talent for telling jokes or mimicking, but does not realize that an interview, board meeting, or funeral is not the place to shine. Likewise, expertise in a particular area, such as cars or poetry, for example, does not give license to wax lyrically in every company.

Finally, people can also acquire inappropriate emotional responses through *observation*. Young children will be affected by repeated exposure to violent, frightening, or sexually inappropriate domestic scenes. Movies and the media are also important, at all ages, in terms of both their emotional and informational impact. For example, naive observation of sexy bodies jumping in and out of sports cars, swimming pools, beds, and relationships can make some people believe that this is what their life should be like. This can lead to unrealistic expectations and to frustration and loss of confidence in themselves and others.

INTERNAL SOURCES OF STRESS: FAULTY THINKING

Everyone develops a set of beliefs about the world, which shapes their life and influences their perceptions. The way in which people *interpret* events plays a huge role in determining their *behavior,* and this, in turn, effects how they *feel*. The personal meaning of a life event, a hassle, an illness, or a bad habit will influence how it is handled. If thinking is faulty, the consequences can be particularly far-reaching, both in terms of how one responds and how one reacts emotionally. Faulty thinking can act as a stressor in two main ways:

1. By biasing one's interpretation of everyday situations and events.
2. By biasing one's outlook, through erroneous or maladaptive beliefs.

Biased Interpretations Of Everyday Events

As explained in chapter 1, thinking is largely a matter of self-talk. People talk to themselves, inside, all the time, silently telling themselves things about themselves and their world. This is the outcome of a developmental process that takes place over a number of years. Because people are such creatures of habit, they consistently respond to and interpret situations in particular ways. Sometimes, unknown to themselves, people get into the habit of consistently *misinterpreting* situations—of seeing everything in exaggerated, anxiety-provoking, pessimistic, or depressing ways. There can also be isolated bad days in an overall happy existence. Such days are often caused by the person deciding early on that "its going to be one of those days," effectively adopting a negative cognitive set, and then fulfilling the prophecy.

A substantial body of research over the last 15 years has highlighted the degree to which people are creators of their own moods and feelings (Beck, 1976; De Rubeis & Beck, 1988; Meichenbaum, 1977). A look at the "alphabet of the mind" will illustrate. This alphabet consists of just three letters; A, B, and C. "A" stands for Antecedent—an event; "B" for Blob or Blank—thoughts; and "C" for Consequence—mood and feelings. When something happens (A), people often find themselves in poor or low spirits (C) later, and do not know why. Changes of humor or mood often seem to "just happen." Joe saw an old friend this afternoon (A), and is now feeling miserable (C). What he and people in general are unaware of is the thinking, the self-talk (B), that takes place between (A) and (C).

For example, seeing an old friend might, under review, have elicited the following sequence of thoughts: "If I greet Dave, he may not remember me. . . . he may snub me . . . it's been so long. . . . we won't have anything in common. It won't be like old times. Anyway, he looks as young as ever, and I have put on so much weight. He looks as if he has done well, too; that's an expensive suit. Gee, they were such great times . . ." It is the *thoughts* that evoke the sad feelings. There is nothing inevitable about seeing an old friend and feeling sad.

Take the other side of the coin: Dave is standing in line at the bank, and a neighbor walks by. She looks straight at him but does not say hello. He is surprised and feels like going after her, but he does not want to lose his place in the line. On the way home, he turns the incident over in his mind: "She can't not have seen me; why did she snub me? Maybe she has heard some gossip about me . . . Maybe there is some rumor going around about me. Why didn't I go after her and question her? Oh yes, I was in line . . . but maybe I was just afraid to? Come to think of it, I am not very assertive with people. What would I have said? I find it hard enough to make small talk. Maybe she sees through me . . . or thinks I am boring . . . maybe she always has. Maybe *everyone* thinks I am just a jerk. I am not even worth stopping to say hello to . . . Gee, I'm really fed up."

Granted, this is an exaggerated example. But the point again is that *between* an event and a change in mood there is always a train of thoughts. These thoughts flow so quickly and silently that people are generally unaware of them and suddenly find themselves angry or upset. Let's call the event (old friend passing by) A; the train of thoughts (did not see me . . . snubbed me . . . rumor . . . unassertive . . . difficulty with small talk . . .) B; and the resulting mood (fed up) C. Dave would generally be unaware of the train of thoughts between A and C; but finds that his humor has changed, and he does not know why. If he examined the thought sequence, he would see that he has jumped to several conclusions on the basis of little or no evidence. Each conclusion has led to further jumps. His day is ruined. He is angry and upset, because an old friend had things on her mind and did not want to stop and chat, or forgot to put in her contact lenses and did not even see him. It sounds ridiculous, but it happens all the time.

Things people say and do can be interpreted in any number of ways. How often has an innocent remark made by a colleague or friend put you in a bad mood? It is not the remark, but the thoughts (B) that *follow* the remark that determine the outcome: "Why did my husband offer, out of the blue, to cook dinner tonight? Does he think my cooking is getting boring? Come to think of it, I have not tried out any new recipes in a long time. But then, he has been working late so much, and eating out in all those fancy restaurants . . . I can't keep up . . . And he always seems to have so much energy. He is in particularly good form these days . . . despite the late hours. His new secretary has relieved him of a lot of the pressure and frustration. He said she is really efficient and nice . . ." (B). Gloom (C).

Unfortunately, people can get into the bad habit of *consistently* misinterpreting situations, reading too much into things, and putting themselves and others down in the process. Aaron Beck, a well-known American psychiatrist, has listed a number of these "cognitive distortions", or common ways in which people distort their reality and thereby create more stress for themselves (Beck, 1976).

Over Generalization.   Here, the individual draws some general conclusion as a result of one or a few isolated incidents. The conclusion is then applied across the board to similar or even dissimilar circumstances; for example, responding to a friend who is apparently ignoring you, or not saying hello, by concluding that people in general find you boring.

Selective Abstraction.   This error in thinking involves concentrating on some detail, taken out of context, while concurrently ignoring more conspicuous features of an event. The experience is conceptualized on the basis of this detail; for example, burning the toast and concluding that the whole day is going to be disastrous, while ignoring the fact that you are up early and showered, have a pot of fresh coffee brewing, and have just received a very gratifying letter from an old friend.

Arbitrary Inference.   Here, the individual makes a specific inference in the absence of evidence to support the conclusion. The evidence may even be to the contrary; for example, concluding that because your partner did not kiss you on arriving home this evening, he does not love you anymore— despite the fact that he was laden down with the week's groceries and a large bouquet of flowers, both of which he had planned as a surprise.

Magnification.   This type of distortion can be seen when the individual grossly magnifies and gives excessive prominence to *one* aspect of an event. For example, a minor error in your work is interpreted as an indication that you are beginning to show signs of age or stress and, furthermore, that the consequences of the error will be enormous.

Minimization. Here, the individual distorts the significance of an event by grossly playing down it's importance. For example, you are the only one to pass an examination or to be singled out for praise, and you conclude that it was nothing, just luck or a fluke.

Dichotomous Thinking. Here, all experiences are placed in one of two categories: impeccable or defective, brilliant or crass. Usually the individual classifies himself in the most negative way. For example, thinking back over a social occasion, you conclude that everyone else was sophisticated, well groomed, and witty, whereas you were out of your depth in all these ways.

Personalization. This type of cognitive distortion refers to the proclivity to associate various external events, especially negative ones, to oneself, when there is no rational basis on which to make such a judgment. For example, you feel personally responsible for the fact that a dinner party that you attended in a *friend's* house did not go well.

Misinterpretation of any *one* situation can involve a number of these distortions; and *hundreds* of minor events and situations constitute an average day. Consequently, the more that people misinterpret, the more they set themselves up for further misinterpretations. The ensuing mood and behavioral spiral can either plummet into feelings of depression or accelerate into high anxiety and tension.

Finally, it is important to point out that, although most people respond to situations with a sequence of thoughts or self-talk, some respond with *visual images.* For example, one woman, listening to a radio report of a traffic accident involving a bus, realized, in retrospect, that she had been panic-stricken at the time because what had gone through her head was: "Oh, my God, that could be my children's school bus; it was their route home." Another person, with a similar panic reaction to the *same* news might remember vivid *images* of the school bus toppling over a ravine at the side of the road and of her children lying motionless in a pool of blood. Images can be even more upsetting and emotion-provoking than self-talk. It is always important, therefore, when discussing emotion-laden material with clients, to establish whether they experience and remember things in pictures and images or in words. Many people report experiencing *both* (Lazarus, 1984; Tower & Singer, 1981).

Erroneous and Maladaptive Beliefs

Albert Ellis, another well-known American psychologist, and founder of *rational emotive therapy,* maintains that in the course of growing up in Western society, many people develop a set of ideas that are, in fact, irrational. These beliefs result in perfectionistic and overly judgmental thinking.

This, in turn, leads to unrealistic expectations of oneself and others and, in turn, to emotional experiences such as frustration, anger, disappointment, and guilt.

According to Ellis (1962), these commonly held but irrational beliefs are as follows:

1. The idea that it is a dire necessity for an adult human being to be loved, or approved of, by virtually every other significant person in his or her community.
2. The idea that one should be thoroughly competent, adequate, and achieving in all possible areas if one is to consider oneself worthwhile.
3. The idea that certain people are bad, wicked, or villainous, and they should be severely blamed and punished for their villainy.
4. The idea that it is awful and catastrophic when things are not the way one would very much like them to be.
5. The idea that human unhappiness is externally caused and that people have little or no ability to control their sorrows and disturbances.
6. The idea that if something is, or may be, dangerous or fearsome, that one should be terribly concerned about it and should keep dwelling on the possibility of it occurring.
7. The idea that it is easier to avoid than to face certain life difficulties or responsibilities.
8. The idea that one should be dependent on others and need someone stronger than oneself on whom to rely.
9. The idea that one's past history is an all-important determinant of one's present behavior and that because something has strongly affected one's life, it should indefinitely have a similar effect.
10. The idea that one should become quite upset at other people's problems and disturbances.
11. The idea that there is invariably a right, precise, and perfect solution to human problems and that it is catastrophic if the correct solution is not found.

Ellis suggested that the *degree* to which a person tends to label situations in accordance with one or more of these irrational beliefs will determine maladaptive behavioral and emotional responses.

This may all sound a bit exaggerated. Most people do not immediately see themselves in these examples at all. This is not surprising, as people do not go around *consciously* telling themselves such extreme things. The point is, however, that because of the overlearned, automatic nature of such beliefs, people *do,* in fact, switch on such silent "tapes" in many everyday situations.

These extreme beliefs, of which they are unaware, often underlie their reactions; they are at the root of many emotional responses, experiences, and, particularly, overreactions. In other words, although they may seem extreme and unfamiliar, in many cases, such beliefs are found nestling there, below the surface. Frequently, when uncovered, people's underlying beliefs can be surprisingly extreme, rigid, and maladaptive.

All of this will become more plausible after taking a look at some commonly held ideas and tendencies, which are, in fact, just less extreme versions of the preceding beliefs:

The Myth of Happiness. This is the widely held idea that one *should* be happy all the time; and, if not, there is something wrong. Basically, people put the best face forward. They try to at least *look* as if they are enjoying themselves at a party, because everyone else seems to be. If a friend approaches and says, "Hi, how are you doing?," they probably smile and say, "Great, I'm doing just fine." In this way, everyone meets smiling faces, so everyone is inclined, understandably, to believe that everyone *else* is happier than they. Have you ever observed someone in apparently fine spirits, to discover later that they were feeling awful at the time? How often has a friend come smiling into your room, only to later reveal the saddest of personal problems or conflicts and to seek your advice?

As a consequence, many people believe that they *should* be happy all the time, because everybody else seems to be. This can lead to a futile search for constant happiness. I say "futile" because happiness means different things to different people; but, more importantly, because a certain amount of pain, disappointment, frustration, and despair is an inevitable part of life and must be accepted as such (Lazarus, 1985). Indeed, it is the very element of spontaneity and unpredictability—the unexpected character of happy moments—that gives life its spice.

Happiness is always a transitory experience. Efforts to make it endure or to pursue it as a goal in living only result in disappointment and frustration. Even in moments of real happiness many people worry about losing it—the "this is too good to be true" feeling. It is already gone. Similarly, people blame themselves for not being able to attain what is unattainable or to avoid what is unavoidable—all of which leaves them stressed, frustrated, and *unhappy*. Happiness comes with an understanding of oneself and one's limitations. It comes with the feelings of self-confidence and self-efficacy that result from developing a set of personal coping skills for dealing with the inevitable stresses and changes of life.

Assumed Similarity. This is the tendency to assume that other people do, or should, see the world and respond to it in the same way as oneself (Ross, Greene, & House, 1977). This belief can lead to many problems, particularly in the area of interpersonal relationships. For example, A might find it impossible to believe that B really does prefer to stay in at night, rather than going out on the town. B wonders why A cannot appreciate the peace and privacy of home, instead of having to constantly socialize. Problems arise when either party *goes on* to infer that the other is deficient in some way, that they are just being selfish, *or* that, with some gentle persuasion, they will "see the light" and change. People are very different. Everyone has their own habits and preferences, their personal view of the world. Fortunately, different things appeal to different people. However, the tendency to assume similarity is very strong, and it can create havoc in otherwise promising relationships and friendships.

Explanatory Attributions.   People try to make sense of their world. They try to understand the causes of their behavior, as well as the behavior of others. But, research has shown that the ways in which people explain the behavior of *others* is very different from the ways in which they explain their own behavior. People think of their own behavior in terms of immediate circumstances—what was going on at the time—whereas they explain the behavior of others in terms of ongoing characteristics, traits, and attributes (Jones & Nisbett, 1971). Imagine, for example, that you have a disagreement with a friend or partner. In thinking it over, you might conclude that: "He's *always* in a bad mood; and anyway, he's very insensitive and unreliable." You, on the other hand, had a headache *at the time,* and only said the things you said on provocation.

Viewing other's behavior as arising from traits and attributes can result in feelings of anger and resentment. It can put you on the boil for hours and may also make you touchy with other people you come into contact with in the course of the day. If, later, you both sit down and discuss the incident, explanations usually make both parties realize that the other's behavior was also surrounded by a whole web of circumstance. You both immediately feel forgiving, because you now understand. However, besides all the time that was wasted in disagreeing and making up, you may now also feel guilty about the things you thought. You may have criticized the other person to friends and regret this also. Your work for the day may have suffered, and you may well have made others suffer too.

The Myth of Unchangeability.   This is the belief that people cannot change, that lifelong patterns of behavior and thinking are laid down in early childhood. If this were the case, there would be no point in writing a book such as this or in attempting to understand people's problems in order to help them make the necessary changes. Childhood *is* extremely important, but recent research has shown that children are psychologically far hardier and more adaptable than used to be believed. They can accommodate, without great trauma, to large changes in their psychosocial world (Clarke & Clarke, 1976). In the same way, adults also have a capacity to institute changes in their lifestyle and thinking right into old age. For example, a middle-aged businessman whose diary is always crammed with engagements, who walks only as far as his car, and overindulges in food, alcohol, and tobacco gets a serious health warning—the distinct possibility of a coronary—unless he changes his lifestyle. Within a month or two, he has pruned his commitments, taken up sports, cut down on his intake of unhealthy substances, and feels like "a different person."

Why, then, do many people go on believing that change is impossible? Because, in many ways, it is a convenient belief. Firstly, change takes planning, effort, and time; and it is always easier to leave until tomorrow what does not have to be done today, especially if the task is unpleasant. Secondly, and more important, is the fact that changes, however small, are frightening; they carry a risk of failure, a threat to self-esteem. Furthermore, because people are such creatures of habit, they can only handle a small amount of change at any time. Before moving house, changing job, or even hairstyle, there is always a moment when the little voice in one's head pleads to stick with the familiar, the well tried and tested. Finally, the belief in unchangeability provides a plausible way out of many situations; people blame laziness, overtiredness, overeating—indeed, almost any bad habit—on things that happened in the dim and distant past or on their genetic inheritance. Phrases like "it's in the blood" or "it runs in the family" are used as passports to total inertia or decadence. What determines change does not run in the family nor does it reside in the past. It lies in one's approach to change itself, and in one's belief in oneself.

Those are four commonly held beliefs and tendencies. Most people, on some level, believe and operate as if they *should* be happy all the time, and that others *should* have the same likes, dislikes, beliefs, and values as them. Furthermore, they tend to forget that other people's behavior also occurs in a web of personal circumstances and does not just spring from inflexible traits; and consequently, that they are also capable of personal change.

So, if these ongoing beliefs, like the more extreme listing of Ellis, serve only to color (and often to distort) people's perceptions of other people and events *and* their enjoyment of life, why are they so prevalent? As explained in chapter 1, people need to use strategies to make sense of their own behavior and that of others; hence, the tendency to assume similarity and to explain other's behavior in simple, global terms. People also have a need to feel secure and in control of their lives, to be understood, approved of, and loved by others. This provides them with a sense of self-esteem, or self-worth and self-confidence; hence, the search for happiness and the reluctance to change.

SUGGESTED FURTHER READING

Theory and Research

Anderson, M. P. (1980). Imaginal processes: Therapeutic applications and theoretical models. In M. J. Mahoney (Ed.), *Psychotherapy process: Current issues and future directions* (pp. 211–248). NY: Plenum Press.

Bandura, A. (1985). Model of casuality in social learning theory. In M. J. Mahoney & A. Freeman (Eds.), *Cognition and psychotherapy* (pp. 81–99). NY: Plenum Press.

Bandura, A. (1986). *Social foundations of thought and action: A social-cognitive theory.* Engelwood Cliffs, NJ: Prentice-Hall.

Cohen, S., & Syme, L. (1985). *Social support and health.* NY: Academic Press.

Compass, B. E. (1987). Stress and life events during childhood and adolescence. *Clinical Psychology Review, 7,* 275–302.

Cronkite, R. C., & Moos, R. H. (1984). The role of predisposing and moderating factors in the stress-illness relationship. *Journal of Health and Social Behavior, 25,* 372–393.

Dryden, W., & Ellis, A. (1988). Rational-emotive therapy. In K. Dobson (Ed.), *Handbook of cognitive-behavioral therapies* (pp. 214–272.). NY: Guilford.

Goldfried, M. R. (1980). Psychotherapy as coping skills training. In M. J. Mahoney (Ed.), *Psychotherapy process* (pp. 89–119). NY: Plenum Press.

Harvey, J. H., & Galvin, K. S. (1984). Clinical implications of attribution theory and research. *Clinical Psychology Review, 4,* 15–33.

Harvey, J. H., Ickes, W. J., & Kidd, R. F. (Eds.). (1976–1981). *New directions in attribution research* (Vols. 1–3). Hillsdale, NJ: Lawrence Erlbaum Associates.

Holahan, C. J. & Moos, R. H. (1987). The personal and contextual determinants of coping strategies. *Journal of Personality and Social Psychology, 52,* 946–955.

Le Bovits, A. H., Baum, A., & Singer, J. (Eds.). (1986). *Advances in environmental psychology (Vol. 6): Exposure to hazardous substances.* Hillsdale, NJ: Lawrence Erlbaum Associates.

Meichenbaum, D. (1977). *Cognitive behavior modification* NY: Plenum Press.

Meichenbaum, D. & Jaremko, M. (Eds.). (1983). *Stress management and prevention: A cognitive-behavioral perspective.* NY: Plenum Press.

Miller, S. A. (Ed.). (1981). *Nutrition and behavior.* Hillsdale, NJ: Lawrence Erlbaum Associates.

Nicholson, J. (1978). *Habits: Why you do what you do.* London: Pan Books.

Paykel, E. S. (1978). Contribution of life events to the causation of psychosomatic illness. *Psychological Medicine, 8,* 245–253.

Rachman, S. (Ed.). (1978). Perceived self-efficacy: Analysis of Bandura's theory of behavioral change (Special Volume). *Advances in Behavioral Research and Therapy, 1,* 137–269.

Schradle, S. B., & Dougher, M. (1985). Social supports as a mediator of stress: Theoretical and empirical issues. *Clinical Psychology Review, 5,* 641–661.

Schulberg, H. C. & McClelland, M. (1987). Depression and physical illness: The prevalence, causation, and diagnosis of co-morbidity. *Clinical Psychology Review, 7,* 145–167.

Skinner, B. F. (1972). *Beyond freedom and dignity.* London: Jonathan Cape Ltd.

Smith, T. W. (1982). Irrational beliefs in the cause and treatment of emotional distress: A critical review of the rational-emotive model. *Clinical Psychology Review, 2,* 505–522.

Waksman, S. A. (1983). Diet and childrens behavior disorders: A review of the research. *Clinical Psychology Review, 3,* 201–214.

Whitney Peterson, L. & Knapp, T. J. (1980). Biomedical and health factors in psychotherapy. In M. J. Mahoney (Ed.), *Psychotherapy process: Current issues and future directions* (pp. 255–277). NY: Plenum Press.

Zastrow, C. (1979). *Talk to yourself.* Englewood Cliffs, NJ: Prentice-Hall.

Zimmerman, M. (1983). Methodological issues in the assessment of life events: A review of issues and research. *Clinical Psychology Review, 3,* 339–370.

3

The Stress Response

Problems, pressures, surprises, and disappointments are an inevitable part of life. Consequently, in the course of evolution, man developed a mechanism to help out in adversity. This is called the "fight or flight" response. Effectively, it is an inbuilt coping kit that automatically comes into operation in times of pressure and emergency. It makes people function, *temporarily,* even more effectively and efficiently than they normally would in all three areas of functioning—physical, behavioral, and cognitive.

THE NORMAL STRESS RESPONSE

The *body* automatically musters up its resources and works to it's own advantage when the sudden need arises. Bodily reactions to stress are complex, and they involve the autonomic part of the nervous system. A hormone called *adrenalin* is produced by the adrenal glands. This acts on the muscles, blood vessels, skin, sweat glands, and the digestive system and prepares the body for "fight or flight." Adrenalin makes the muscles relax in order to facilitate the flow of blood to them, because they require more blood than usual for action. To compensate for this extra blood supply to the muscles, blood vessels in other areas are constricted—thus, the pale face of the stressed person. There is also increased pressure on the body's pump, the heart; so the heart rate is increased. This, in turn, creates a greater need for oxygen, and breathing therefore becomes more rapid. All this autonomic activity results in a depletion of the body's water supply; people perspire when under pressure (e.g., sweaty palms) and when cooling down after action. Water is drawn from other parts of the body, the most familiar consequence being a dry mouth. Everyone has experienced some or all of these symptoms when surprised, frightened, or in an emergency. These reactions are *normal* and they help people cope with the inevitable stresses of life.

On a *behavioral,* or motor level, pressure makes people "get their act together" more quickly and efficiently than they normally would. They respond more vigorously and adeptly. If, for example, you had to prepare a meal for eight people at very short notice, you might find yourself skillfully and purposefully moving around the kitchen, chopping vegetables, preparing the table, stirring pots, watching pans, and perhaps listening to the radio in the background—all your actions being comfortably coordinated.

On a *cognitive* level, the same applies. In the short term, there is an increase in speed and efficiency. In a crisis situation, for example, people can find themselves surprisingly calm, their thoughts efficiently and quickly guiding the appropriate coping responses, for example, "phone police," "don't touch anything," "take exact time." Likewise, when well-prepared at a pressurized interview, people find that they can think clearly and quickly, all the relevant facts and figures springing to mind. They can take in details of the interviewers and the immediate surroundings, and even anticipate questions. All their mental gears are working in harmony.

Up to a certain point, then, pressure improves one's performance on all levels. Behavior is speedy and coordinated, the mind is quick and alert, and the body works in synchrony. This is what is *meant* to happen. This mechanism is what has helped people survive and evolve in as comfortable and dignified a fashion as possible. However, when people are under too much pressure for too long—be it in a particular, isolated situation, or on an ongoing basis—this healthy, adaptive short-term coping response is just not enough. At this point, it can, in fact, work to one's disadvantage. It can become problematic and self-defeating.

THE PROBLEMATIC STRESS RESPONSE

The Body

If the body is under excessive or chronic strain, the normal adaptive response can become a problem in itself. There can be uncomfortable and unpredictable outbursts of autonomic activity, such as heart palpitations or shortness of breath, occurring out of context or out of proportion to the situation or triggering event. The most extreme example is a "panic attack," where, suddenly and for no apparent reason, the heart begins to pound, the person starts to perspire and perhaps shake, the chest feels tight, and there is usually a desire to run, although legs can also feel weak (see chapter 4). Likewise, when people are under prolonged pressure, they can get to a point where they feel constantly or chronically anxious and stressed and find it hard to relax in almost any situation. People vary enormously in the sensitivity and reactivity of their bodies. Some labile people, the very minute they receive unexpected news (good *or* bad) can get a headache, lose their appetite, or feel queasy. Others get physically wound up only in *particular* situations; shy people can find themselves blushing or trembling in social situations that, to others, are enjoyable recreations. Some people dread the idea of speaking in public or asking questions in class or at a board meeting, for fear that their voice will quiver or that their heart will pound so furiously everyone will hear.

The most immediate, and commonly recognized, reaction of the body to pressure, is, as described, to "wind up." There is, however, another side to the coin. Some people "wind down." This *can* occur as a consequence of the physical neglect that sometimes accompanies stress; when people eat less, they lose weight with a concomitant loss of energy. However, when a person continues, unsuccessfully, to try to cope with what comes to be construed as a hopeless life situation, depression can also set in. Lack of energy, little appetite for food or sex, and sleep disturbances are some of the ways in which the body slows down, signaling that it has had enough (see chapter 5).

Looking at the body's response to stress in a wider context, it is now recognized that if people are subjected to prolonged or excessive stress, there can be significant consequences for *general health* (Ader, 1980; De Longis et al., 1982; Verbrugge, 1976). Prolonged stress considerably increases the risk of developing a number of serious diseases, such as colitis, arthritis, and heart disease. Ulcers, migraine and tension headaches, asthma, backaches, and constipation are also stress-related. There is also another, less direct connection between physical health and stress. Stress interferes with the efficient functioning of the immune system, lowering the body's resistance to infection and thereby increasing susceptibility to many common physical ailments (Fabris, Garcia, Hadden, & Mitchinson, 1983; Jemmott & Locke, 1984; Woolfolk & Richardson, 1978). You may have noticed that people tend to get colds or flu when they are already under pressure. "Now, of all times, I get the flu," we hear; it is no coincidence.

Finally, unresolved stress can lead to drug-taking of various kinds. For many, this is self-prescribed, in the form of tobacco, alcohol, and other mood-altering drugs such as cocaine and "crack." For others, it is tranquilizing drugs, such as those prescribed by their general practitioner. As well as coping with the inevitable plummet to reality when the effects wear off *and* the expense of an increasing tolerance, drugs can also take their toll on the body. The relationship between cigarette smoking and increased risk of lung cancer is well established, but drugs have numerous less obvious effects on brain tissue and general health. As described in chapter 2, cocaine—besides being the most potent of the widely used anxiety-producing drugs—can also cause panic attacks. At the very least, drugs deplete the system of vital energy. Even the theoretically "safe" (i.e., prescribed) drugs can lead to over-dependence and abuse, as well as to vitamin deficiency (see Shiffman & Wills, 1985).

Behavior

If, while preparing for the unexpected dinner guests, the phone rings again to say they will be there, not in 30 minutes but in 10, what happens? Panic. There is just not enough time. "How typical and inconsiderate. What will they think of me? I look a mess." Suddenly, the pans all start to boil at the same time, the oven timer buzzes, the telephone rings again, the radio starts to blare, and the carving knife slices silently into one's finger, sending a trickle of the most visible red onto the newly laundered white linen table cloth. In other words, if the pressure is too intense, the adaptive coping mechanism simply breaks down. People become fussed, flustered, and clumsy; their movements lack coordination and effectiveness. In short, every-thing seems to fall apart.

This is one isolated incident. What happens when a person is pressur-ized—from business, an upcoming evaluation or exam, or a bad relation-ship—over an extended period of time? Here, the situation is more complex. As with the physical reactions to stress that have already been described, many people have a tendency to "wind up." They do more of everything. They find that they cannot sit still. They are restless and uncomfortable unless occupied, whether at home or at work. This usually leads to overdoing things and to genuine tiredness and exhaustion. "Nervous energy" contains no magic ingredient; a tired body and brain do not function to capacity. Others eat more, drink more, or smoke more than usual, and this can compound their stress by overspending money or adding extra pounds to the body. Others go out more, socializing, in an effort to take their mind off things, and this can result in increased spending, as well as late nights and loss of sleep.

On the other hand, some people find themselves slowing down, even grinding to a halt. There is a decrease in the usual activity level, which in turn effects some or all areas of living. If the energy and enthusiasm to do things is just not there, work piles up, and this adds to the feelings of pressure and helplessness. Sometimes, ordinarily gregarious people find themselves making excuses not to go out; they avoid social activities and curtail outside contact to a minimum. Some find that they are eating less or have no appetite for the usual beer or cigarette, for exercise or sex. For many, also, sleep can become a problem—waking very early in the morning, tired but unable to go back to sleep.

These are *general* descriptions of how people respond to stress, in terms of changes in behavior and activity level. What, in fact, happens in the *individual* case, as with the body, is that personal weak spots and vulnerabilities are highlighted and exacerbated. The people who *generally* find social situations difficult now find them impossible. People who have problems with decision making and problem solving now find themselves in a panic when faced with the smallest decision. The poor time-keepers and money-managers are totally overwhelmed. Anything that *normally* makes a person anxious or nervous will do so now to a much greater extent. Advoidance behavior increases accordingly. Likewise, people who tend to overeat find themselves bingeing too frequently; the same goes for the smokers and drinkers. The conscientious workers stay later than ever in the office. The perfectionists become unraveled and panicky as they feel time closing in on them. Sensitive people can be moved to tears by a sentimental movie or an evocative piece of music, or get overly upset by some minor tragedy in the news.

The Mind

Under a certain amount of pressure, the mind is equipped to cope. People function more effectively than usual; thinking is quick and clear. Under excessive or prolonged pressure, however, people can experience any of a number of disconcerting stress symptoms. Many complain of not being able to think straight, concentrate, or recall even familiar names or telephone numbers. Others find it hard to follow conversations or to remember what was said 5 minutes earlier, or the details of a television program seen the previous evening. Even efforts to read can result in distress; getting to the end of a page and realizing that nothing has been retained. Others find themselves going "blank," or feeling strangely distant from things, as if in a trance or a daze, or "in another world." Understandably, people often worry that there may be something physically wrong—a brain tumor or dementia—that is interfering with their thinking; and *this* is not a cheering thought.

These are, in fact, all examples of the mind's reactions to excessive stress. Unlike physical and behavioral tendencies to wind up, the mind tends to wind down, or, more appropriately, to slow down. If people try to sort through too much growing confusion over too long a period of time, they get to a point where they just cannot take in any more. It may help to think of the mind as a vessel, normally half full of thoughts about everyday things ("Must go to the bank", "Hope Bob calls."). The other half attends to all that is happening around it in the outside world—what a friend is saying, that he is wearing a new shirt, that it looks as if it may rain, *and* the really sexy woman who just wafted by. When people are worried, tired, stressed, or overstretched, they simply do not have this extra space, this openness to attend to the outside world. They are engrossed in other things and in themselves. This is the real meaning of being "preoccupied." Furthermore, a mind "full of care" cannot sort through all that is in there with the same speed as usual. Thinking and mental reactions are slower, and, frequently, this is obvious to others. "What's wrong with Dave? He left his cash card in the machine, and then he nearly walked out in front of a bus."

There are also people who, when under pressure, experience an *increase* in cognitive activity, similar to that described of body and behavioral reactions. These people lie awake at night, going over and over things that happened during the day, or perhaps a long time ago. They worry in advance about possible mishaps the next day or in the distant future. Such ruminations can seriously interfere with sleep, and let little concerns grow totally out of proportion. Some find it impossible to switch off during the day, either, repeatedly thinking over a problem or worrying excessively about a job in hand—which further effects their work perfor- mance and concentration. One client said that he felt his mind was like a slave driver, urging him to complete things that realistically would have been best left until the following day.

As well as the wind-ups and slow-downs, there is another very important aspect of the cognitive response to stress. When under pressure, people are much more likely to *misperceive* and *misconstrue* situations and to *misinterpret* the remarks of others—in effect, to distort their experiences in various ways and to varying degrees. Here, I refer to the cognitive distortions discussed in chapter 2. When under pressure, tendencies to exaggerate, personalize, and overgeneralize all increase. A person who is normally in- clined to look on the gloomy side of things might become thoroughly depressed after hearing news of price increases on the radio: "Soon we won't even be able to run the car . . . I can see us all starving." Someone with a tendency to exaggerate might, when already stressed, become completely panicked by the arrival of two regular bills in the mail: "This afternoon there will be *more,* and tomorrow *more.* Where will the money come from? We will have to go into debt . . . deeper and deeper into debt." When under pressure, people in general are more likely to misperceive and distort events, thereby adding to the stress spiral. However, the exaggerated response of the cognitively vulnerable person under pressure can make things a thousand times more stressful a thousand times a day.

Finally, just as people "tighten their belts" when times are tough, they similarly tighten their beliefs when under pressure. You may have noticed how people in disagreement become progressively more rigid and dogmatic the more prolonged and heated the debate. They narrow their conceptual goggles. Opinions become facts; requests become demands; suggestions become orders. "Shoulds" and "musts" outnumber "coulds" and "mights." "Sometimes" becomes "always" or "never." Occasional behaviors become traits; the world is seen in black and white. There is no room for other people's points of view. They are "wrong." Furthermore, there are often excessive, and sometimes offensive, efforts to clarify and establish one's own views and then to impose them on others. These are, in effect, desperate attempts to secure personal validation, which, however temporary, provides a fragile sense of control and efficacy.

People need to make sense of their world. At times of stress, things often (correctly) appear to be unraveling. Ambiguity generates more anxiety; clarity generates security. People under pressure, therefore, cling rigidly to the familiar, well tested and well known. Change presents a threat. The unpredictability of other people's actions and demands becomes more and more frightening. Not surprisingly, stressed people find themselves getting *into* disagreements more frequently than they normally would; so their existence becomes more and more stressful. People under prolonged pressure, therefore, become progressively more inflexible and unapproachable. Furthermore, realizing that they are not happy, that things have changed, makes them even more unhappy. Other people are not behaving as they expect or wish; and this can make them feel powerless and isolated, or angry and resentful. Everyone suddenly seems to be turning out to be selfish and insensitive: "Can't he see the situation I'm in? Why am *I* always expected to change and compromise? What's wrong with everyone?"

MIND, BODY, AND BEHAVIOR

People function on three different levels—physical, behavioral, and cognitive. So far, each system has been dealt with separately, for the sake of clarity. But, in reality, they do not operate in isolation. People interact with the world constantly on all levels; and consequently, if a problem arises in one area, it can quickly effect functioning in the other two, and in one's relationship with the outside world. Theoretical questions concerning these interactions and, specifically, as to the *primary* of thought, action, or affect, have become a source of major controversy in recent years (R. Lazarus, 1982, 1984b; Zajonc, 1980, 1984); the debate continues.

What we know is that, on a day-to-day basis, these three systems are not perfectly correlated; they do not work in complete harmony (Hugdahl, 1981; Lang, 1968). For example, a person can be very "wound up" on a physical level and *feel* extremely tense and anxious while *behaving* efficiently and *thinking* quite clearly. Furthermore, although everyone experiences and responds to the world in these three ways, there are large individual differences

in modes of response. Some people, when stressed, consistently have difficulty in getting their thoughts together, or can feel like running—but do not
experience any uncomfortable physical symptoms, for example. Another
person might feel physically like a time bomb, but, at the same time, be able
to think clearly and get on with their work. In other words, people have
characteristic *ways* of responding to stress. Some people are more physical,
whereas others are more cognitive or behavioral.

Such habitual styles of response have nothing to do with intelligence or
background; nor do they result from conscious deliberations or choices.
People do not, for example, decide early on in life to have panic attacks,
rather than muzzy thoughts, when upsetting things occur. Response patterns
develop over time and reflect the individual's personal vulnerabilities and
unique learning experiences. These individual differences are extremely important in understanding both one's own patterns of stress response and
those of the people around one. It can be difficult, for example, for the type
of person who responds to stress by feeling ill or shaky, to understand
another person who complains of not being able to concentrate, think
straight, or get any work done; or yet another who rushes around doing
even *more* than usual while claiming to be so pressurized that he or she
cannot cope.

There are also large individual differences in people's *areas* of vulnerability. Some people develop fears and phobias, others get depressed, and yet
others turn to food or alcohol. These differences are related to the nature of
the stressor, but even more so to the individual's unique genetic make-
up, learning history, and experiences. What generally happens, as already
explained, is that existing tendencies to wind up or down—physically, behaviorally, or cognitively—come to the fore when under stress. A person who
tends to overindulge will be particularly likely to eat or drink to excess after
a shock, a disagreement, or when dissatisfied with a work situation, for
example. Someone who normally likes to keep her surroundings neat and
tidy, might find herself being excessively fussy at times when a relationship
is not going well or when worried about financial or marital prospects. A
person who normally has a tendency to err on the side of pessimism, might,
under pressure, react to bills, a slight weight increase, or an interpersonal
letdown as if it were the end of the world. A person with a sensitive stomach
might find that, coming up to exams or deadlines, they cannot eat or keep
food down at all. One such client said that he felt as if his stomach had been
invaded by an army of butterflies. Everyone has such weak spots, which can
give rise to problems, as well as greatly *adding* to the situation when pressure
is coming from other areas. Unfortunately, one of the most insidious aspects
of stress is its self-escalating nature. What starts off as a problem in one area
can quickly get lost in a web of confusion. Imagine, for example, that Barry
is preoccupied about his job. As a result, he is not great company, and even

puts people off by being uncharacteristically irritable or unduly reserved. Little support is offered from a spouse who has been embarrassed by a public outburst or retreat, which also caused upset for others. Marital and sexual relations then suffer. Preoccupation over this renders Barry even less efficient at work, which leads to financial losses and threats from a boss or partner. Because things at home are becoming more frosty, a habit of staying late at the office or going for a few beers sets in. This results in a neglect of eating and, subsequently, weight loss. He then feels even more tired, listless, and unhappy, as well as more vulnerable to illnesses, both major and minor. Tension headaches and stomach upsets perpetuate an increasingly stressful existence. Sensing that things are unravelling adds to the pressure and panic. Not feeling in control colors his perception and interpretation of situations, making him increasingly dogmatic and unreasonable, and so on.

Whether the initial *stressor* is an external event, ill health, or faulty behavior or thinking, and whether the initial problem *response* is physical, behavioral, or cognitive, it is in this way that problems gradually accumulate. They slowly grow and feed into one another in complex and subtle ways. The fact that people are such bad observers of themselves facilitates the process. Problems build up without their awareness. The time when they most need to take stock is when it is hardest to do so, because they are just too caught up in themselves.

When things finally do reach a level where a person can no longer cast a blind eye and is *forced*—by a boss, a massive panic attack, a significant weight change, or an exam failure, for example—to acknowledge that there is a problem and to take a look at things, it can be at a disaster area. Health, social relationships, and finances can all have taken a bruising. At this point, professional assistance, such as that of a clinical psychologist, is usually sought. The first step in helping any client to cope is to get them to simply *stop and think*. The next is to *define* exactly what is wrong, and to identify the problem or problems, and the sources of stress. The necessary changes then have to be carefully *planned*. This takes time and perseverance, but the skills acquired along the way serve for life.

SUGGESTED FURTHER READING

Theory And Research

Ader, R. (Ed.) (1981). *Psychoneuroimmunology*. NY: Academic Press.

Ader, R. (1985). Conditioned immunopharmacological effects in animals: Implications for a conditioning model of pharmacotherapy. In L. White, B. Tursey & G. E. Schwartz (Eds.) *Placebo: Theory, research, and mechanism* (pp. 316–320). NY: Guilford.

Baum, A. & Singer, J. E. (Eds.) (1987). *Handbook of psychology and health (Vol. 5): Stress*. Hillsdale, NJ: Lawrence Erlbaum Associates.

Beck, A. T. (1976). *Cognitive therapy and the emotional disorders.* NY: International Universities Press.

Beck, A. T. (1984). Cognitive approaches to stress. In R. Woolfolk & P. Lerner (Eds.), *Principles and practice of stress management* (pp. 255–305). NY: Guilford.

Beck, A. T. (1985). Cognitive therapy, behavior therapy, psychoanalysis and pharmacotherapy: A cognitive continuum. In M. J. Mahoney and A. Freeman (Eds.), *Cognition and psychotherapy* (pp. 325–347). NY: Plenum Press.

Beck, A. T. & Emery, G. (1985). *Anxiety disorders and phobias: A cognitive perspective.* NY: Basic Books.

Folkman, S. & Lazarus, R. S. (1982). Stress and coping theory applied to the investigation of mass industrial psychogenic illness. In M. J. Collingan, J. W. Pennebaker, & L. R. Murphy (Eds.), *Mass psychogenic illness: A social-psychological analysis* (pp. 237–255). Hillsdale, NJ: Lawrence Erlbaum Associates.

Glaser, R., Rice, J., Sheridan, J., Fertel, R., Stout, J., Speicher, C. E., Pinsky, D., Kotur, M., Post, A., Beck, M., & Kiecolt-Glaser, J. K. (1987). Stress-related immune suppression: Health implications. *Brain, Behavior, and Immunity, 1,* pp. 7–20.

Goldenberger, L. & Breznitz, S. (1982). *Handbook of stress: Theoretical and clinical aspects.* NY: The Free Press.

Greenberg, L. S. & Safran, J. D. (1987). *Emotion in psychotherapy.* NY: Guilford.

Greenberg, L. & Safran, J. (1984). Integrating affect and cognition: A perspective on the process of therapeutic change. *Cognitive Therapy and Research, 8,* 559–578.

Kiecolt-Glaser, J. K., & Glaser, R. (1988). Psychological influences on immunity: Implications for AIDS. *American Psychologist, 43,* pp. 892–898.

Kuiper, N. A. & MacDonald, M. R. (1983). Reason, emotion and cognitive therapy. *Clinical Psychology Review, 3,* 297–316.

Lerman, C. E. (1987). Rheumatoid arthritis: Psychological factors in etiology, course and treatment. *Clinical Psychology Review, 7,* 413–425.

Mandler, G. (1984). *Mind and body: Psychology of stress and emotion.* NY: W. W. Norton.

Rachman, S. (1981). The primacy of affect: Some theoretical implications. *Behavior Research and Therapy, 19,* 279–290.

Safran, J. D. & Greenberg, L. S. (1982). Cognitive appraisal and re-appraisal: Implications for clinical practice. *Cognitive Therapy and Research, 6,* 251–258.

Safran, J. D. & Greenberg, L. S. (1986). Hot cognitions and psychotherapy process: An information-processing, ecological approach. In P. C. Kendall (Ed.), *Advances in cognitive behavioral research and therapy* (Vol. 5, pp. 143–177). NY: Academic Press.

Sammons, M. T., & Karoly, P. (1987). Psychosocial variables in irritable bowel syndrome: A review and proposal. *Clinical Psychology Review, 7,* 187–201.

Woolfolk, R. L., & Richardson, F. C. (1978). *Stress, sanity and survival.* NY: New American Library.

Young, T. (1988). Substance use and abuse among native Americans. *Clinical Psychology Review, 8,* 125–138.

PART II
SPECIFIC PROBLEM AREAS

Anxiety, Fears, and Phobias

An event is said to be stressful if it poses "a real or perceived threat to a person,"—that is, when they feel unable to cope or that they are not in control. Stress is, and always has been, an integral part of living, one of the basic ingredients of life. For this reason, as already explained, man has developed an adaptive coping mechanism—the "fight or flight response"— to deal with these inevitable pressures and problems. Up to a certain point, stress adds a dash of spice to life. It keeps us on our toes. It makes people perform even more efficiently on all levels—physically, behaviorally, and cognitively.

What happens beyond this point, however, is not so desirable. Most people have experienced the discomfort—maybe even embarrassment—of a dry mouth, shaky voice, pounding heart, sweaty hands, or wobbly legs, at some time or another. Everyone knows what it is to be frightened or worried about something; the "something" can be concrete, like a bill or illness, or less tangible, like the anticipation of a future unpleasantness—an exam, interview, or work deadline, for example. People can even get worked up at the prospect of something pleasant, such as a wedding, party, or date. Likewise, everyone has spent the occasional night lying awake, thinking over and over something that happened during the day or that might happen in the future. Most people occasionally avoid things, places, or people that make them feel uncomfortable or nervous.

For many people, however, fear and anxiety are a major problem. A large number of research studies (of psychiatric populations, general medical practices, and community surveys) suggest that about one third of the adult population suffers constantly from nervous complaints, especially anxiety, and that about 5%, or 1 in 20, have a constitutional predisposition to anxiety (Lader, 1975). Fortunately, in *most* cases, nervous reactions and anxiety-related difficulties can be attributed to things *other* than constitutional factors, such as an inability to cope with an unconducive or threatening environment, an unhealthy lifestyle, bad habits, faulty learning, or distorted thinking. Generally speaking, anxiety is most common among women, the poor, and the aged, but the reasons for these trends are complex.

Anxiety is present in the mildest to the most severe emotional disturbances, from transient distress to mental illness. Consequently, fear and anxiety are present in all the major problems of living—fears and phobias, depression, obsessionality, interpersonal difficulties, marital and sexual problems, and problems of overindulgence. Five basic kinds of fear have been identified: fear of things and places, fear of internal fears (i.e., fear of bodily sensations of anxiety), fear of one's own thoughts, interpersonal and social fears, and derivative fears (i.e., fears and anxieties that arise as a result of other problems). This chapter focuses on the first two of these—fear of things and places (phobias) and fear of internal fears (agoraphobia). The remaining fears are dealt with in the following chapters, in the context of the other major problems of living.

FEARS AND PHOBIAS

When a person is fearful of something to an extent that would be generally regarded as out of proportion to the stimulus, they are said to be *phobic*. For example, one young man I treated was so afraid of dogs that it totally curtailed his social life and, eventually, his professional life. His fear was irrational.

Facts and Figures

The most common phobias and fears are of animals, heights, spiders, thunder, fire, darkness and night, noise, storms, and lightning. A fear of flying is also quite prevalent and can occur in experienced passengers and even crew members. People can also develop phobias about illness, disease, and death, and other bodily things, such as swallowing, blood, or medical procedures in general. I could also list snakes, enclosed spaces, water, dirt, cancer, fire, birds; suffice it to say that people can become phobic of almost anything, from flies to tomatoes. Basically, it is a fear of the potential of the object to harm one. The number of people who suffer from phobias to the extent that it interferes with their getting on with life is relatively few (about 8% of the population). However, there are many people who, although not clinically "phobic", fear certain ordinary things in their environment much more than they realistically should (Marks, 1969; Rachman, 1978a). The Fear Survey Schedule (see Table 4.1) was developed to measure responses to such commonly occurring fears.

Causes, Signs, and Symptoms

Seligman, an American psychologist, is of the opinion that humans have an in-built fear of certain things, for example, snakes; and that people are much more likely to develop phobias of these things (Seligman, 1971; Seligman & Hager, 1972). Be that as it may, the *main* way in which fears and phobias develop is through traumatic or faulty learning. As explained in chapter 1, we learn in three ways—by association, by consequence, and by observation. Fear can often be triggered by a single traumatic event or experience, such as being bitten by a dog or sexually assaulted. The anxiety so generated can then lead to avoidance of the same or similar objects, persons, or situations thereafter. Anxieties can also arise as a consequence of vicarious conditioning. In other words, people can become fearful of things through observation, without even being directly involved. Sometimes, because certain phobias run in families, it can look as if they are genetically transmitted—for example, if all the children in a family are afraid of birds. The more reasonable explanation is that children *learn* to be fearful of the same things as their parents are, by a process of association, reinforcement, and observation.

Physiological.   The physical symptoms of anxiety are dealt with in more detail in the following section on agoraphobia. The basic phobic response includes all the autonomic concomitants of anxiety, outlined in chapter 3—heart palpitations, muscular tension, shaking, blushing, trembling, perspiration, nausea, numbness, tingling in the hands and feet, a desire to urinate, and stomach upsets. These symptoms can occur not only in the presence of the feared object but also at the mere *thought* or anticipation of it. When people are in a constant or prolonged state of anxiety, sleep, appetite, and general health can suffer.

Behavioral.   The most immediate behavioral reaction is that of "flight," which, in time, can develop into an avoidance response. Avoidance is self-defeating, because it feeds the anxiety; the *temporary* relief that is experienced makes it more likely for the same and similar situations to be avoided again. People can get to a point where their whole life is tailored by their avoidance of an increasingly large number of everyday situations, objects, and events. Their social, emotional, and professional lives take the toll.

Cognitive.   There is a large cognitive component in phobic reactions because, objectively speaking, the stimulus or object of the fear is, to most other people, innocuous. It is what the source of the fear *means* to the

Below are 51 different stimuli which can cause fear in people. Please rate how much fear you feel using the following rating scale and record your answer in the space provided:

Table Key:

1 = None
5 = Much fear
2 = Very little fear
6 = Very much fear
3 = A little fear
7 = Terror
4 = Some fear

Table	4.1: Fear Survey Schedule			
__	1.	Sharp objects	__ 27.	Being with drunks
__	2.	Being a passenger in a car.	__ 28.	Illness or injury to loved ones
__	3.	Dead bodies	__ 29.	Being self-conscious
__	4.	Suffocating	__ 30.	Driving a car
__	5.	Failing a test	__ 31.	Meeting authority
__	6.	Looking foolish	__ 32.	Mental illness
__	7.	Being a passenger in an airplane	__ 33.	Closed places
__	8.	Worms	__ 34.	Boating
__	9.	Arguing with parents	__ 35.	Spiders
__	10.	Rats and mice	__ 36.	Thunderstorms
__	11.	Life after death	__ 37.	Not being a success
__	12.	Hypodermic needles	__ 38.	God
__	13.	Being criticized	__ 39.	Snakes
__	14.	Meeting someone for the first time	__ 40.	Cemetries
__	15.	Roller coasters	__ 41.	Speaking before a group
__	16.	Being alone	__ 42.	Seeing a fight
__	17.	Making mistakes	__ 43.	Death of a lovedone
__	18.	Being misunderstood	__ 44.	Dark places
__	19.	Death	__ 45.	Strange dogs
__	20.	Being in a fight	__ 46.	Deep water
__	21.	Crowded places	__ 47.	Being with a member of the opposite sex
__	22.	Blood.	__ 48	Stinging insects
__	23.	Heights	__ 49.	Untimely or early deaths
__	24.	Being a leader	__ 50.	Losing a job
__	25.	Swimming alone	__ 51.	Auto accidents
__	26.	Illness.		

person—their perception of the object or situation, and what they are saying to themselves about it—that keeps the anxiety alive: "It will bite me." "We are going to crash, I know we are." Unfortunately, such preoccupation makes it even more difficult for the individual to think straight, to concentrate, and to be objective. Likewise, many phobics experience vivid visual images of themselves in their feared situations—being savaged by a dog, surrounded by screaming people in a plummeting airplane, or going totally blank at an exam or interview. Such images can be even more disturbing and less easily dismissed than anxiety-provoking self-talk.

Treatment

The recognized treatment of choice for phobias is called *systematic desensitization*. It is one of a family of flexible exposure techniques for overcoming fears (see Appendix IV: Exposure). As with all the interventions described in later chapters, the therapist starts off with a thorough evaluation interview or *behavioral assessment*. When a clear picture of the problem has been formed—and this may take a couple of consultations—an assessment of the client's motivation to change is carried out (Appendix I: Motivation Analysis), after which the change plan is set up (see Appendix I: Change Plan).

The client's ongoing diary-keeping then provides detailed information about the situations in which the problem occurs and the degree of anxiety generated. It also gives the therapist a feel for the client's "life space" (Appendix I: Self-Monitoring Behavior). This information facilitates the construction of a realistic and personalized hierarchy of increasingly more anxiety-provoking situations. The person is then trained in deep muscular relaxation (Appendix III: Relaxation) and, over a number of therapy sessions, is systematically exposed to each item until the pinnacle of the hierarchy is reached. Systematic desensitization can be carried out in imagination (Appendix V: Desensitization in Imagination) but, more often, real-life, or *in vivo*, exposure is preferred (Appendix IV: Systematic Desensitization).

If, as with many phobias, part of the client's fear stems from ignorance (lack of information), he or she is supplied with reading material on the subject. For example, a thanatophobic—somebody who is phobic of thunder—might be supplied with easy-to-read literature about thunder and how harmless it really is. Children's books can be ideal in delivering simple facts in an unthreatening way.

As important as the behavioral part of the intervention is the cognitive part. From their diary-keeping, clients are taught to identify and then to dispute the validity of maladaptive, anxiety-provoking self-statements, which occur *during*, as well as *before* and *after*, exposure to their feared objects or situations: "I know it's going to bite me," "I escaped this time—next time I won't be so lucky." They gradually learn to replace their negative self-talk with a new, more objective internal dialogue, which they can then utilize *in* the feared situations. This effectively breaks the fear spiral by replacing negative thoughts with incompatible, realistic, and reassuring appraisals (Appendix V: Self-Disputation). Sometimes, underlying beliefs, such as, "Because I am afraid of dogs, I am inferior," also have to be uncovered and explored (Appendix V: Vertical Arrow). Finally, if the client's fear is generated and maintained by anticipatory visual images, strategies for dismissing and distracting have to be acquired (Appendix V: Distraction), as well as guidelines supplied on how to utilize their imaginal capacity as a general coping tool (Appendix V: Coping Imagery).

AGORAPHOBIA

Agoraphobia merits consideration in its own right, because it differs greatly from other fears and phobias. Unlike phobias of mice or spiders, where the fear is of the potential harm that the object causes, the fear in agoraphobia is of one's own internal feelings and body sensations—fear of (internal) fear.

Facts and Figures

The term *agoraphobia* comes from the Greek and may be translated *not* as a "fear of open spaces," as is often thought, but as "fear of the market place" (Marks, 1969). This is because agoraphobics fear crowded, public places from which they cannot easily escape if they feel panicky. People *can* also have panic attacks in large, empty places and open spaces, where they suddenly feel acutely self-conscious, exposed, and aware of themselves and of their heightened body sensations. In both cases, the person's focus of attention is on himself or herself, and more specifically, what is going on in his (or her) body.

In a panic attack, there is an intense outburst of autonomic activity, producing any number of symptoms, ranging from a rapidly pounding heart, "jelly" legs, sweaty palms, dry mouth, an inability to breathe, and dizziness. People typically report not being able to think straight and wanting to run. Panic attacks frequently occur unpredictably and out of context. They leave the person feeling physically drained and, understandably, confused about what has happened. Many worry that they have had a heart attack. There is also concern as to when the next attack will occur; and, in fact, this fear generally becomes a primary preoccupation. *Secondary anxiety,* or fear of panic, becomes integral to the problem itself and, thus, makes it *more* likely for another attack to occur. It can even unwittingly bring one on (Weekes, 1984).

Agoraphobia commonly begins in young adult life, between the ages of 18 and 35. It usually starts with a severe panic attack, which is then compounded by retrospective worry, apprehension, and fear of a second and third attack, and so on. There is often a gradual process of withdrawal from all places that are likely to induce panic. These are usually crowded places, like supermarkets and movie theaters, from which it is difficult to make a speedy and invisible exit. It is the *anticipatory anxiety* that leads to gradual withdrawal; people simply go out less and less. One client, when I first met her, had only gone as far as her front door to take in the newspaper in 20 years.

Agoraphobia is a common condition. In the United States and Great Britain, roughly 6 in every 1,000 people suffer from a severe form of it.

Many, although they never seek professional help, experience milder forms that can temporarily or permanently interfere with their lifestyle. Agoraphobic attacks can happen to almost anyone and are not related to intellectual ability, education, or socioeconomic status. Men and women get attacks with equal frequency, but they are more likely to *persist* in women. The percentage of people who consult professionals is heavily weighted towards females.

Causes, Signs, and Symptoms

Recent findings suggest that some people are genetically more predisposed to panic attacks than others. Furthermore, anxiety-producing drugs, such as cocaine, can produce panic attacks and lead to agoraphobic avoidance. Be that as it may, the first attack usually comes on during or after an episode of stress—a life event, an illness, or prolonged pressure—and is remembered clearly many years later. Some researchers suggest that the onset occurs in a climate of conflict, which is usually, but not necessarily, of an interpersonal nature (Goldstein & Chambless, 1978). There is frequently no *obvious* trigger for the first attack, which comes "out of the blue." The unpredictable nature of panic attacks is one of their most important features, because it induces feelings of vulnerability and of not being in control. People cannot tell when the next attack will occur, and this makes them feel helpless and frightened. Many understandably become overly self-vigilant, which produces a vicious and self-perpetuating cycle.

Physiological. The physical concomitants of panic attacks are their most significant aspect. There is a sudden, unexpected outburst of autonomic activity such as heart palpitations, rapid breathing, "air hunger," hot or cold flashes, dizziness, sweating, and trembling. Sometimes people feel that the pavement is coming up to meet them, or that they are falling backwards. The first attack usually comes on suddenly and does not last very long. Most panic attacks are over in a minute or two, but the person can remain in a heightened state of anxiety for hours. Panic attacks do not damage the system; they do not lead to heart attacks or weaken the heart, or induce strokes or epileptic fits. They *are,* however, extremely disturbing experiences, and they leave the person physically exhausted and psychologically drained. Fear of a repetition is therefore understandable. Unfortunately, people gradually become hypersensitized to their own body sensations—even to small changes in heart rate or breathing—which they then misinterpret as a sign of impending catastrophe (Beck & Emery, 1985).

Behavioral. The most immediate behavioral response to the sensations of panic is to run. This is why the security of home is so important to the agoraphobic person—it is often the one place in which they feel completely

safe. The usual pattern is one of gradual withdrawal and increasing avoidance of places where panic attacks are likely to occur, those being crowded
places and places with limited outside access. Shopping is done either very
early or very late—at times when there are few people around, when lines
are short, and exits are clearly visible. The same goes for bars, restaurants,
buses, movie theaters, and churches. If the person avails of these facilities at
all, it is at off-peak times, and they position themselves near a door or an
exit. Confined places or situations, such as heavy traffic, elevators, and visits
to the hairdresser or dentist, are usually also avoided.

Air travel is frequently abandoned for the same reasons, and also because
of the additional fear of being away from home. Vacation plans are often
shelved—although, ironically, if these people do manage to get away, they
are often fine while actually on vacation. Why? Because none of the custom-
ary associations that trigger attacks are present. They are fine *until* they
return home; which can be an awful disappointment to those who think
they have somehow magically shaken off their problem. Not just vacations,
but planning ahead in general usually decreases, due to the build-up of
anticipatory anxiety that it generates. There is also an increased reliance on
others—spouse, children, or friends—who can find themselves accompany-
ing the person more and more, or actually doing various errands and chores
for them. This gradual surrendering of independence can have major psychological consequences, especially to self-confidence. Finally, there can be
avoidance of substances and activities that could potentially induce sensations even vaguely similar to those of panic—alcohol, caffeine, active sport,
or sex.

Cognitive.   At the time of the first attack, thinking is usually in a spin.
People report not being able to think at all, feeling unreal, or feeling that
something awful was about to happen. Others remember thinking that they
might lose control, collapse, or go mad. Some have clear visual images of
themselves choking, or lying in a coffin, or of their own heart not beating.
Over time, as well as these initial thoughts and images, there is the added
and ongoing fear of future attacks: "What if? When?" This secondary, or
anticipatory, anxiety frequently takes over. For this reason, agoraphobia is
often referred to as the "portable phobia." It is carried around in the body
and in the mind.

There is frequently also frustration, due to lack of understanding of the
problem, and this is compounded by inhibition about discussing it with
others ("What's happening to me? I must be going crazy. I can't tell anyone
I'm afraid to go shopping; they would think I was weird."). A fear of being
alone can also develop—fear of having an attack when alone, even in one's
own home. But, the more time the person spends inside and alone, the more
anticipatory anxiety that is generated—with obvious results. Finally, due to

curtailment of social life and contacts, feelings of helplessness and depression can set in.

Treatment

The *final* element in the treatment of agoraphobia and panic disorder is systematic, live exposure (Appendix IV: Systematic Desensitization). Clients must eventually learn to enter situations that normally induce panic attacks and to remain there until their anxiety subsides. Before getting to this point, however, a number of therapeutic hurdles have to be crossed.

After a detailed intake interview, it is especially essential with agoraphobic clients to carry out a thorough analysis of their motivation to change (Appendix I: Motivation Analysis). This is particularly important if the problem is of long standing and their existence has been curtailed for a considerable period of time. The therapist helps these clients take a realistic look ahead and anticipate the wider consequences of overcoming their problem. Generally, the idea of freedom of movement acts as a significant motivator: "Imagine *me* being able to dress up and go out again." However, the fact of being very out of practice or out of date, either socially or with changes in the environment, can be daunting. Sometimes also the problem, although objectively crippling, has had its hidden pay-offs, or *secondary gains*—not having had to go to work or even do the grocery shopping in years, for example. More significantly, it may have masked, or even developed to help them "cope" with, a long-standing social phobia or marital discord. If such compensations, large or small, are identified, they have to be explored and included in the change plan (Appendix I: Change Plan).

Because physical symptoms are so integral to the problem of agoraphobia, they are tackled first. Clients are educated about the psychological nature of their symptoms—the role of the autonomic nervous system and the relationship between sensations, their *misinterpretation,* and panic. They are then reassured that their feelings of impending doom, intense vulnerability, and copelessness are ill-founded and part of the problem.

Therapy can then proceed with the therapist inducing panic attacks in his or her office; this can be done by getting the client to deliberately hyperventilate, for example. In other words, the body sensations, images, and cognitions that occur in a panic attack are elicited in the place of consultation. Clients are asked to focus on their specific sensations, images and thoughts and on what they *mean* to them. They identify the symptoms they fear the most and their worst fears of what might happen. As well as providing the therapist with a wealth of information for cognitive intervention, clients are also learning that they can produce panic sensations at will, and that nothing catastrophic happens. To help them consolidate these feelings of being in control, they are then trained in controlled breathing, whereby they adopt a smooth, relaxed pattern of breathing, with which it is difficult to overbreathe. They are usually also trained in deep muscular relaxation (Appendix III: Relaxation).

Cognitive intervention is integral to the effective alleviation of panic disorder, because a basic misinterpretation of sensations is primary in inducing panic. Accordingly, the focus at the next stage of the intervention is on getting clients to *reattribute* their body sensations, that is, to change from the catastrophic interpretation to a more objective one. The thoughts and images that accompany panic attacks—before, during, and after—are also examined. As explained, these cognitive concomitants can be elicited during an in-office panic induction. Self-statements, such as: "I can feel it coming on—maybe I will die this time," or "What if I lose control or go crazy?" are carefully explored, disputed, and replaced with more reasonable, reassuring, and objective ones (Appendix V: Self-Disputation). Likewise, panic images are examined, especially for their personal relevance and meaning. These can then be replaced with incompatible coping imagery (Appendix V: Coping Imagery).

In some cases, it is necessary to do a deeper analysis of underlying beliefs concerning personal vulnerability or independence, or what the problem *means* to the individual. Many clients erroneously believe, for example, that they could die in an attack. Likewise, beliefs such as that they will never be cured or will never be able to live a normal life or that they are not the same as everybody else are quite common (Appendix V: Vertical Arrow). If the problem is of long standing, self-esteem and self-confidence may also have suffered, or depression may have set in due to feelings of helplessness and hopelessness. These kinds of feelings also have to be gently eased (Appendix V: Uncovering The Shoulds). Some clients who have been confined for a long time need assistance in getting started again, whether this involves simply structuring their day (Appendix IV: Daily Activity Schedule) or organizing their time (Appendix IV: Managing Time).

As with the treatment of phobias with systematic desensitization, a personal hierarchy of progressively more difficult situations is then constructed (Appendix IV: Systematic Desensitization), using the client's self-report, Weekly Panic Log (see Figure 4.1), and diary-keeping records (Appendix IV: Self-Monitoring Behavior). This is gradually worked through. What treatment usually involves is going further and further away from home, into smaller and more crowded situations, standing on lines at supermarket check-outs at peak shopping times, or driving or taking public transport through heavy traffic. The items obviously vary according to the client's specific fears. The therapist normally accompanies the person into such situations at the beginning of the intervention but then gradually "fades out" by perhaps walking a distance ahead or behind, or meeting them in the situation when they have already been there alone for some time. Family

FIGURE 4.1 Weekly Panic Log:

Name: _____   Date: _____

WEEKLY PANIC LOG

Date, Time and Duration of the Panic Attack	Situation in which Panic Attack occurred and Severity of the Panic Attack (1-10)	Description of the Panic Attack Symptoms and Sensations Experienced	Interpretation of Sensations and Accompanying Thoughts and Images	Was This a Full-Blown Attack? Yes/No If No, Explain Why	Your Response to Panic Attack. What Did You Do? (Specify any medication taken and dosage.)
1.					
2.					
3.					
4.					
5.					
6.					
7.					
8.					
9.					
10.					

Please indicate any additional Panic Attacks on another sheet.

members and friends can also be enlisted in the therapy (Appendix II: Enlisting Friends). This is especially relevant for clients who live a long distance from the place of consultation, as it makes more sense for them to practice in their own territory. Eventually however, they must go it alone.

Not quite as essential, but also worth mentioning, are eating habits. Sometimes, vulnerability to panic attacks can be exacerbated by a habit of going for long periods without food. When blood sugar levels drop, people can experience jittery, nervous feelings, which, in many ways, resemble pre-panic sensations. Likewise, a habit of consuming either a lot of coffee or cigarettes is unwise, because it stresses the body and, particularly, the autonomic nervous system (Appendix III: Body). Exercise is also encouraged—for general fitness, but more so because of increasing evidence of the beneficial effects that exercise (particularly aerobic exercise) has on both depression and anxiety-related disorders (Appendix III: Exercise). Finally, clients are advised, when feeling totally mobile, to explore new recreational, educational, and social facilities, rather than sticking with the environment they knew before; effectively, they are encouraged to expand their new life space (Appendix II: Utilizing Environmental Resources).

SUGGESTED FURTHER READING

Theory And Research

Barrios, B. A., & Shigetomi, C. C. (1979). Coping skills training for the management of anxiety: A critical review. *Behaviour Therapy, 10,* 491–522.

Beck, A. T. (1976). *Cognitive therapy and the emotional disorders.* NY: International Universities Press.

Beck, A. T., & Emery, G. (1985). *Anxiety disorders and phobias: A cognitive perspective.* NY: Basic Books.

Beck, A. T., Epstein, N., Brown, G., & Steer, R. A. (1988). An inventory for measuring clinical anxiety: Psychometric properties. *Journal of Consulting and Clinical Psychology, 56,* 893–897.

Clark, D. A. (1986). A cognitive approach to panic. *Behavior Research and Therapy, 24,* 403–411.

Dobson, K. S. (1985). The relationship between anxiety and depression. *Clinical Psychology Review, 5,* 307–324.

Eysenck, H. J. (1975). Anxiety and the natural history of neuroses. In C. D. Spielberger & I. G. Sarason (Eds.), *Stress and anxiety* (Vol. 1, pp. 51–94). NY: Wiley.

Foa, E. B., & Kozak, M. J. (1985). Treatment of anxiety disorders: Implications for psychopathology. In A. H. Tuma & J. Maser (Eds.), *Anxiety and the anxiety disorders* (pp. 421–452). Hillsdale, NJ: Lawrence Erlbaum Associates.

Foa, E. B., Steketee, G., & Young, M. C. (1984). Agoraphobia: Phenomenological aspects, associated characteristics, and theoretical considerations. *Clinical Psychology Review, 4,* 431–457.

Freedman, A. M., Dornbush, R. L., & Shapiro, B. (1981). Anxiety: Here today and here tomorrow. *Comprehensive Psychiatry, 22,* 44–53.

Jansson, L., & Lars-Goran Ost. (1982). Behavioral treatments for agoraphobia: An evaluative review. *Clinical Psychology Review, 2,* 311–336.

Kendall, P., & Watson, D. (1989). *Anxiety and depression: Distinctions and overlapping features.* NY: Academic Press.

Marks, I. (1969). *Fears and phobias.* London: Heineman.

Meichenbaum, D., & Turk, D. (1976). The cognitive-behavioral management of anxiety, anger and pain. In P. O. Davidson (Ed.), *The behavioral management of anxiety, depression, and pain,* (pp. 1–34). NY: Brunner Mazel.

Ottaviani, R., & Beck, A. T. (1986). Cognitive aspects of panic disorders. *Journal of Anxiety Disorders, 1,* 15–28.

Rachman, S. J. (1978). *Fear and courage.* NY: W. H. Freeman.

Rachman, S. J., & Maser, J. (Eds.). (1988). *Panic: Psychological perspectives.* Hillsdale, NJ: Lawrence Erlbaum Associates.

Vandereycken, W. (1983). Agoraphobia and marital relationship: Theory, treatment, and research. *Clinical Psychology Review, 3,* 317–338.

Popular and Self-Help

Charlesworth, E. A., & Nathan, R. G. (1982). *Stress management.* NY: Ballantine.

Fensterheim, H., & Baer, J. (1977). *Stop running scared.* NY: Rawson Associates.

Hodgson, R., & Miller, P. (1982). *Self-watching: Addictions, habits and compulsions: What to do about them* (Chapter 5). London: Century Publishing Company.

Marks, I. (1978). *Living with fear: Understanding and coping with anxiety.* NY: McGraw-Hill.

Meichenbaum, D. (1985). *Coping with stress.* London: Century Press.

Weekes, C. (1981). *Hope and help for your nerves.* NY: Bantam Books.

Weekes, C. (1981). *Simple effective treatment of agoraphobia.* NY: Bantam Books.

Whitehead, T. (1988). *Fears and phobias.* London: Sheldon Press.

Wilson, R. R. (1986). *Don't panic.* NY: Harper & Row.

Wolpe, J. (1988). *Life without fear.* Oakland, CA: New Harbinger.

Woolfolk, R. L., & Richardson, F. C. (1978). *Stress, sanity and survival.* NY: New American Library.

Zane, M. (1984). *Your phobia.* NY: Warner.

Depression

Everyone has felt "down," "fed up," or "blue" at some time or another. We have all experienced times when we have had no great appetite for anything, when we did not want to bother going out or dressing up, when we had no "get up and go." In fact, such mild feelings of depression are so common as to suggest that if you have never felt low, then there is something wrong! One reason for the commonness of such feelings is the nature of life itself. We all get put down and let down from time to time. We all experience disappointments and losses; relationships and friendships break up, loved ones die or move away, possessions and jobs are sometimes unexpectedly taken from us. Sometimes, a number of circumstances combine to create a depressing overall life situation.

FACTS AND FIGURES

As with anxiety, and the other problem areas to be discussed, there is a difference between the normal lows that everyone experiences and the crippling, incapacitating depression that makes many people seek professional intervention and sometimes leads to hospitalization. Compared to most other problems, depression is very common, and is often referred to as the "common cold of mental disorders." At least 4% of the adult population is sufficiently depressed at any given time to meet the most rigorous of diagnostic criteria. Figures also suggest that the percentage of people likely to experience an episode of depression at some stage during their lifetime may be estimated at between 25% and 50% of the population. In 1973, a report by the National Institute of Mental Health indicated that depression accounted for 75% of all psychiatric hospitalizations and that, during a given year, 15% of all adults between the ages of 18 and 74 suffer significant symptoms of depression.

People also seem to be more vulnerable to depression at different times of life. These, by and large, are times of change. The prevalence of depression is relatively low in early childhood but increases during adolescence and tends to peak between the ages of 20 and 40. Beyond this, the rate is fairly stable, and it even declines slightly. Figures also suggest that women get depressed more than men—two to three times as many females report having depression. However, these figures must be interpreted with caution, because many people who experience a depressive episode appear to remain vulnerable to relapse, and this elevates the statistics (see Lewinsohn, Hoberman, Teri, & Hautzinger, 1985). As stated in chapter 2, young working-class mothers are particularly at risk. It is important to point out also, however, that most people have relatively short-lived episodes of depression, and many are able to cope without professional assistance.

CAUSES, SIGNS, AND SYMPTOMS

What causes depression? This question has been much debated; and both psychology and psychiatry have provided explanatory theories to account for its many faces. Different theories emphasize the importance of biochemical, environmental, behavioral, interpersonal, and cognitive factors, respectively.

The type of depression that comes from within is called *endogenous* depression. There is evidence of a genetically transmitted predisposition to depression that renders some individuals more vulnerable than others. In other words, depression and manic depression (also called bipolar depression) run in families. Depression can also result from biochemical changes within the body; if someone suddenly becomes depressed for no apparent reason, the depression is more likely to be chemically determined (see McKeon, 1986). Other physical causes of depression include illness, some prescribed and "recreational" (i.e., mood altering) drugs, and such hormonal changes as premenstrual syndrome, childbirth, and menopause (see chapters 2 and 3).

As important are environmental and psychological precipitants. As explained in chapter 2, significant life events, such as bereavements, separations, children leaving home, illness, retirement, financial worries, redundancy, and old age can be depression-inducing (Benjaminsen, 1981). Recent research also indicates that the *perception* of the event, that is, the meaning of the event for the individual, will determine whether or not depression is experienced. Ongoing, chronic microstressors and daily hassles can also wear people down over a period of time. Heightened vulnerability is perhaps best understood in terms of perceived helplessness; when people feel they cannot cope, that they are not in control, they experience a loss of self-esteem and self-confidence (Seligman, 1975).

Behavioral factors are emphasized by those who attribute depression to a decrease in the amount of *reinforcements* the person receives from his or her environment. The idea here is that a decrease in pleasant events and/or an increase in unpleasant events will lead to dysphoria. Interpersonal interactions and relationships obviously play a significant causal role here (Lewinsohn, 1975).

Particularly important in recent years are *cognitive* explanations of depression. Such theories, and particularly that of Aaron Beck, suggest that depression results from biased and negative cognitive structures, that is, how a person thinks about himself, the world, and his future. When depressed, people distort their experiences. They view the world as a threatening place and themselves as unworthy. Thinking is particularly laced with automatic negative thoughts, cognitive distortions, and erroneous beliefs (see chapter 2). This leads to the type of self-perpetuating misinterpretations described in chapter 3. One negative event, or even an event misconstrued negatively, can lead to a downward spiral (Beck, Rush, Shaw, & Emery, 1979).

Undoubtedly, all five sets of factors play a causal role. Probably the best way of viewing depression is as *multicausal* (Billings & Moos, 1982). More often than not, it is due to a combination of factors; life is complex, and one thing leads to another. So, one of the most obvious features of depression is its multicausality. Another is its *symptom heterogeneity*. In other words, the *key* symptom of depression is dysphoria; but, beyond that, there can be any of a large number of diverse symptoms that include emotional, cognitive, behavioral, and somatic factors. Furthermore, there are large individual differences in the number and severity of the symptoms that are experienced.

Physiological. When people are depressed, sleep is often affected. Some tend to sleep an abnormally large amount, whereas others wake early and are unable to return to sleep. There is usually also a decrease in energy level, appetite, and sex drive, combined with feelings of tiredness and lethargy. Some people experience pains in the back of the head, and constipation. Others become emotionally labile and can find themselves bursting into tears for little or no reason.

Behavioral. Depression can also bring a shift in activity level; people can become either lethargic or agitated—usually the former. As well as feeling tired, some find that they are actually walking and talking more slowly than they normally would. There is a general slowing down. Eating and drinking patterns can also change. Some eat more than usual and put on weight, but more find that they have little or no appetite for food. Even the most appetizing dishes can taste like sawdust. Lack of appetite, combined with reduced energy to shop for and prepare food, often results in significant weight loss, especially for those living alone. Others turn to alcohol to drown their sorrows. Unfortunately, as well as the problem of increasing dependence *and* the expense, alcohol is, chemically, a depressant; so, ultimately, the situation is compounded even further. When in company, depressed people can be very irritable; but a greater problem is the desire to withdraw from the world, to hide away from people, to become invisible. This provides more time to brood and often also results in neglect of personal appearance, dress, and hygiene. Old hobbies lose their attractiveness. Normal daily activities, such as dressing, washing, eating, and chatting, become a chore. Getting through the day can be a huge, and sometimes impossible, task. Overall, the spark has gone out of life.

Cognitive. When people are depressed, they often have difficulty concentrating and remembering things. They can look as if they are in a daze or stupor. There is a general slowness and indecisiveness in thinking. Along with this, there are usually recurrent negative thoughts about themselves, the present, and the future. Situations tend to be interpreted in very biased and negative ways. This makes the person feel even more depressed and perpetuates the ever-descending spiral. Depressed people can feel worthless or guilty about minor faults or trivial mistakes made even years before. They can ruminate and torture themselves about such things for hours on end. These gloomy thoughts are generally accompanied by a sad, apathetic mood and feelings of helplessness. Resulting hopelessness, in turn, often leads to feelings of despair and thoughts of suicide. Overall, there is a huge feeling of loss—loss of confidence, loss of enthusiasm, loss of purpose, loss of meaning, loss of life.

TREATMENT

A number of urgent questions must be addressed before a therapist can or should proceed with therapy for depression. First and foremost is whether the client is feeling suicidal, or contemplating suicide. The Beck Depression Inventory is a quick, well-validated, and effective method of establishing the degree of a client's depression—mild, moderate, or severe. However, it is advisable for therapists to also administer any or all of the following questionnaires developed by Beck and his team: the Hopelessness Scale, the Scale for Suicide Ideation and the Cognition Checklist Scale (Table 5.1). In cases where a client is severely depressed or there is any indication of suicide risk, a psychiatrist should be hastily consulted and hospitalization arranged.

Another related issue concerns the *cause* of the depression. If a client's depression is of recent onset, there is no obvious external precipitant, and they are complaining of loss of appetite and libido and of early morning wakening, it is likely to be endogenous, or biochemical. This is particularly true if there is a family history of depression. Here again, a cross-referral to a psychiatrist should be speedily effected. There are now many effective psychotropic medications for dealing with both endogenous and bipolar depressive disorders. On the other hand, if a client complains primarily of physical symptoms, they may be physically ill and their psychological symptoms may be secondary (see chapter 2). Here, a thorough check-up with their general practitioner or a specialist is the action priority, and again, this should be carried out as quickly as possible. Because depression can effectively involve dealing with life and death, the importance of speedy and appropriate action at this assessment stage cannot be overstressed.

If the therapist is satisfied that a client is not at risk for suicide and that their depression is clearly attributable to psychological factors, such as a recent life event (e.g., bereavement or redundancy) or on-going stress, then therapy proceeds as follows. Because attitudes and feelings change more slowly than behaviors, the therapist will usually start by getting a depressed client to *do* things. It is important to keep in mind that depression presents unique problems for the therapist. The apathy, which is integral to depression itself, can make it difficult for clients to muster up the energy and enthusiasm to help themselves—to motivate themselves to even keep a diary. A Motivation Analysis (Appendix I) can be a bruising experience; so, I usually begin by helping clients construct a simple, realistic Daily Activity Schedule (Appendix IV). Once even a minimal routine is operating on a regular basis and it looks as if there is some gradual acceleration in activities from day to day, then cognitive intervention can be initiated.

Firstly, the relationship between thinking and mood is explained. Then, clients are taught to monitor their thinking (Appendix I: Self-Monitoring Thinking) and to identify and examine their negative self-talk. They learn to connect "low" times of the day or certain activities that depress them with the cognitive activity that accompanies them. When examined, their self-talk is usually found to be permeated with exaggerated, pessimistic, negative, and self-denegrating thoughts: "I'm no good; I can't even make a cup of coffee," "I'm a burden on everyone." With the help and encouragement of the therapist, these negative self-statements are examined and disputed (Appendix V: Self-Disputation). Typical errors of thinking (see page 40) are identified and repeatedly pointed out to the clients who gradually begin to see and understand the effect that their repeated, habitual negative thoughts are having on their mood.

It is usually necessary to then go on to more in-depth cognitive therapy and to explore underlying beliefs of worthlessness, helplessness, or hopelessness:

TABLE 5.1
Cognition Checklist

Name: _____   Date: _____ / _____ / _____

Instructions: Please rate how often you have each of the thoughts that are described below during each of the following situations.

	Never	Rarely	Sometimes	Often	Always
When I have to attend a social occasion I think:					
1. I'm a social failure.	0	1	2	3	4
2. I'll never be as good as other people are.	0	1	2	3	4
When I am with a friend I think:					
3. People don't respect me anymore.	0	1	2	3	4
4. No one cares whether I live or die.	0	1	2	3	4
5. I'm worse off than they are.	0	1	2	3	4
6. I don't deserve to be loved.	0	1	2	3	4
7. I've lost the only friends I've had.	0	1	2	3	4
8. I'm not worthy of people's attention or affection.	0	1	2	3	4
9. There's no one left to help me.	0	1	2	3	4
When I feel pain or physical discomfort I think:					
10. What if I get sick and become an invalid?	0	1	2	3	4

	Never	Rarely	Sometimes	Often	Always
When I feel pain or physical discomfort I think: *(cont'd)*					
11. Something might be happening that will ruin my appearance.	0	1	2	3	4
12. I am going to be injured.	0	1	2	3	4
13. What if no one reaches me in time to help?	0	1	2	3	4
14. I'm going to have an accident.	0	1	2	3	4
15. I might be trapped.	0	1	2	3	4
16. I am not a healthy person.	0	1	2	3	4
17. There's something very wrong with me.	0	1	2	3	4
Please rate how often you have the following thoughts regardless of the situation.					
18. Life isn't worth living.	0	1	2	3	4
19. I'm worthless.	0	1	2	3	4
20. I have become physically unattractive.	0	1	2	3	4
21. I will never overcome my problems.	0	1	2	3	4
22. Something awful is going to happen.	0	1	2	3	4
23. I'm going to have a heart attack.	0	1	2	3	4
24. I'm losing my mind.	0	1	2	3	4
25. Something will happen to someone I care about.	0	1	2	3	4
26. Nothing ever works out for me anymore.	0	1	2	3	4

"I'm a complete failure," "I've made such a mess of my life—I feel so guilty," "Nobody loves me—how could they?" (Appendix V: Vertical Arrow; Uncovering The Shoulds). If a significant life event, such as a bereavement or children leaving home, triggered the depression, the thoughts and feelings related to this must be explored also. Contrary to appearances, depressed people are often very angry inside, because—rightly or wrongly—they believe that life has been unfair to them or that they have been used or exploited, for example. If such feelings and beliefs are identified, they must be worked through.

On a more general level, if the precipitating factor was not an event as such, but chronic stress—from an unconducive environment, an unsatisfactory job or relationship, or a lack of social skills—this must be dealt with; otherwise, depression will recur. By helping clients to explore other aspects of their environment (Appendix II: Utilizing Environmental Resources), to increase their social contacts or social skills (Appendix VI: Making Conversation), to become more assertive (Appendix VI: Assertion), or to learn communication or problem-solving skills in order to ameliorate marital disharmony (Appendix VI: Problem-Solving; Communicating Emotions), their vulnerability can be decreased.

Not as essential but also important in the treatment of depression are the following. Because depression is frequently accompanied by feelings of anxiety or fear, depressed clients often benefit from relaxation training (Appendix III: Relaxation) or from taking up some sport, preferably aerobic (Appendix III: Exercise). Diet and eating patterns may also need to be changed or reestablished, especially if they have not recently been bothering to eat regular or nourishing meals (Appendix III: Eating). Alcohol is a chemical depressant and is therefore especially inadvisable for people who are depressed or prone to depression. Although sleep patterns usually revert to normal when depression lifts, some advice may be needed to facilitate regular sleep again, particularly if the person's entire routine has been disrupted or if they have become overly anxious about not being able to sleep (Appendix III: Sleep). At this advanced stage of therapy, they may also benefit from some guidelines on organizing time in order to build up and maintain a normal routine and activity level and to get things done (Appendix IV: Managing Time).

Social supports are also of immeasurable value right through a depressive episode—be they family or friends (Appendix II: Enlisting Friends). I do find it worthwhile, however, to advise these caring people to spend their precious time with the client *doing* things—rather than talking about the problem or listening to long depressing monologues. This is counterproductive for all concerned. It can be particularly difficult for the socially isolated and those living alone to pick up from depression, especially if loneliness was a causal factor. A good relationship with the therapist is obviously a distinct advantage here, in terms of feeling cared for and understood and in maintaining morale and generating enthusiasm for life. Such clients can sometimes *also* benefit from attending a social skills training group. This puts them in direct contact with other people, as well as facilitating the development of friendships on a wider scale (Appendix VI: Making Conversation).

SUGGESTED FURTHER READING:

Theory and Research

Beck, A. T. (1987). Cognitive models of depression. *Journal of Cognitive Psychotherapy, 1,* 5–37.

Beck, A. T., Hollon, S. D., Young, J. E., Bedrosian, R. S., & Budenz, D. (1985). Treatment of depression with cognitive therapy and amitriptyline. *Archives of General Psychiatry, 42,* 142–148.

Beck, A. T., Rush, A. J., Shaw, B. F., & Emery, G. (1980). *Cognitive therapy of depression.* NY: Guilford.

Beck, A. T., & Young, J. E. (1985). Cognitive therapy of depression. In D. Barlow (Ed.), *Clinical handbook of psychological disorders: A step-by-step treatment manual* (pp. 206–244). NY: Guilford.

Blaney, P. H. (1977). Contemporary theories of depression: Critique and comparison. *Journal of Abnormal Psychology, 86,* 203–223.

Burbach, D. J., & Borduin, C. M. (1986). Parent-child relations and the etiology of depression: A review of methods and findings. *Clinical Psychology Review, 6,* 133–154.

Coyne, J. C. (1986). Studying the role of cognition in depression: Well-trodden paths and cul-de-sacs. *Cognitive Therapy and Research, 10,* 695–705.

Dobson, K. S. (1985). The relationship between anxiety and depression. *Clinical Psychology Review, 5,* 307–324.

Dobson, K. S., & Shaw, B. F. (1986). Cognitive assessment with major depressive disorders. *Cognitive Therapy and Research, 10,* 13–29.

Evans, M., & Hollon, S. D. (1988). Patterns of personal and causal inference: Implications for the cognitive therapy of depression. In L. B. Alloy (Ed.), *Cognitive processes in depression* (pp. 344–377). NY: Guilford Press.

Fennell, M. J. V., & Teasdale, J. D. (1986). Cognitive therapy for depression: Individual differences and the processes of change. *Cognitive Therapy and Research, 10,* 225–236.

Kendall, P., & Watson, D. (eds.). (1989). *Anxiety and depression: Distinctions and overlapping features.* NY: Academic Press.

Kovacs, M., Feinberg, T. L., Crouse-Novak, M. A., Paulauskas, S. L., & Finkelstein, R. (1984). Depressive disorders in childhood: I. A longitudinal prospective study of characteristics and recovery. *Archives of General Psychiatry, 41,* 643–649.

Krantz, S. E., & Moos, R. H. (1988). Risk factors at intake predict nonremission among depressed patients. *Journal of Consulting and Clinical Psychology, 56,* 863–869.

Levitt, E. E., Lubin, B., & Brooks, J. M. (1983). *Depression: Concepts, controversies and some new facts* (2nd Ed.). Hillsdale, NJ: Lawrence Erlbaum Associates.

Olinger, L. J., Kuiper, N. A., & Shaw, B. F. (1987). Dysfunctional attitudes and stressful life events: An interactive model of depression. *Cognitive Therapy and Research, 11:1,* 25–40.

Rush, A. J., Weissenburger, J., & Eaves, G. (1986). Do thinking patterns predict depressive symptoms? *Cognitive Therapy and Research, 10:2,* 225–236.

Simons, A. D., McGowan, C. R., Epstein, L. H., Kupfer, D. J., & Robertson, D. J. (1985). Exercise as a treatment for depression: An update. *Clinical Psychology Review, 5,* 553–568.

Simons, A. D., Murphy, G. E., Levine, J. L., & Wetzel, R. D. (1986). Cognitive therapy and pharmacotherapy for depression: Sustained improvement over one year. *Archives of General Psychiatry, 43,* 43–48.

Popular and Self-Help

Burns, D. (1981). *Feeling good: The new mood therapy.* NY: New American Library.

Emery, G. (1981). *A new beginning: How you can change your life through cognitive therapy.* NY: Simon and Schuster.

Hodgson, R., & Miller, P. (1982). *Self-watching: Addictions, habits and compulsions: What to do about them* (Chapter 6). London: Century Publishing Company.

Lewinsohn, P., Munoz, R., Youngren, M. A., & Zeiss, A. (1978). *Control your depression.* Engelwood Cliffs, NJ: Prentice-Hall.

McKeon, P. (1986). *Coping with depression and elation.* London: Sheldon Press.

Rush, J. (1983). *Beating depression.* London: Century Press.

Werthman, M. (1979). *Self-psyching.* London: Bachman & Turner.

6

Obsessive-Compulsive Problems

Many people like to keep themselves and their surroundings clean and tidy, to check that plugs are out and switches are off before going to bed and that doors are locked before going out. Many people feel uncomfortable in a room where pictures are slightly askew on the walls or color combinations in fabrics or decor do not match; likewise, if books are not returned to their shelves, or files are not put away in the appropriate order. Many people cannot sit down and relax until they have finished household or professional chores. Many people make lists of jobs to be done and tick them off with satisfaction as they go. It is common for people to experience a thought going around in their head at night of something that happened during the day that they felt they could have done better or of an interaction that did not go as well as they had expected. Nagging doubts that one did not address an envelope correctly or lock the safe before leaving the office are also quite common. These are all normal experiences of what are clinically referred to as *obsessive-compulsive* problems.

Normal levels of obsessionality are healthy; they ensure that desirable standards of hygiene, efficiency, safety, and organization are maintained. There is a difference, however, between these normal levels of efficiency, concern, and drive and the degree beyond—the point of diminishing returns—where the helpful mechanism becomes self-defeating and sometimes incapacitating.

FACTS AND FIGURES

What are obsessive-compulsive disorders? The name is self-explanatory, indicating two distinct but commonly interrelated components—the obsessive, or cognitive, and the compulsive, or behavioral. Compulsive rituals can develop on their own, but they more frequently occur in conjunction with obsessions. The general course of events is as follows: An individual experiences a particularly unpleasant thought (image or impulse) that keeps recurring; and the anxiety generated by this can most effectively be reduced by carrying out some ritual, or routine behavior. Usually, both components go together.

Clinical *obsessions* are repeated intrusions of thoughts, images, or impulses that are difficult to dismiss. Because the content of these intrusions is generally unpleasant, or even repugnant to the person (e.g., sex or violence), they generate anxiety. Research has indicated that most people experience these kinds of thoughts or ideas from time to time *but* can dismiss them easily, and consequently, they do not generate too much discomfort. In other words, most people occasionally have a disturbing thought or an unpleasant image of themselves doing or saying something uncharacteristic or crude; but it does not last or cause undue anxiety, and it is therefore less likely to recur. Those for whom obsessions are a problem become overly preoccupied with these unacceptable thoughts, which consequently return again and again, become progressively harder to dismiss, and thereby generate more distress—a vicious circle. One gentle lady client was tortured by a fear that she might use profane language in public. She gradually restricted her contact with the outside world—including answering the telephone, opening the front door, or even going to the local store. Another client could spend up to 2 hours deciding whether to switch on the television with his right or his left hand. Obsessions can occur alone, but, generally speaking, they are tied to a compulsive ritual, such as checking or washing (see Rachman, 1978b).

Compulsions can range from the normal urge to do things well to the totally incapacitating rituals that are experienced by some clients. The logic behind these rituals is illustrated by the old joke about "keeping the elephants away." *A* comes across *B*, who is busy clapping his hands three times at regular intervals. *A* questions *B* as to the purpose of the activity, and *B* replies that it is "to keep the elephants away." *A*, in amazement, says: "But there are no elephants;" and *B* calmly replies that this is because he is keeping them away! The same type of "logic" characterizes many compulsive rituals. It is fear of the consequences of *not* carrying out the ritual that keeps the person doing it. If you believe, for example, that your spouse will crash the car on the way home *unless* you wash your hands at 15-minute intervals during the day, you will ensure that you wash your hands. If you fear that, *unless* you check all the electrical appliances in the house six times before going to bed, the whole house and neighborhood will burn down, you will make very sure that you check them. These neutralizing rituals can be cognitive as well as behavioral; for example, saying a quick prayer following a "bad thought." Carrying out the compulsive ritual serves to *temporarily* reduce anxiety. Rituals therefore become reinforcing in themselves and are, in turn, more likely to increase in frequency. Well-known examples of people whose lives were entirely controlled by such compulsions were Lady Macbeth, with her compulsive handwashing, and the millionaire Howard Hughes, whose fear of contamination made him restrict his entire lifestyle and carry out the most complicated rituals for eating, washing, and other everyday activities.

The main obsessional compulsions are probably very common, but just how common is not known. Those whose difficulties reach such a disruptive level that they have to seek professional help is quite small, estimated at 1% to 5% of the psychiatric population in the United States and the United Kingdom. Usually, such difficulties start in late adolescence and early adulthood. Until relatively recently, it was believed that obsessive-compulsive problems occurred with equal frequency in both sexes. A new finding, however, indicates a clear preponderance of females with cleaning rituals. The reasons are not fully understood and await further research (see chapters 2 & 3 in Rachman & Hodgson, 1980).

CAUSES, SIGNS, AND SYMPTOMS

What do we know of predisposing factors? Both obsessive thinking and compulsive rituals tend to occur more often in people who have always had meticulous and perfectionistic personalities, but they *can* occur in the most disorganized of individuals. There is also a relationship between obsessional compulsions and depression, but the nature of the association is unclear. In some cases, obsessional difficulties indicate the existence of an underlying depression; in others, obsessional difficulties lead to feelings of helplessness and, consequently, to depression. Regarding background, my clinical experience suggests a causal role for authoritarian parents, who praise or express affection primarily in response to behaviors such as cleaning and tidying. It is also likely that observational learning is important; a child who observes a very perfectionistic parent or parents over a number of years may understandably model himself accordingly (Rachman & Hodgson, 1980, chapters 4 through 7). The obsessional personality is excessively concerned with having things "under control," and is therefore overly self-disciplined, conscientious, and perfectionistic. Their lives are ruled by "shoulds" and "musts." They worry and wonder about what others think of them, and often drive themselves to attain unrealistic standards and goals. Obsessive-compulsive behaviors range from the clinically significant and disruptive levels of some clients to the slightly fussy ways that are common to many people.

Physiological. Obsessive-compulsive disorders primarily effect behavioral and cognitive aspects of functioning. Nonetheless, it is important to acknowledge that such problems can also lead to high levels of somatic or physical anxiety. When people are *prevented* from carrying out a ritual, gross bodily discomfort can be experienced, such as palpitations, nausea, and tightness in the chest. This can be due to fear of the consequences of *not* completing the compulsive ritual or to frustration over not being able to get something "finished." Beads of perspiration can also appear while lying awake at night, ruminating: "Did I lock the front door?" "Did I switch on the alarm?" Going over and over such things or trying to generate a clear visual memory of the questioned activities only makes them get totally out of proportion.

Behavioral. The main compulsions are those of checking, cleaning, and washing. Checking of household apparati can range from the quick glance that most people give, to spending hours every day checking and rechecking—that the stove is switched off or electrical appliances are unplugged, for example. Cleaning rituals can range from having a daily or weekly routine that keeps the house in order to spending *hours* of every day repeatedly washing sinks or scrubbing floors. Likewise, with personal hygiene, there is a continuum ranging from normal levels of self-grooming to hours spent meticulously and laboriously washing hair, skin, or nails.

Hours can also be spent completing complicated cleaning or disinfecting rituals, which are usually related to fear of contamination or of contaminating others. Generally speaking, these rituals become gradually more detailed and elaborate and, consequently, consume greater and greater amounts of time. One client said that he felt he was "painting himself into a corner," as his cleaning rituals became more time-consuming and self-defeating. Cleaning rituals are frequently accompanied by avoidance of the supposedly contaminating substances.

Obsessional people also characteristically do things in a particular order or sequence. Due to rigidity and perfectionism, they are often perceived as slow workers. Tasks are completed in minute detail; work is checked and rechecked. Procrastination is also quite common (i.e., putting things off until "tomorrow"). This occurs because most tasks, however small, can seem huge because of the excessive amount of time and effort that the person is compelled to expend. There can also be rigid dressing and undressing rituals, where clothes are folded and put away in a certain order. Another manifestation of obsessive-compulsive behavior, which occurs to varying degrees, is fussiness, such as in matching colors in decor or dress. An inability to tolerate things being out of place is also common. Many find it hard to throw things out, and they hoard useless pieces of junk for many years.

Workaholics and "Type As" also fit in here—unable to leave the office until the desk is cleared, even though it would be better left until tomorrow. The compulsive person will also insist on doing things himself—to ensure that they are "done, and done well." The purpose of all this organization and routine is to provide a feeling of control, and therefore security. Compulsive people consequently find changes, however small, very difficult to handle. They can be very upset and put out by even small changes in routine—when things do not go according to plan.

Cognitive. Two common cognitive features of obsessional people are doubting and overconscientiousness. Here, again, there is a continuum from the healthy level of doing a job well and being reliable to the extreme where, no matter how many times an item is checked, there is still a nagging doubt or dissatisfaction that it could have been done better or *should* be checked again. The excessive conscientiousness and the very high, self-imposed standards are often related to fear of failure. There are unrealistic expectations of others as well as of themselves. Frequently, they will go to excessive trouble for others and are then disappointed when these people do not live up to their expectations of perfection.

Indecision—vacillating over even the most trivial choices—is another problem area. Realizing just how silly the dithering is can further exacerbate already high levels of anxiety and frustration. One client, having spent two hours in a supermarket trying to decide what to buy for dinner—fish or meat—said that she felt like the proverbial starving donkey between two bales of hay. Another client was perpetually late for social engagements, due to her inability to decide what to wear; invariably, both she and her husband would arrive very late *and* in poor spirits. Obsessional people also find larger decisions, such as whether to move house or change jobs, very hard to make.

Indecision is usually related to excessive analyzing of the respective consequences of one course of action as opposed to another. Everyone indulges in such necessary evaluations, but they do not lie awake at night ruminating over minor decisions made during the day. Obsessional people, because they are so analytic, often let things get grossly out of proportion—"What would happen if?" This is doubly relevant when one considers their fear of failure, overconscientiousness, and inability to handle change. Difficulty in coping with change is also reflected in conservative, rigid beliefs and attitudes; frequently, extremely moralistic stances are taken on personal affairs and public issues. Such people are often very religious and scrupulous. This again reflects the need to maintain structure and control. Thus, the "shoulds," "musts," and "guiltys" that often permeate the obsessional person's talk and self-talk.

Finally, as explained, many are disturbed by intrusive thoughts, images, or impulses. The content is usually unpleasant and frequently either violent or sexual in nature (e.g., stabbing one's child or flirting with the local pastor). Such intrusions are particularly unacceptable to these people of "tender conscience;" and they can be followed by elaborate, time-consuming efforts to *generate* a counterimage or thought (e.g., of cuddling the child or being blessed by the pastor). These are attempts to put things right. Likewise, when unsure of whether or not they have checked that a plug is out, for example, obsessional people can spend large amounts of time trying to retrieve a clear image or visual memory of the action to put their mind at ease.

In sum, such people indulge in a lot of cognitive activity. The content can be simply pleasant but *excessive,* as in constant daydreaming. More often, however, it is intrusive, unpleasant, and personally unacceptable. Efforts *not* to think about these disturbing things generate anxiety, as well as increasing the likelihood of the unwanted thoughts, images, or impulses returning. Obsessional people think too much, in the same way as they tend to do too much. In the extreme, it becomes totally counterproductive—often producing the very situation they set out to avoid.

TREATMENT

Obsessional people find change particularly threatening and hard to handle. Therefore, before embarking on therapy, it is essential for the therapist to carry out a detailed analysis of the client's motivation and openness to change (Appendix I: Motivation Analysis). Unlike the other problem areas already discussed, the main purpose of this exercise with obsessional clients is to point out the *negative* consequences of things remaining as they are—or getting worse. On the other hand, because of the nature of their problems and their general need for approval, obsessional people are normally very cooperative and committed clients. They keep *obsessionally* neat and detailed diaries and usually arrive half an hour early for their appointments. Some are perpetually late.

Obsessive-compulsive difficulties generally involve *both* a behavioral and a cognitive component. From their diary-keeping (Appendix I: Self-Monitoring Behavior), the therapist first identifies the stimulus or stimuli that repeatedly trigger the compulsive response and notes the frequency of these occurrences. The sight of dirt in different parts of a house—kitchen, study, bathroom—might lead to laborious cleaning rituals several times a day, for example. Likewise, "bad thoughts" might recur throughout the day and lead to innumerable prayers or trips to the church to say confession.

Because the obsessional's anxiety is related to fear of the consequences of *not* carrying out the neutralizing activity, the therapist then focuses on this core fear. This is done by repeatedly exposing the client to the triggering stimulus or stimuli and preventing him or her from performing their ritual. The rationale is to show them that their fear is unfounded, that is, that the feared consequence does not occur. The technique is called *response prevention,* and it is another variant of the flexible continuum of *exposure* techniques for overcoming fears (Appendix IV: Response Prevention). Because exposure often leads to high levels of somatic anxiety, clients are generally also trained in deep muscular relaxation (Appendix III: Relaxation).

Severe compulsive difficulties are sometimes treated in a hospital setting, on a Response Prevention Ward specifically designed for dealing with such problems and where a high ratio of trained nursing staff supervise the patients. If carefully planned and executed, response prevention programs— whether carried out in a hospital, in the therapist's consulting room, or in the client's home—can have dramatic and almost immediate positive effects. The important and difficult thing is to prevent the client from carrying out the ritual for as long as it takes for them to see that the feared consequence does *not* occur, and for the contingent anxiety to decrease. Depending on the particular problem, the response prevention phase of treatment is sometimes *preceded* by getting the client to repeatedly expose himself or herself to their unacceptable *thoughts or images*. This type of *satiation* can take several hours of exposure over several sessions, until the anxiety generated by the thought or image is lessened, along with the urge to neutralize.

The same general approach is applied to checking rituals. Clients are prevented from checking when the compulsion is triggered. Alternatively, if therapy is carried out on an outpatient basis, frequency of checking can be gradually reduced over a period of time (Appendix IV: Cutting Down on Checking; Appendix V: Fading). Therapists also sometimes model the feared behavior for the client; a dirty cloth might be handled without washing the hands, and the client would be encouraged to do likewise. Obviously, the patient–client relationship is very important, especially if the person really believes that he or she could, for example, die, if they do not carry out the ritual.

On the topic of beliefs, many obsessional people do believe—totally illogically, but nonetheless firmly—that the feared consequence will occur unless they carry out their ritual (i.e., that "the elephants will come"). Consequently, cognitive intervention is an essential ingredient in therapy. It is particularly important for the therapist to establish—on, for example, a 1 to 100 scale—the client's *degree of belief* in the possibility of the feared consequence occurring, and to work at reducing this. Such beliefs are ex- plored and challenged (Appendix V: Vertical Arrow). Obsessional people are also frequently rigid and unrealistic in their personal expectations and standards and in their expectations of others. Consequently, uncovering these underlying beliefs, and showing them how they are driving themselves unnecessarily, can lessen feelings of guilt about their own limitations. It can also reduce repeated disappointments in others who cannot live up to their unrealistic expectations (Appendix V: Uncovering The Shoulds).

Exploration of the self-statements and images that trigger and accompany the ritualistic behavior is also imperative. Self-talk such as, "If I can get my hands *absolutely* spotless, I'll be okay," are examined and disputed (Appendix V: Self-Disputation). Likewise, cognitions are examined for their personal acceptability. Anxiety is frequently alleviated by informing the person of the statistical frequency of such intrusions, that is, that *most* people experience such thoughts, images, or impulses from time to time, but that it does not worry them at all. People who suffer from intrusive impulses—to stab their child, for example—also benefit from reassurance that the likelihood of such feelings *actually* leading to, or resulting in them carrying out the feared behavior, is negligible.

Some find it useful to exaggerate their fears. It gives them a perspective on how unrealistic and illogical their concerns really are (Appendix V: Exaggerating). On the other hand, training clients in distraction and dismissal techniques can be very effective in helping them cope on a day-to-day basis—if an image or thought intrudes in the middle of a board meeting or while chatting to a friend, for example (Appendix V: Distraction). Other essential techniques are those for overcoming the indecision that plagues the lives of many obsessionals (Appendix V: Indecision), and for reducing excessive daydreaming (Appendix V: Daydreaming).

If the problem is a more *general* one of perfectionism, this can be tackled in various ways. Some perfectionistic people find it hard to get started (Appendix IV: Getting Finished), whereas others need to learn how to speed up (Appendix IV: Speeding Up). Sometimes, people feel they are being controlled by the rigidity of their own rituals and routines and benefit from advice on delaying and disrupting (Appendix IV: Delaying and Disrupting). They are also frequently encouraged to experience the freedom of being someone totally different (Appendix IV: Role Characterization). "Type As" especially need to learn how to slow down (Appendix IV: Type A). Finally, sometimes obsessional people, due to their need for approval, find it hard to assert themselves, and they need to acquire basic assertions skills (Appendix VI: Assertion).

SUGGESTED FURTHER READING

Theory and Research

Beech, H. R. (Ed.). (1974). *Obsessional states*. London: Methuen.
Beech, H. R. & Vaughan, M. (1978). *Behavioral treatment of obsessional states*. Chichester: John Wiley & Sons.

Foa, E., Steketee, G., & Milby, J. B. (1980). Differential effects of exposure and response prevention in obsessive-compulsive washers. *Behavior Research and Therapy, 48:1,* 71–79.

Garamoni, G. L. & Schwartz, R. M. (1986). Type A behavior patterns and compulsive personality: Toward a psychodynamic-behavioral integration. *Clinical Psychology Review, 6,* 311–336.

Gordon, P. K. (1983). Switching attention from obsessional thoughts: An illustrative case study. *Journal of Psychiatric Treatment and Evaluation, 5,* 171–174.

Haaga, D. A. (1987). Treatment of the Type A behavior pattern. *Clinical Psychology Review, 7,* 557–574.

Rachman, S. J. (1976). The modification of obsessions: A new formulation. *Behavior Research and Therapy, 14,* 437–443.

Rachman, S. J. and Hodgson, R. J. (1980). *Obsessions and compulsions* (Century psychology series) Engelwood Cliffs, NJ: Prentice-Hall.

Popular and Self-Help

Dyer, W. (1983). *Your erroneous zones.* London: Sphere Books.

Ellis, A., & Harper, R. A. (1975). *A new guide to rational living.* Hollywood, CA: Wilshire Book Company.

Emery, G. (1982). *Own your own life.* NY: New American Library.

Freudenberger, H. J. (1980). *Burnout.* London: Arrow Books.

Friedman, M., & Rosenman, R. H. (1974). *Type A behavior and your heart.* NY: Knopf.

Hodgson, R., & Miller, P. (1982). *Self-watching: Addictions, habits, and compulsions: What to do about them* (Chapter 15). London: Century Publishing Company.

Knaus, K. (1979). *Do it now.* Englewood Cliffs, NJ: Prentice-Hall.

Lazarus, A. & Fay, P. (1975). *I can if I want to.* NY: Warner Books.

Marks, I. (1978). *Living with fear* (Chapter 9). NY: McGraw-Hill.

Roskies, E. (1987). *Stress management for the healthy "Type A."* NY: Guilford.

Relating

One thing that people cannot avoid is other people. Getting along with people, being able to talk and listen to them and laugh and cry with them is an essential part of living. Research has repeatedly highlighted the importance of even *one* close, confiding relationship as a buffer against depression and other psychological problems. In other words, it is the quality of relationships, rather than the quantity, that really counts. So, what is "relating" all about? When, where, why, and how can it go wrong?

Many ways of viewing and labeling interpersonal difficulties have been proposed. One is along a continuum ranging from those who are extremely timid—terrified at even the prospect of meeting people—to those who are excessively loud and brash. Problems of relating can also be seen along a continuum of depth: from those who can only make superficial conversation and small talk that does not go beyond the trivial to those who can relate on a deeper level and have intimate relationships but are very poor at informal chat and casual socializing. Another continuum is that of assertiveness—spanning those who are excessively passive and are always being taken for granted to those who consistently overreact in an aggressive fashion.

FACTS AND FIGURES

Using *shyness* as a broad term to encompass all these types of difficulties, how common are such problems? The results of a large-scale survey carried out by an American psychologist, Philip Zimbardo, are surprising (Zimbardo, 1981). The most basic finding on shyness in the United States was that it is "common, widespread, and universal" (p. 26). More than 80% of those questioned reported having been shy at some stage in their life. Furthermore, 40% considered themselves to be presently shy—roughly 4 out of every 10 people. About a quarter reported themselves to be chronically shy (i.e., now and always). Of these, a lonely 4% of what he termed "true blue shys" (p. 26) said that they were shy all of the time, in all situations, and with virtually all people. Their discomfort was strong enough to effect every aspect of their lives.

The last group constitutes a small minority, but many people find that in particular *situations* they react with the kind of thoughts, feelings, and actions that usually characterize the shy person. *Situationally shy* people do not see themselves as shy; rather, they see external events as causing temporary discomfort (e.g., walking into a room full of strangers). This type of problem may take the form of blushing and obvious embarrassment, or it may be concealed behind an offensive attack with negative consequences. It is worth remembering that a person's outward behavior is not always a reliable indicator of how he or she really feels.

There is no difference between the sexes in the prevalence of shyness, but shyness is more common among children than adults; most adults probably manage to overcome their shyness in the course of growing up. But, for those who do not, there are many consequences of an inability to relate—perhaps the most important being that of loneliness. Shy people are generally not "asked back," because they are not noticed at all or because they are remembered as being unpleasant and unfriendly *or* excessively loud and aggressive. Consequently, many people with interpersonal difficulties spend a lot of time alone. As well as loneliness, this provides ample opportunity to ruminate about the problem, thereby rendering them even less confident about approaching people in the future. Other consequences of shyness are alcoholism and drug abuse. Some shy people get into the habit of taking a couple of drinks before going out, for Dutch courage. Spending a lot of time alone can also feed a habit of taking a drink or two for company. A drink or two can somehow turn into three or four, or more.

Another, broader consequence of shyness is interference with career plans and the realization of potential in professional areas. A person who is afraid to speak at meetings or in class for fear of going blank, blushing, or shaking will miss out on opportunities to make an impression or be noticed. Likewise, not knowing how to assert oneself can create major difficulties when trying to ask for a well-earned wage increase or promotion. An inability to *take* criticism without overreacting aggressively can militate against consideration for promotion. Not being able to *offer* constructive criticism—another assertive skill—can determine whether or not one will be able to handle the demands of a promotion, if offered. People who find it difficult to make small talk often avoid even the everyday social activities related to work life, such as coffee or lunch breaks in the cafeteria. As well as creating the wrong impression, this can lead to extreme frustration, despondency, and depression (see Trower et al, 1978, Part I).

CAUSES, SIGNS, AND SYMPTOMS

Are some *situations* more difficult than others? For many, the worst possible situation imaginable would be something like having to give an assertive speech to a large group of people who are evaluating the effort. The types of *people* most likely to induce discomfort are strangers, especially those of the opposite sex, and authority figures, but even familiar people can sometimes induce shyness. It is important to emphasize again that, for many people, shyness is limited to certain situations and certain kinds of people.

Like the other problems discussed, shyness is experienced in all three areas of functioning—physiological, behavioral, and cognitive. Some people experience shyness in all three ways and in all situations. Shy people do not experience different kinds of things from those who are not shy. They experience the *same* symptoms but with greater intensity; the difference is quantitative rather than qualitative.

Physiological. The physiological experience of shyness can include all the symptoms of anxiety that have already been described—blushing, palpitations, hands or voice trembling, jelly legs—as well as the overpowering feelings of embarrassment and self-consciousness that can go with these. Some people experience these physical sensations just in the presence of others, or even at the thought of meeting people. Such people are defined as *primary social phobics*. Others get physically anxious only in specific situations, for example, when about to make a speech or enter a crowded room. The arousal response of blushing is a huge problem for many people— enough to make some avoid going out at all. Physiological arousal is also very much part of the experience of anger. Anger usually results from frustration, which, in the case of the shy person, is frequently related to a lack of assertion skills.

Behavioral. Many people's problems in relating stem from their behavior, which can be either excessive or deficient in various ways. People communicate with their body in subtle ways, often without even realizing it (Argyle, 1978). The body—particularly the face—sends out all kinds of messages before people even open their mouths. Body language and *nonverbal communication* are, therefore, very important. Some examples will illustrate. There is a comfortable distance at which to stand when talking to people; standing too far away or too near can make the other person feel uncomfortable. Dress is also revealing—casual or formal, clean or scruffy, trendy or frumpy. Rapid manual gesticulations and tapping feet can also be giveaway signs of anxiety.

The face is a world of its own. Timid people usually do not give adequate eye contact; they look down or away. The angry person, on the other hand, prolongs eye contact beyond the point when it remains comfortable and unthreatening. The right amount tells the other person that one is interested in what they are saying and that one is listening. Facial expression and emotion is read from the mouth too—the happy smile, sarcastic smirk, tight-lipped indication of disapproval, or sexy pout.

Nonverbal messages are also conveyed by the voice. Both rate of speech and pitch or tone of voice can alter a communication entirely. When people are anxious, they are inclined to speak quickly and in a higher pitch; when depressed, more slowly and in low, monotonous tones. Tone of voice is also very important in shaping the meaning of a communication. Any message can be said in a thousand different ways—to express enthusiasm, sincerity, boredom, sarcasm, cynicism, or optimism. How loudly people speak is also informative. As a rule, timid people speak in low tones and are often difficult to hear, whereas confident people speak up; however, shy people sometimes overcompensate in an excessively loud and boorish fashion.

Problems can arise on a *behavioral* level as well, both when people do not have the necessary social know-how, and when they have the skills but use them excessively or inappropriately. Examples of the former are: waiting for the other person to speak, come over, or keep the conversation going; making it difficult for people to approach by averting one's eyes when someone tries to make eye contact; speaking so quietly that people cannot hear; and not listening to the other person because one is so preoccupied about what one is going to say next oneself. Some people get into the habit of avoiding all social situations because they feel so anxious and unable to cope.

The opposite situation also arises, that is, where social skills have been acquired but are used excessively. Examples are when a person overdresses, monopolizes the conversation, or speaks too long or is too loud. At other times, behavior can be *situationally* inappropriate—telling jokes at a funeral or trying to have a meaningful conversation about life at a loud disco, for instance.

Cognitive.   Cognitive problems in relating are frequently caused by people's evaluations of themselves or others, or of the particular situation they find themselves in. In other words, what goes through people's minds at any time is extremely important in determining their behavior. An internal dialogue such as "I can't face this," "He's going to find me boring," "I'll go blank," will, at the least, not instill great confidence; and *might* make a person leave or avoid a feared situation entirely.

Self-statements such as "She's going to get angry," "I can feel myself on the boil, too," frequently create self-fulfilling prophecies. Faulty cognitions can also give rise to problems in the area of assertion. Particularly relevant here are the underlying assumptions and erroneous beliefs that were discussed in chapter 2. If a person believes that they *must* be loved and approved of by everyone and in every situation, it will be extremely difficult for them to assert themselves or to say "no" without feeling guilty. If they believe that everyone is out to get them, they will be much more likely to respond aggressively rather than assertively.

TREATMENT

When a client is referred with social difficulties, it is essential for the therapist to first establish whether the problem is one of *primary* or *secondary* social phobia. In other words, does the person possess adequate social skills but is too *anxious* to perform socially and to communicate, or do they *not know* what to do in social situations and are anxious as a result of the frustration and negative feedback generated by their ineffective social behavior? This can be established from the results of questionnaires like the one in Table 7.1, but even more important are the client's self-report and the therapist's observations during the intake interview. A unique feature of dealing with social difficulties is that *interviewing* socially anxious clients effectively provides a live demonstration of the problem: amount of eye contact, trembling hands or quivering voice, verbal fluency, facial expression, body language. The problem speaks for itself. Therapy is then tailored accordingly. More detailed information on whether the problem is a general one or is specific to certain situations, people, or places is also necessarily acquired from the client's ongoing diary keeping over the following weeks (Appendix I; Self-Monitoring Behavior).

Before embarking on any intervention however, and irrespective of whether the problem is one of primary or secondary social phobia, the therapist also carries out an in-depth evaluation of the client's motivation to change (Appendix I: Motivation Analysis). It is very important for such people to look ahead at the wider consequences of being able to mix and mingle socially, without fear. This can be a very motivating exercise; but, more importantly, it can serve to avoid the common mistake of thinking that newly acquired social skills and confidence will magically transform every aspect of their life (e.g., a bad marriage, or long-anticipated promotion).

If the problem is clearly one of primary social phobia, therapy consists of

Table Key:

0 No difficulty
1 Slight difficulty
2 Moderate difficulty
3 Great difficulty
4 Avoidance if possible

Table	7.1: Social Situations Questionnaire	
		Difficulty
1.	Walking down the street	---
2.	Going into shops	---
3.	Going on public transport	---
4.	Going into pubs	---
5.	Going to parties	---
6.	Mixing with people at work	---
7.	Making friends of your own age	---
8.	Going out with someone you are sexually attracted to	---
9.	Being with a group of the same sex and roughly the same age as you	---
10.	Being with a group containing both men and women of roughly the same age as you	---
11.	Being with a group of the opposite sex of roughly the same age as you	---
12.	Entertaining people in your home, lodgings etc.	---
13.	Going into restaurants or cafes	---
14.	Going to dances, dancehalls or discoteques	---
15.	Being with older people	---
16.	Being with younger people	---
17.	Going into a room full of people	---
18.	Meeting strangers	---
19.	Being with people you don't know very well	---
20.	Being with friends	---
21.	Approaching others - making the first move in starting up a friendship	---
22.	Making ordinary decisions affecting others. e.g. what to do together in the evenings	---
23.	Being with only one other person, rather than a group	---
24.	Getting to know people in depth	---
25.	Taking the initiative in keeping a conversation going	---
26.	Looking at people directly in the eyes	---
27.	Disagreeing with what other people are saying and putting forward your own views	---
28.	People standing or sitting very close to you	---
29.	Talking about yourself and your feelings in conversation	---
30.	People looking at you	---

training the client in deep muscular relaxation (Appendix III: Relaxation), and then constructing an exposure hierarchy like that used in the treatment of other phobias by systematic desensitization (Appendix IV: Systematic Desensitization). The client is gradually and systematically exposed to increasingly more anxiety-provoking situations on the hierarchy. This can be done first with the therapist in imagination (Appendix V: Traditional Desensitization), but live exposure is the ultimate goal.

More frequently, people are referred with *secondary social phobias*, or skills deficits. Although social difficulties of this type can be dealt with effectively in individual therapy sessions, more often therapy takes place in a group setting, with 8 to 10 people who have similar problems. Social skills groups carry the advantages of providing an arena for live practice before going out into the real world, as well as people with whom to practice. Observing others with similar difficulties can be very reassuring, as well as allowing clients to see where they and others are going wrong and that it is possible to put things right.

Social skills training programs can cater to the whole range of social behaviors, from making conversation (Appendix VI: Making Conversation) to complex assertive interactions (Appendix VI: Assertion). These skills are acquired by the therapist modeling, and participants then role-playing, problem situations (e.g., introducing oneself at a party, or asking someone out on a date). A flexible hierarchy of progressively more difficult social situations is gradually worked through (Appendix IV: Behavioral Rehearsal).

Groups generally meet on a weekly basis for about 2 hours, over a period of 8 to 10 weeks. Relaxation training is also included (Appendix III: Relaxation). Video-taped feedback is usually used in later sessions, when the level of performance has improved somewhat; in early sessions, it can be counterproductive and depressing for clients who do not realize the full extent of their social deficits.

Finally, education in cognitive techniques has become an integral part of comprehensive social skills programs. This is particularly true over the last 10 years, when the shortcomings of purely behavioral programs were increasingly recognized. Clients are supplied with information, including written handouts, on the role of self-statements such as "I can't make small talk," "I can't say no to his request—even though I know it is unreasonable," "People will see how tense I am—I *should* be happy and relaxed," in maintaining their difficulties. Taking examples from participants' self-reports and diary-keeping (Appendix I: Self-Monitoring Thinking), they are taught, in group, to dispute these negative self-statements (Appendix V: Self-Disputation). They also learn to identify underlying maladaptive beliefs and to challenge and change them (Appendix V: Vertical Arrow; Uncovering The Shoulds).

Homework assignments between sessions are an essential part of the self-help element of any social skills program. These tasks—for example, to strike up conversation with someone on a train or bus—are reviewed at the beginning of each session, and any problems that arose are discussed and integrated into the role-play and cognitive exercises on that day's agenda. The resolution and repeated practice of such examples from people's lives and recent experiences are enormously helpful for all. Depending on the needs of the particular group, which is generally planned with problem *homogeneity* in mind, supplementary techniques include developing visual imagery (Appendix V: Coping Imagery) and cognitive rehearsal (Appendix V: Cognitive Rehearsal). Similarly, people who, through nervousness or lack of know-how, are inclined to talk too long benefit from learning how to get to the point (Appendix VI: Defining The Problem). I also frequently include clients referred for primary social phobias in a social skills group, once their anxiety has been alleviated. This provides them with an opportunity to relax in the company of others and to explore their new-found confidence in an unthreatening atmosphere.

Finally, because an ability to form friendships and to relate to and get along with people is such a vital ingredient in healthy living, *and* because the consequences of not having adequate social contacts and supports can be so disastrous (see Chapter 2), when clients are feeling more confident, I encourage them to acquaint themselves with their environment. This means exploring it and identifying areas and facilities of potential interest; especially recreational activities that involve meeting other people (Appendix II: Utilizing Environmental Resources). Many also need guidelines on environmental planning, that is, on how to defuse potentially anxiety-provoking social situations in advance (Appendix II: Advance Preparation). Finally, members of some of my groups, on their *own* initiative, have continued to meet socially after the formal termination of the course. They continue to offer one another social support and an opportunity to practice their skills. When this happens, spontaneously, it also speaks for itself.

SUGGESTED FURTHER READING

Theory and Research

Blankstein, K., Pliner, P., & Polivy, J. (Eds.). (1980). *Advances in the study of communication and affect: Assessment and modification of emotional behavior* (Vol. 6). NY: Plenum Press.

Burns, D. (1985). *Intimate connections*. NY: New American Library.

Buss, A. H. (1980). *Self-consciousness and social anxiety*. San Francisco, CA: W. H. Freeman.

Fiske, S. T., & Taylor, S. E. (1984). *Social cognition*. Hillsdale, NJ: Lawrence Erlbaum Associates.

Gilmour, R., & Duck, S. (Eds.). (1986). *The emerging field of personal relationships*. Hillsdale, NJ: Lawrence Erlbaum Associates.

Goffman, E. (1956). *The presentation of self in everyday life*. Edinburgh: University Press.

Hartman, L. M. (1983). A metacognitive model of social anxiety: Implications for treatment. *Clinical Psychology Review, 3,* 435–456.

Hollin, C. R., & Trower, P. (1988). Development and application of social skills training. A review and critique. In M. Hersen, R. Eisler, & P. M. Miller (Eds.), *Progress in behavior modification* (pp. 166–214). CA: Sage.

Horowitz, L. M., & Vitkus, J. (1986). The interpersonal basis of psychiatric symptoms. *Clinical Psychology Review, 6,* 443–469.

Horowitz, L. M., Weckler, D. A., & Doren, R. (1983). Interpersonal problems and symptoms:

A cognitive approach. In P. Kendall (Ed.), *Advances in cognitive-behavioral research and therapy* (pp. 81–125). London: Academic Press.

Jones, W. H., Hobbs, S. A., & Hockenbury, D. (1982). Loneliness and social skills deficits. *Journal of Personality and Social Psychology, 42*, 682–689.

Liberman, R. P., King, L. W., De Risi, W. J., & McCann, M. (1975). *Personal effectiveness.* NY: Plenum Press.

Mead, G. H. (1934). *Mind, self and society.* Chicago: University of Chicago Press.

Novaco, R. (1975). *Anger control: The development and evaluation of an experimental treatment.* Lexington, MA: Lexington Press.

Peplau, L., & Perlman, D. (Eds.). (1982). *Loneliness: A sourcebook of current theory, research, and therapy.* NY: Wiley Interscience.

Schneider, B. H., Rubin, K. H., & Ledingham, J. E. (Eds.). (1985). *Peer relationships and social skills in childhood: Issues in assessment and training.* NY: Springer-Verlag.

Shatz, M. (1978). The relationship between cognitive processes in the development of communication skills. In C. B. Keasy (Ed.), *Nebraska symposium on motivation: Social cognitive development* (Vol. 26, pp. 1–42). Lincoln: University of Nebraska Press.

Staub, E. (Eds.). (1980). *Personality: Basic aspects and current research.* Englewood Cliffs, NJ: Prentice-Hall.

Popular and Self-Help

Alberti, R. E., & Emmons, M. (1975). *Stand up, speak out, talk back.* Pocket Books.

Argyle, M., & Trower, P. (1980). *Person to person: Ways of communicating.* London: Harper and Row.

Gabor, D. (1981). *How to start a conversation and make friends* (A Fireside Book) NY: Simon and Schuster.

Garner, A. (1981). *Conversationally speaking.* NY: McGraw-Hill.

Hauck, P. (1980). *Calm down.* London: Sheldon Press.

Hodgson, R., & Miller, P. (1982). *Selfwatching: Addictions, habits, compulsions: What to do about them* (Chapter 7). London: Century Publishing Company.

Miller, S., Wackman, D., Nunnally, E., & Saline, E. (1982). *Straight talk.* NY: New American Library.

Smith, M. J. (1975). *When I say no I feel guilty.* NY: Bantam Books.

Zimbardo, P. (1981). *Shyness.* London: Pan Books.

8

Marriage

Dramatic social changes have taken place in the last 20 years, the impact of which has been both positive and negative. More women are working and earning income, and this has led to a new status as well as greater independence. Contraception and divorce also, in theory, suggest increased freedom in relationships. On the negative side, however, many people fear that these changes may result in the initial decision to marry not being taken as seriously as it used to be. Some even voice a concern about the survival of the institution of marriage and of family life itself.

There are two main types of relationship problems: difficulties in the couple's interpersonal exchanges and in their sexual interactions. Sexual problems often give rise to marital and communication difficulties and, likewise, marital difficulties can produce problems on the sexual side. Because both marital and sexual problems frequently go hand in hand, which should be examined first? Because of the greater trust demanded by sexual exchanges and habits, it is generally recommended that sexual difficulties be approached *after* the relationship has been strengthened. Accordingly, this chapter examines marriage and marital problems, and the following chapter covers sex and sexual difficulties.

FACTS AND FIGURES

How common are marital difficulties? American figures suggest that the rate of marriage remains, more or less, constant. However, between 8% and 14% of married couples admit to problems severe enough to contemplate separation or divorce, and *actual* divorce rates have accelerated dramatically in the last 20 years (Stuart, 1980b). Problems can arise during the early years of a marriage, if the couple fails to establish the necessary minimum ability to relate both physically and emotionally. Breakdown at a later stage can occur for any number of reasons—unfaithfulness, deterioration in communication, partners changing at different rates, or developing in different directions.

CAUSES, SIGNS, AND SYMPTOMS

Marriage is a complex contract. Many things can cause tensions at *any* stage—external pressures, health problems, problem behaviors, or changes in the attitudes of one or both parties.

Environmental.   The external environment can create stresses in many ways. There can be pressures from work or from financial commitments. Problems often arise if both parties are working, especially if both are career-oriented or if one party's job necessitates spending a lot of time away from home (Tryon & Tryon, 1982). On the other hand, marriage can sometimes result in a woman having to give up her job—if, for example, she moves to her husband's neighborhood or part of the country. This can also mean that she becomes financially dependent again, which is another big change. Moving house or changing neighborhood can cause other problems—especially if the new home is smaller, noisier, or less attractive than either party's previous accommodation. Interference from one or both extended families often causes a conflict of loyalties. The arrival of children, and the inevitable change in lifestyle that their existence imposes, is a very common cause of disharmony. In later years, when children leave home and the couple find themselves alone together—perhaps for the first time in many years—they can discover that they are "strangers;" this can, obviously, be very traumatic.

Physiological.   The health of one or both parties can also test a relationship. Major physical and mental illnesses can obviously have a huge impact on a marriage. Premenstrual syndrome, pregnancy, and post partum depression also have significant effects. Less extreme in it's impact, but nonetheless important, is general health. If one partner is physically unwell or overworked, it can affect both energy and irritability levels. In fact, differences in normal energy levels—which sometimes only become apparent after marriage—can play havoc. Some people are constantly "on the go," whereas others simply have less energy. There are also large individual differences in people's daily, or diurnal, rhythm: Some are "morning people," whereas others "come alive" at night. Physical changes, which occur over time, can also be important; sometimes one partner ages more obviously and quickly than the other. This can also affect their energy level, attractiveness, and self-confidence. Changes in appearance—weight gain due to overindulgence, child-bearing or self-abuse, for example—can tip the balance in an already turbulent situation.

Behavioral.   Living with someone is not the same as dating. The habits of a partner that were regarded as pleasant little idiosyncrasies during court-ship can become major sources of irritation within a marriage. Differences in standards of hygiene and tidiness, for example, are a common source of tension and disagreement. Differences in food preferences or the fact that one smokes or drinks alcohol can lead to bickering and tension. Habits as basic as eating biscuits in bed, snoring, or leaving the cap off the toothpaste can become triggers for major outbursts.

Differences in social needs and independence are also very important. One partner might like to go out every night and spend a lot of money, whereas the other might prefer to go out only occasionally and see the money invested in practical, household things. A lack of assertion or a tendency to be aggressive are other common sources of marital tension, as are differing needs for privacy and time spent alone. Shyness in one can lead to overdependence, and resentment on both sides. Often, one partner is less communicative, less talkative, or less demonstrative than the other—something that may not have been apparent before marriage—and this can lead to feelings of loneliness or rejection.

Another major cause of marital breakdown is lack of communication. Inability or unwillingness to listen to a partner's point of view or to express one's opinion on, or feelings about, things as mundane as grocery shopping or baby-sitting can create havoc in an otherwise well-suited partnership. Over time, people also get used to one another. Time itself often results in a decrease in verbal and nonverbal communication and affectionate gestures. Even in a good relationship, communication can sometimes gradually deteriorate to a point where both parties feel that they are being completely taken for granted.

Equally important are changes that are external to the relationship itself; particularly in the case of couples who marry young. For example, a young man, in the process of building up his career, can change quite dramatically in his level of self-confidence and sophistication. A partner who has spent the equivalent years at home, rearing children, can understandably feel threatened and left behind. Conversely, the fact that women are generally becoming more assertive and independent (continuing to work after marriage, and returning to work after having or rearing children) can meet with resistance from a traditional spouse. Finally, infidelity and affairs usually lead to problems, even in the most "liberated" of partnerships.

Cognitive.   The early days of marriage are especially important for getting to know and understand a partner's attitudes, beliefs, flash points, and weak spots. Many people enter marriage with unrealistic expectations of themselves, of their partner, or of marriage as a whole. This inevitably leads to disappointments and resentment. Differences in attitudes to things as basic as sex, contraception, child-rearing practices, or finances—which, ironically, are often *not* discussed in advance—can lead to major outbursts.

Some people are more emotional than others. Personal insecurities are often highlighted within a relationship in the shape of unfounded jealousy, suspicion, or excessive demands for attention and reassurance (Margolin, 1981). Opposites do attract, but these very personality differences can often result in misunderstandings or in a genuine inability to understand and empathize with a partner's fears or anxieties. There is a tendency, as already explained, to assume similarity. Partners can also differ in their ability to handle change: Support can be needed even when pleasant things, like a vacation or the purchase of a new house, are being planned.

As in the other areas discussed, people also change psychologically over time. Finding that a partner's attitude to something as fundamental as divorce, adoption, or religion has altered significantly can, in some cases, lead to insecurity on a wider level: "Is he going to change his attitude toward me also?"

TREATMENT

Over the last 10 years there has been a distinct trend towards broadening the conceptual and technical domains of behavior marital therapy to include cognitive and affective factors. Tackling relationship difficulties is a complex undertaking. Two independent people are involved; people who frequently see their shared situation very differently. The therapist must establish, as early as possible, what the basic problem is and whether or not both parties are prepared and motivated to work at improving their joint situation. Establishing exactly where the difficulties lie is not always easy.

I have found it useful, on the first consultation, or intake interview, to start off by talking to the couple *together*. This provides an opportunity to assess the *feeling tone* of the relationship (the vibes)—whether they look at one another directly or sit closely together, who does the talking, and so on. Both parties are then interviewed *separately* to get a clearer picture of how they independently view the situation, and also to allow for confidential disclosures about how motivated, or hopeless, they feel about their future together. Sometimes, at this point, one party will reveal the existence of, for example, an ongoing extramarital affair of which their partner is unaware, and their consequent reluctance to work at improving the marriage.

Assuming that no such major obstacles arise, communal discussion is then resumed. Both parties are asked to keep *two* separate diaries *each* over the following weeks (Appendix I: Self-Monitoring Behavior). The first is a daily record of situations, times, and themes (e.g., lack of time, money, or sex) that are constant sources of irritation or that consistently lead to disagreements. As well as this *mutual monitoring*, they also keep independent records of things their partner does, or does not do, that repeatedly annoy or upset them—like habits of breaking arrangements, coming home late or intoxicated, or procrastinating over household chores. Questionnaires such as the Beier-Sternberg Discord Questionnaire (Table 8.1) are also frequently used to identify areas of marital conflict and unhappiness.

At the next session, 2 to 3 weeks later, both sets of diaries are independently reviewed and discussed. The therapist notes the most obvious sources of conflict and upset, and *prime problem times*. A thorough analysis of the couple's readiness and willingness to work at changing is then carried out (Appendix I: Motivation Analysis). Both parties independently analyze their reasons for wanting to stay in the relationship and to work at the marriage. It sometimes becomes obvious, at this juncture, that the possibility of separation or divorce should be discussed. If both parties *do* decide to try again, there must be a clear agreement that they are both prepared to work at it, and that they realize what is at stake if they do not. When the major areas of change have been identified from the diaries and discussed, a change plan, with realistic goals and time span, is devised (Appendix I: Change Plan). If communication is very deteriorated, it is sometimes useful to institute written behavioral contracts at this time to get things started (Appendix VI: Contracts). Continued monitoring is also essential.

The subsequent sessions focus primarily on increasing communication. This includes working on skills of relating, listening, expression of feelings, problem solving, and assertion (Appendix VI: Listening; Problem Solving; Feeling Expression; Assertion). The results of these sessions—which can span a number of weeks or months—and the contingent between-session homework assignments usually lead to changes in the couple's schedules. For example, the need for more socializing or for more time together might become obvious. These planned changes—which must be small, concrete, and easily observable—are written down. There are also a number of effective techniques for increasing positive exchanges, such as "love days" and "caring days" (Appendix VI: Increasing Positive Exchanges), which are put into operation during this time also.

When behavior changes have started, both parties usually find it beneficial to begin cognitive work. They are taught how to recognize their negative

TABLE 8.1 Beier-Sternberg Discord Questionnaire.

DQ

With these scales, we want to find out what you believe are the areas of agreement or disagreement in your marriage. We also want to find out if these areas of agreement and disagreement make you feel happy, sad, or indifferent. For example, if money is a topic of much disagreement in your marriage, you could make a mark in Scale 1: *Degree of Agreement* under the numbers 5, 6, or 7 depending on the extent of your disagreement. If you were to make a mark under the number 7, this would mean that you feel there is much disagreement about money in your marriage. If you were to mark under the number 5, this means you feel there is some disagreement about money.

With *Scale 1* we want to find out how you differ from your spouse in looking at things. In *Scale 2* we want to find out how you feel about these differences. If, for example, a disagreement were to make you very unhappy, as in the "Money" example given above, you would mark 6 or 7 on *Scale 2: Results of Agreement or Disagreement*. Please check each item in both scales. Remember, the *higher* the number the more disagreement or conflict over a particular topic, the *lower* the number, the *more* agreement.

	Scale 1: Degree of Agreement							Scale 2: Results of Agreement or Disagreement						
	Agree						Disagree	Happy						Unhappy
	1	2	3	4	5	6	7	1	2	3	4	5	6	7
1. Money														
2. Children														
3. Sex														
4. Concern and love														
5. Doing things together (in spare time)														
6. Friends & social life														
7. Getting ahead, ambition														
8. Politics														
9. Children's education														
10. Religion														
Other(s): please specify														

thinking in problem situations: "He's doing it on purpose," "Why doesn't she notice my new shirt—she wants me to ask her if she likes it," "Surely he must *know* that I'm tired; he always wants sex at the wrong time." The next step is to learn how to examine and dispute these negative self-statements on paper (Appendix V: Self-Disputation) and *then* to practice applying the objective, new appraisals *in* the problem situations. They are also encouraged to *share* their problematic self-talk by discussing these self-defeating "tapes" with their partner—who, very often, turns out to have been totally unaware that they were annoyed, disappointed, frustrated, or tired at the time the problem arose. A partner's *actual* motivation and thinking, when discussed in retrospect, frequently turns out to be much simpler and less malicious than was interpreted or concluded at the time. *Mind reading* is usually a long way off the mark, and assuming similarity only leads to further misunderstandings (see Assumed Similarity, p. 72).

When the relationship is genuinely on firmer ground, and communication is less defended, it frequently becomes obvious from honest interchange that both parties need to take a hard look at areas of *personal* functioning. They might benefit, as individuals, from losing weight, improving general punctuality, or becoming more assertive or less fussy, for example. These can be things that their partner has repeatedly pointed out, or that they had been privately planning to get around to "sometime." Likewise, one or both parties may need to look at underlying cognitions in relation to independence, unfulfilled expectations, or self-esteem; and to spend some sessions alone with the therapist working through these, or similar, long-standing areas of personal conflict or uncertainty (Appendix V: Vertical Arrow; Uncovering the Shoulds).

Finally, as things continue to improve, the couple may find it timely to increase shared activities (Appendix VI: Increasing Positive Exchanges) or to explore their environment anew together, and to develop some areas of common interest (Appendix II: Utilizing Environmental Resources).

SUGGESTED FURTHER READING

Theory and Research

Beck, A. T. (1988). *Love is never enough.* NY: Harper and Row.

Bradbury, T. W., & Fincham, F. D. (1987). Assessing the effects of behavioral marital therapy: Assumptions and measurement strategies. *Clinical Psychology Review, 7,* 525–538.

Halweg, K., & Jacobson, N. S. (Eds.). (1984). *Marital interaction: Analysis and modification.* NY: Guilford.

Holtzworth-Munroe, A. (1988). Causal attribution in marital violence: Theoretical and methodological issues. *Clinical Psychology Review, 8,* 331–344.

Jacobson, N. S., & Margolin, G. (1979). *Marital therapy.* NY: Brunner Mazel.

O'Leary, K. D. (Ed.). (1987). *The assessment of marital dischord.* Hillsdale, NJ: Lawrence Erlbaum Associates.

Stuart, R. B. (1980). *Helping couples change.* NY: Guilford.

Wills, R. M., Faitler, S. L., & Snyder, K. D. (1987). Distinctiveness of behavioral versus insight-oriented marital therapy: An empirical analysis. *Journal of Consulting and Clinical Psychology, 55,* 685–690.

Wilson, G. L., & Bornstein, P. H. (1986). The assessment of marital interaction. In P. H. Bornstein, & M. T. Bornstein (Eds.). *Marital therapy: A behavioral-communication approach* (pp. 34–52). NY: Pergamon Press.

Wood, L. F., & Jacobson, N. S. (1985). Marital distress. In D. Barlow (Ed.), *Clinical handbook of psychological disorders: A step-by-step treatment manual* (pp. 344–416). NY: Guilford.

Popular and Self-Help:

Dominian, J. (1968). *Marital breakdown.* Baltimore: Pergamon Press.

Hodgson, R., & Miller, P. (1982). *Selfwatching: Addictions, habits, compulsions: What to do about them* (Chapter 7). London: Century Publishing Company.

Markman, H. J., Floyd, F. J., Stanley, S. M., & Storaasli, R. D. (1988). Prevention of marital distress: A longitudinal investigation. *Journal of Consulting and Clinical Psychology, 56,* 210–217.

Miller, S., Wackman, D., Nunally, E., & Saline, E. (1982). *Straight talk.* NY: New American Library.

9

Sex

It is ironic that, in this so-called "liberated" age, there is more nonsense written and spoken about sex than almost any other topic. Part of the reason is the surprising degree of ignorance and misinformation that still abounds. Unfortunately, because people are not taught about sex in the same way as they are taught about literature or geometry, what is learned is often acquired by *personal* associations, *personal* consequences and *personal* observations. The associations and consequences are often best forgotten, and the observations can be misleading or damaging. Yet everyone is expected to know about sex, have lots of it, and enjoy it enormously.

The result is a presumption of knowledge, experience, and expertise; and a reality of misinformation, ignorance, and anxiety. People feel they *should* know, and are therefore often embarrassed to ask. People feel that sex *should* be consistently exciting, tender, and satisfying to both partners; and so, they often erroneously believe that they are missing out or are inadequate.

Sex is a core symbol in a relationship, and an important part of most people's lives. It is a way of communicating feelings that are sometimes difficult to put into words. Enjoyable sex is both stimulating and relaxing. It refreshes the body and the mind; it can soothe tensions, misgivings, and even disagreements. Good sex between people who really care for each other is what *making love* is all about.

On the other hand, the bedroom can become an arena for wrestling with emotions and personal conflicts. Sex necessitates openness and vulnerability. Therefore, it can be abused as a vehicle for establishing power. Love and fidelity are often also tested through sex. In sum, it can become a trigger for, or an end point of, a whole panoply of interactions—sexual and marital, social and emotional.

FACTS AND FIGURES

Various researchers, like Masters & Johnson, suggest that about 50% of all couples experience sexual difficulties at some stage in their married life (Masters & Johnson, 1970). This is understandable, because successful sex demands a considerable degree of communication, cooperation, and coordination—sexual and otherwise—between partners. People need a period of time together to get to know one another sexually, as well as in other ways. Consequently, many sexual problems arise in the early days of a marriage or partnership, when the couple are still getting habituated. However, sexual problems can also arise at a later stage—even in a well-matched partnership where sex has hitherto been unproblematic and satisfying to both partners. An occasional episode of sexual difficulty is no cause for alarm, although problems can arise if one party is blamed for the change. It is always best to view sexual difficulty as a problem of the *couple*. Masters and Johnson (1970) contended: "There is no such entity as an uninvolved partner" (p. 2).

CAUSES, SIGNS AND SYMPTOMS

When and why do sexual problems arise? There are many reasons. The four areas of functioning—environment, body, behavior, and thinking—are all important. An equally important cause of sexual difficulties, however, is ignorance and misinformation. There is still an incredible amount of ignorance about sexual anatomy and basic sexual functioning, about what is fact and what is fiction in relation to sexual practices, and about how much and how often is "normal."

There are no hard and fast rules about sex, no recommended daily (or weekly) allowances. Neither wanting lots nor wanting only a little is abnormal, and it is pointless for people to compare themselves against some kind of average. Essentially, it does not matter if a couple make love twice a day or twice a year. Problems arise where there are *discrepancies* in the needs, tastes, or appetites of both parties; and there is *also* a lack of communication or compromise.

Environmental.   As with marriage, a stressful external environment is not conducive to good sex. If one or both parties are under pressure—at work or at home—this can put strain on the relationship, which can, in turn,

RESEARCH

Our knowledge of sexual practices and norms has been built up gradually and primarily through the findings of a number of large-scale surveys and laboratory investigations. The first survey of significance was carried out by Alfred Kinsey in the United States in the late 1940s (Kinsey, Pomeroy and Martin, 1948). His results highlighted, among other things, the wide variety in people's sex lives, and extraordinary differences between people. Some men had sex more than twice a day, whereas others only reported one sexual experience in a lifetime. Women were even more variable; some consistently had very large amounts of sex, whereas others not only had no sexual experience at all, but had never felt any kind of sexual need or desire (Kinsey, Pomeroy and Martin, 1953).

More recent American data, provided by Masters and Johnson, has confirmed these wide individual differences (Masters & Johnson, 1970). These researchers also accumulated a reliable base of factual information about the normal sexual response cycle and exploded a number of widely held erroneous beliefs and myths. For example, in men they found that variation in the size of the erect penis is very small; and furthermore, that sexual satisfaction is unrelated to size. They claimed that intercourse during menstruation does not harm women, and is largely a matter of personal preference. They also asserted that it is not possible to differentiate between clitoral and vaginal orgasm, as had been previously believed. They suggested that simultaneous orgasm is not a necessary goal for love-making—and can even cause difficulties, because it encourages self-awareness, which, in turn, can dissipate the spontaneity of love-making. Regarding aging, they validated the idea that old age is associated with changes in sexual response but that it need not be a cause of loss of potency or interest. Finally, they reported that masturbation is quite common, especially among males, and does not do any harm to the vast majority (Masters & Johnson, 1966).

Ironically, although this information was available over 20 years ago, many of these myths still abound, and still lead to unrealistic expectations and unnecessary anxieties.

affect sex. Sex can also be hindered by a lack of privacy, realistic fears of interruption, or simply a lack of time. On an even more mundane level, an environment that is too cold, too warm, too dirty, or too noisy can also act as a "turn-off."

Physiological. The body is obviously a crucial part of good sex, and if it is not functioning properly, sex will be affected (Kolodny, Masters, & Johnson, 1979). Sexual problems can arise from anatomical defects in the reproductive system and various urological, endocrine, and cardiovascular disorders. Deficient hormonal functioning, circulatory problems, and the aging process can also effect libido and sexual performance. Many of the sexually transmitted diseases can also influence sex, both directly and indirectly. Other important factors are general ill health and physical exhaustion and tiredness.

Formal psychiatric difficulties, such as endogenous depression and schizophrenia, will also create difficulties. A high level of somatic anxiety, although not a "mental illness" as such, can indirectly affect sex in a number of ways. Highly anxious people often have difficulty relaxing and switching off; and, the rapid breathing that accompanies sexual arousal can sometimes trigger an association with pre-panic attack sensations, thereby producing anxiety and apprehension. Prescribed drugs can also, ironically, affect sexual functioning (e.g., hypotensives, some antidepressants, and some forms of the contraceptive pill). Although some people find that alcohol relaxes them, excessive consumption effects sexual potency and performance, especially in men. Menopause and postpartum depression are also important. Libido can also vary significantly at different phases of the menstrual cycle; while weight loss or worry can also effect the menstrual cycle and lead to decreased interest on a more general level. Finally, vaginal infections often result in painful intercourse for women.

A less direct but also very important physical factor is appearance. A body that is very thin or very fat will not be as provocative or stimulating as one that is well proportioned. Other details of external appearances are items like hair curlers, face masks and creams, dowdy night attire, or a 2-day growth of beard. General hygiene is also important; bad breath or dirty hands and fingernails can make a big difference.

Behavioral.   Good sex is a fine balance of communication on many levels. Lack of experience can lead to excessive eagerness to prove adequacy or stamina; and to decreased attentiveness to the other's needs. Sex is a skill, and, therefore, it requires practice, as well as knowledge of one's own likes and dislikes and those of one's partner. People vary enormously in their sexual tastes and needs. Problems can arise if one party is too rough or too quick, too demanding or too aggressive, too gentle or too slow. In many partnerships, one person—usually the man—tends to take the initiative more often than the other. If "the initiator" would like the other party to take a more active and spontaneous role, and they, due to disinterest or inhibition, fail to do so, resentment and frustration can build up.

What leads up to sex and what occurs afterwards are also very important. A woman who likes gentle pillow-talk and cuddling after sex may feel disappointed by a partner who is snoring, oblivious to the world, 2 minutes after intimate disclosures and love-making. Generally speaking, women need more foreplay and also have a greater need to feel "loved" in a more general sense.

It is imperative, therefore, that a couple develops adequate communication skills, both verbal and nonverbal, so that they can share their experiences, likes and dislikes, needs, and preferences—and not just "assume similarity."

Cognitive.   The belief that sexual problems indicate deep-seated psychopathology is simply wrong (Wright, Perreault, & Mattieu, 1977). What is at the root of many sexual difficulties is anxiety. Anxiety and sex do not mix. In other words, whatever is going on in one's head will affect what goes on in bed. This includes general attitudes and beliefs, as well as specific anxieties and worries.

Very often, problems arise early in a relationship, because of real or perceived pressure to perform. This can result in performance anxiety, fear of failure, and "spectating." What frequently happens is that a small problem arises and one or both parties become over-concerned, self-conscious, and goal-oriented. Then the spontaneity—so integral to good sex—is replaced with anxiety, and this sets in motion a vicious cycle of self-fulfilling prophecies. Each time the couple goes to bed they hope that things will be better. This anticipatory anxiety makes it *less* likely for things to run smoothly; and the next time, they are both a little bit *more* apprehensive. In the early days of a relationship, anxiety can also be generated by ignorance—which, in turn, can lead to shyness and embarrassment. Ignorance can also produce unrealistic expectations, which can result in disappointment in a partner or in personal feelings of inadequacy.

Reality-based anxieties—such as fear of pregnancy or an intense desire to become pregnant—can also interfere with sex. Differences in attitudes and expectations—about religion, contraception, or pornography—can also generate tension. Partners often differ in their levels of curiosity and adventurousness. One person might like to try out different positions, whereas the other—for any number of reasons—might not. Sexual trauma (in childhood or at a later stage) can also precipitate problems, such as fear of the sight of the genitalia or the act of penetration itself. On the other hand, people sometimes feel guilty about *enjoying* sex; and this can, in turn, lead to emotional inhibition. Another factor that can produce guilt is indulgence in sexual fantasies; some find that fantasizing during sex makes it more exciting, but they feel guilty and reluctant about disclosing the fact to their partner.

Sex can also be affected by time itself. Over time, repeated sex with the same person loses its novelty and can become monotonous. There can also be decreased interest in the partner, as a sexual object or on a wider scale. Problems can also arise if the relationship as a whole is not going well. Marital or interpersonal difficulties can give rise to feelings of aggression,

---

WHAT ARE THE COMMON SEXUAL PROBLEMS?

The most common problems in *men* are:

1. *Impotence.* This is the inability to attain or maintain an erection of sufficient strength to enable the act of intercourse to take place. Occasional episodes of impotence happen to all men—due to tiredness, ill health, drugs, or excess alcohol consumption. But, if impotence is the rule and not the exception, or if a man has *never* achieved an erection of sufficient strength to enable the act of intercourse to take place (primary impotence), then professional advice should be sought.

2. *Ejaculation Difficulties.* Premature ejaculation is the inability to delay ejaculation for a sufficient period of time for intercourse to take place. Ejaculatory incompetence is the inability of the man to ejaculate while the penis is inserted in the woman's vagina. In either case, professional advice should be sought.

The most common problems in *women* are:

1. *Orgasmic Difficulties.* Some women do not have orgasms at all, and others do not have them frequently enough or when they want them, that is, usually after intercourse. Sometimes expectations are too high, but professional advice may also be needed.

2. *Painful Intercourse (Dyspareunia).* Painful intercourse can be caused by vaginal disease or infection. This should be checked out with one's M.D. It can also be related to having intercourse before the woman is lubricating. There is also a condition called *vaginismus*, where the muscles around the entrance of the vagina go into a painful, involuntary spasm, making penetration impossible. The prognosis for this problem is very positive, but it does require professional guidance to overcome.

---

decreased interest, as already mentioned, or resentment between partners to the extent that sex is used as a weapon.

TREATMENT

The complexities involved in solving sexual difficulties are many. As with marital problems, two independent parties are involved; but, sex also touches on the most intimate and personal aspects of people's lives. Because the causes of sexual difficulties are numerous, it is essential, before starting sex therapy, to ensure that both parties undergo a thorough physical examination, to eliminate the possibility of a medical cause for the problem. Diabetes, for example, can cause impotence in men.

Having done this, the first interview involves more or less the same steps as in marital therapy. In other words, the intake session starts with a short talk with the couple *together*—to see how they relate and to get a general outline of the problem. In this introductory preamble, the therapist also conveys a number of important facts: that sexual problems are common; that, generally speaking, the prognosis is good; and that the couple is not unusual in experiencing sexual difficulties, but in having the good sense to do something about it. Such reassurance is usually necessary, because these people are about to talk to a stranger about the most intimate details of their private life, and because they *also* frequently have erroneous beliefs that sexual problems indicate underlying psychopathology.

Both parties are then interviewed *separately*, to establish what they independently see as the problem and what they think are the reasons for it. At this point, the therapist also excludes other obvious causes—such as severe depression, alcohol or drug abuse, extreme marital discord, ignorance, or extramarital affairs—*and* acquires as much information as possible about the history of the problem and current sexual functioning. If, at the end of the interview, the therapist has a clear picture of the situation and considers that the problem is workable, there is a "round table discussion." The couple are provided with a tentative explanation as to why they are experiencing difficulties in their sexual relationship, and an outline of therapy. Because mutual cooperation is essential for treatment to succeed, a thorough analysis of the couple's willingness to work at changing is carried out at the very beginning of the next session, which usually takes place a week or two later (Appendix I: Motivation Analysis). This exercise serves to make the couple independently aware of how important a good sex life is to their relationship, as well as the advisability of not allowing things to continue as they are.

I have found Masters & Johnson's (1970) approach to the treatment of sexual dysfunction particularly useful in the early stages of interventions for sexual difficulties. The essential components of their program are *graded exposure* (Appendix IV: Systematic Desensitization) and the learning of sexual skills (Appendix IV: Behavioral Rehearsal). The couple first contracts to abstain from full intercourse. Then, through a series of graded tasks—which are approached in a goal-free and relaxed atmosphere over a number of weeks or months—they learn or re-learn what pleases and what displeases their partner.

The first stage of treatment is called *sensate focus*. The couple sets aside time (e.g., 20 minutes several times a week) to caress and touch the other's body without clothes. They learn to give and receive pleasure, without focusing on or touching the genitals or erogenous zones. After a number of weeks, when they are more comfortable and relaxed together, they are encouraged to explore each others sexual organs—again, giving and taking pleasure, *without* moving on to intercourse. By taking away what has hitherto been the "goal," that is, coitus, pressure to perform, fear of failure, and spectating ("Am I doing it right—I hope it goes right this time") are also eliminated. It is essential, however, that people stick to the agreement *not* to have full intercourse. Sometimes this is difficult, as a relaxed couple often find themselves more aroused than they have been in a long time. If they *do* break the rules however, and things do not go well—which is what usually happens because they have not completed treatment—they are back to square one and have the attendant disappointment and regret to cope with also.

During these sessions, the couple is also strongly encouraged to talk, to tell each other how they feel. Communication can be a problem due to ignorance, so I usually advise couples, however overtly sophisticated, to read one of the many informative and widely available books on sex. People simply cannot talk if they do not have the vocabulary. If ignorance is not the problem, but one or both parties are too shy to say how they feel and put their feelings into words, they are encouraged to communicate nonverbally (e.g., with agreeable sighs or by steering and guiding a partner's hand). Finally, couples often express the concern, at this stage, that the program is very artificial. The idea of going to bed for 20 minutes before dinner or their favorite television program, undressing, getting excited, and then returning to their normal routine, strikes them as unrealistic or even amusing. It *does* take a little getting used to, and often also requires perseverance and effort to fit the sessions into an already tight schedule. However, like most other behaviors, after a few days it becomes a habit, and self-consciousness decreases. Furthermore, as the couple becomes more relaxed, these interludes become more of an enjoyable recreation than a chore.

When the couple has progressed satisfactorily through the sensate focus stage of therapy, and they are happy about caressing each other's bodies freely and without anxiety, the therapist goes on to focus on the *particular* problem identified at the intake interview or for which they were referred (e.g., impotence, vaginismus). It is not necessary to go into the specifics of treatment for each of the major problems here. For those interested in reading further, a list of well-written books and manuals is provided in the annotated bibliography at the end of the chapter.

Because people's problems are always unique, any number of other behavioral techniques may also be utilized. For example, the couple may have to develop communication skills on a more general level (Appendix VI: Listening; Problem Solving). One party may need to become more assertive in expressing his or her needs and preferences, to take the initiative more often, or to learn how to give and take compliments (Appendix VI: Assertion). An ability to say "no" without feeling guilty (Appendix V: Uncovering The Shoulds), or to express feelings and accept the other's intimate disclosures without undue embarrassment or self-consciousness (Appendix VI: Expressing Emotions; Accepting Emotions), are also skills that frequently need to be acquired.

Sexual problems have a particularly good prognosis and are no indication of underlying pathology, as used to be suspected. However, as with *all* the problem areas discussed, cognitive intervention is a necessary ingredient in sexual therapy. This frequently consists of examining the kinds of things that go through each party's mind *before, during*, and *after* sex—self-statements such as: "I hope it goes well *this* time," "I wish I could relax—what's wrong with me." Also, thoughts that repeatedly come to mind when sex is suggested are usually very informative ("He wants me to have sex every night, but he won't do anything *I* want. The car is still in the garage"). These problematic internal dialogues can be identified from ongoing diary-keeping (Appendix I: Self-Monitoring Thinking) and then examined and disputed in individual or joint sessions (Appendix V: Self-Disputation). As with marital therapy, it can be very educational for the other party to learn the silent fears or frustrations that their partner carries into the bedroom.

Also, underlying erroneous beliefs and conflicts about sex ("I'm no good at sex; I don't want to do it, it's wrong," "Men are all rough; they don't want to know how I *feel*," "If she doesn't have an orgasm, she'll blame me") *or* traumatic sexual experiences need to be uncovered and explored as to the effects that they are having on the person's enjoyment of sex, as well as on the relationship as a whole. On the other hand, feelings of guilt about enjoying sex or the fantasies that accompany it also need to be worked through (Appendix V: Vertical Arrow; Uncovering The Shoulds). Some therapists, in fact, make a point of *including* imagery training as part of therapy. They encourage the couple to develop visual images and personal fantasies, both for cognitive rehearsal as well as to increase sexual arousal and satisfaction (Appendix V: Coping Imagery; Cognitive Rehearsal). It very much depends on individual tastes and needs; there are no hard and fast rules for everyone.

If one party finds it hard to relax or feels very tense in bed, relaxation training can help greatly (Appendix III: Relaxation). Likewise, people who find it hard to "switch off" cognitively can develop the ability to distract themselves from intrusive thoughts (such as "Did I unplug the heater") or images of themselves tired and puffy-eyed in the office the following morning, or unable to concentrate (Appendix V: Distraction). On a wider level, one or both parties may realize that they need to improve their overall appearance or attractiveness, cut down on alcohol, lose weight, buy some new clothes, or improve personal hygiene. These changes must also be planned to take place over a period of time, using the same tools for change as before (Appendix I: Change Plan). Finally, even when therapy is successful, an effort is sometimes needed to continue to schedule sex as a regular and enjoyable activity; old habits die hard. This is important, as it helps both parties to unwind and relax together and to share their most intimate and personal feelings (Appendix IV: Managing Time). Being loved makes people feel good.

SUGGESTED FURTHER READING

Theory and Research

Annon, J. (1976). *Behavioral treatment of sexual problems: Brief therapy.* Hagerstown, MD: Harper & Row.

Bancroft, J. (1983). *Human sexuality.* Edinburgh: Churchill Livinstone.

Beck, J. G. & Barlow, D. H. (1984). Current conceptualization of sexual dysfunction: A review and an alternative perspective. *Clinical Psychology Review, 4,* 363–378.

Cole, M. (1985). Sex therapy. A critical appraisal. *British Journal of Psychiatry, 147,* 337–351.

Crown, S. (Ed.). (1976). *Psychosexual problems: Psychotherapy, counselling and behavioral modification.* London: Academic Press.

Ellis, E. M. (1983). A review of empirical rape research: Victims reactions and response to treatment. *Clinical Psychology Review, 3,* 473–490.

Haddon, C. (1982). *The limits of sex.* London: Michael Joseph.

Hawton, K. (1985). *Sex therapy: A practical guide.* Oxford: Oxford University Press.

Hite, S. (1976). *The Hite report.* NY: Macmillan.

Hite, S. (1981). *The Hite report on male sexuality.* London: McDonald.

Jehu, D. (1979). *Sexual dysfunction.* NY: Wiley.

Kaplan, H. S. (1974). *The new sex therapy.* NY: Brunner Mazel.

Kaplan, H. S. (1979). *Disorders of sexual desire.* NY: Brunner Mazel.

Kaplan, H. S. (1981). *The illustrated manual of sex therapy.* London: Granada.

Katchadourain, H. & Lunde, D. (1975). *Fundamentals of human sexuality.* NY: Holt Rinehart and Winston.

Lo Piccolo, J. & Lo Piccolo, L. (Eds.). (1978). *Handbook of sex therapy.* NY: Plenum Press.

Munjack, D. J. & Oziel, J. (1980). *Sexual medicine and counselling in office practice: A comprehensive treatment guide.* Boston: Little Brown.

Symons, D. (1979). *The evolution of human sexuality.* Oxford: Oxford University Press.

Popular and Self-Help

Barbach, L. (1983). *For each other.* London: Corgi Books.

Belliveau, F. & Richter, L. (1971). *Understanding human sexual inadequacy.* London: Coronet.

Brown, P. & Faulder, C. (1979). *Treat yourself to sex.* London: Penguin.

Comfort, A. (1972). *The joy of sex.* NY: Simon and Schuster.

Delvin, D. (1975). *The book of love.* London: New English Library.

Heiman, J., Lo Piccolo, L., & Lo Piccolo, J. (1976). *Becoming Orgasmic.* Englewood Cliffs, NJ: Prentice-Hall (Spectrum).

Katchadourian, H. (1974). *Human sexuality: Sense and nonsense.* San Francisco, CA: W. H. Freeman.

Zilbergeld, B. (1979). *Men and sex: A guide to sexual fulfillment.* London: Souvenir Press.

10

Overindulgence

"Go on; one more won't make any difference." "You deserve it; you've had a rough day." Sound familiar? These are the kinds of things people say to themselves when they are trying to justify what they know in their heart is not the right course of action for their mouth—one more ice cream, beer, or cigarette. This chapter covers two major areas of overindulgence that have serious consequences for health and threaten psychological well-being: overeating and smoking. The problem of excessive alcohol consumption is too controversial and complex to deal with in a text such as this. There are numerous comprehensive treatments of the subject, and they are included in the annotated bibliography at the end of the chapter.

The major health problems of modern living are no longer attributable to infectious diseases, but to patterns of behavior, especially bad habits such as eating too much and smoking (Pomerleau, Bass, & Crown, 1975). Why do so many people choose to destroy themselves with excess calories and nicotine? One reason is the constant flow of advertisements on radio and television, in magazines and newspapers; everywhere, people see others doing all the things they are told not to do. The effects of vicarious conditioning, or learning by observation, are very powerful: Despite government health warnings, the 1960s' image of the smoker as sophisticated and "cool" lingers on in some circles. Association learning also plays a major role. People come to associate eating and smoking with certain places, people, situations, or emotional states. Some people reach automatically for the cookie jar or cigarette pack when they are upset or under pressure—or even when they are happy or excited about some positive occurrence. Furthermore, our affluent society trains people to reward themselves, and others, with things that taste nice, that make them feel relaxed, or that provide a quick "buzz." The immediately satisfying effects of food and nicotine are extremely important in understanding why these habits persist. The majority of people know very well what is good and bad for them, but the thought of looking good on the beach in 6 months time or of not having a racking cough in 3 months time is not as compelling as the present desire to eat or smoke. Why not just enjoy life, and let tomorrow take care of itself? Some facts and statistics provide the answer.

OVEREATING

Facts and Figures

Obesity is a major health problem, with multifarious undesirable social and personal consequences. Yet, current estimates suggest that between 40 and 80 million Americans are overweight; and furthermore, that obesity is on the increase. The pattern is the same in the United Kingdom. Major sex and social differences have been identified. Overall, women are more prone to overweight than men; it is normal for adult men to carry about 10% to 20% of body weight in fat, and for adult women to have about 25% fat. Men are more likely to become overweight in their early 30s, whereas women show the pattern later, during their 40s and early 50s. There are also large class differences; obesity is six times more common among lower socioeconomic groups (see Stunkard, 1986).

How fat is fat? An adult is considered overweight if his or her total body weight exceeds "ideal" weight by 20% or more. Insurance companies have developed charts that indicate ideal body weights for height, sex, and body build. However, because the measurements include muscle, skin, water, bone, and fat, these charts are open to misinterpretation. Consequently, experts now suggest that obesity is more properly defined as excess *fat*, as opposed to excess weight. A quick way to establish if you are too fat is to pinch the back of your upper arm, halfway between your shoulder and elbow, using your thumb and first finger. If you can pick up a fold of flesh with a *thickness* of more than an inch, then you are "overweight." However, *really* accurate measures of the fat content of the body require expensive equipment.

The medical consequences of being overweight are well known. Obesity has been associated with heart disease, high blood pressure, strokes, kidney problems, gall stones, diabetes, osteo-arthritis, and breathing difficulties. Operations also carry a greater-than-normal risk. Even examining an overweight person to make a diagnosis can be hampered by layers of fat. Life insurance companies also stress that people 20% above their ideal weight carry a greater risk of dying early. To complicate matters, fat people also seem to get involved in more accidents—both at home and at work—either because they move more slowly, or because their bulk simply gets in the way, or both.

Finally, the psychological consequences of being overweight are very significant. The image of the fat person as jolly and placid, or a "bundle of laughs," is totally wrong. Depression and low self-esteem, social embarrassment, and gross self-consciousness are among the many problems that overweight people experience. These feelings are not just subjective; studies show that the obese actually *do* bear the brunt of significant social discrimination (Tobias & Gordon, 1980); which, undoubtedly, compounds feelings of self-denigration.

Causes, Signs, and Symptoms

If the consequences of obesity are so significant, in terms of both physical and psychological well-being, why does the problem persist? The question of weight and weight control is extremely complex, and involves a number of factors, including environment, body, behavior patterns, and thinking.

Environmental. We all associate particular people and places with eating. Dining with certain friends may mean a heavy meal that is hard to refuse without giving offense, for example. Some environments, such as restaurants, are more food-rich than others. Particular times can become triggers for overeating, such as weekends, vacations, and coffee breaks. It is easy to get into the habit of eating at these times without necessarily feeling hungry. At Christmas, many people eat excessive amounts simply because it's Christmas.

Association learning, therefore, plays a significant role in determining how, when, what, and how much people eat. In many cases, eating is only related in a small way to hunger. This appears to be particularly true of some overweight people; research suggests that these people may be more "external" than normal-weight people. In other words, they may be more sensitive to their surroundings, and therefore less able to exercise self-control in the presence of food and food-related cues (Rodin, 1981).

Physiological. Experts now feel that many people are born with a genuine predisposition to obesity (Stunkard et al, 1986); but will not automatically become overweight unless they overeat and are inactive. In other words, obesity does appear to run in families, but it need not necessarily manifest. Unfortunately, however, the children of overweight parents are often overfed, and they therefore *learn* to overeat from a very early age.

In this context, one focus of research has been childhood eating patterns and the *set point* or *ponderostat* theory (Hirsch, 1973). Although the number of fat cells is genetically determined, it seems that fat cells are also formed during infancy and again in adolescence. People who overeat at these critical times form more fat cells than others, and, as a consequence, are more likely to put on weight, as well as to have more difficulty losing it. Theoretically, then, two people of the same weight may be carrying a different number of fat cells; so, one may have to struggle to maintain a certain weight, whereas the other may be able to eat what he or she wants and still hold a consistent weight (see Brownell, 1984).

Finally, differences in metabolic rate have been a particular focus of investigation in recent years. Generally speaking, the rate of basal metabolism is higher in men and in those of large body build, and it decreases with age. However, significant individual differences have also been identified; some people gain weight predictably when overfed, whereas others do not. The reasons are extremely complex and not fully understood. On average, the metabolic rate of the obese is lower than that of normal-weight persons; they do not burn off excess calories as efficiently as the average person. Recent investigations have also indicated, however, that when people diet their metabolic rate *slows down*. This makes sense in terms of evolution and survival; that is, at times when food was not available, metabolic rate slowed down in order to conserve food and energy. But, what it means in relation to the problem of obesity is that, if someone is *repeatedly* putting on weight and then dieting to lose, over time their body may gradually become less efficient at losing weight (Brownell, Greenwood, Shrager, & Stellar, 1986a; Leibel & Hirsch, 1984). Recent research also suggests that exercise may help to speed up metabolic rate over a period of time (Thompson, Jarvie, Lahey, & Cureton, 1982).

Behavioral.   People develop *patterns* of eating. They get into habits— good and bad—of having regular meals several times a day or of snacking on the way to meetings and eating large meals late at night. Some people eat very slowly; others gulp their food. Some eat a balanced, healthy diet, whereas others maintain themselves on "empty" calories, like candy. For some, eating is just a habitual activity; they have lost track of where hunger fits in. People's eating patterns are extremely different. Some are obviously more healthy than others.

Bad eating habits develop via all the regular learning routes. People come to associate, and respond to, certain faces, places, and moods with eating. They succumb to the short-term "buzz" of an ice cream or burger, rather than focusing on the longer term prospect of confidently strolling along the street in 6 months time. They are seduced by posters and videos of trendy people eating trendy junk food. Finally, many overweight people, due to an inability to assert themselves socially, often feel pressured into breaking a diet, out of unwillingness to offend a hostess who has gone to a lot of trouble.

Cognitive. Research also suggests that overweight people are especially likely to respond to negative emotional states (e.g., anger, fatigue, loneliness, or boredom) by eating (Cummings, Gordon, & Marlatt, 1980). Overindulgence is then often followed by guilt and remorse, which perpetuates the cycle.

Many overweight people also have a very negative self-image (Leon & Chamberlain, 1973). This can be related to embarrassment about their size and shape; but, as often, it is attributable to feelings of helplessness. After many unsuccessful attempts to lose weight, fat people, understandably, can begin to feel that their weight is not under their control (Perri, McAdoo, Spevak, & Newlin, 1984). Apparent lack of willpower and lack of commitment on the part of the overweight person is often due to the development of an erroneous belief that it is *impossible* for them to lose weight. This, in turn, has depressing consequences in terms of self-perceived helplessness and hopelessness. By and large, the overweight are not a happy group of people.

All in all, the subject of weight is extremely complex. None of the theories provide a comprehensive explanation—probably because the overweight are not all of a type. Weight problems can be due to a mixture of heredity, metabolism, learning, environment, and attitude. Therefore, an understanding of why a particular individual is overweight requires a careful analysis of that person's unique environment, body, eating patterns, and personal psychology.

SMOKING

Facts and Figures

In the United States, although smoking is declining in all groups except women, there are still more than 50 million smokers. Four out of 10 adults in the United Kingdom smoke. Tobacco contains several kinds of particles and gases that are detrimental to health—nicotine, tar, carbon monoxide, hydrogen, cyanide, and nitrogen oxide. In the United States alone, it has been estimated that smoking is responsible for 325,000 deaths per year from cancer and diseases of the heart, lungs, and circulatory system. The risk of developing lung cancer is 10 times greater for cigarette smokers. In Britain, almost 10 people die every day from lung cancer. Chronic bronchitis kills 24,000 people per year. Smoking also causes cancer of the mouth and bladder, which, together with cancer of the larynx, account for several thousand deaths per year. Although many people suffer from these diseases without ever having smoked, the risk increases dramatically if one does smoke.

Furthermore, people who share space with smokers effectively smoke the equivalent of about five cigarettes a day by inhaling smoke-filled air. More significantly, it is now suspected that the "side stream smoke" that comes from the cigarette while it is idly smoldering may be more dangerous than the smoke inhaled by the smoker. In other words, "passive smoking" may be even more lethal.

So, if it is that bad for people, why do they smoke? As explained earlier, the reasons for starting something are not always the same as those for continuing. Many people start smoking out of curiosity, because they see prestige figures doing it, or because of peer pressure. Immediate reinforcement makes them continue. After a while, it becomes more than a bad habit; it becomes an addiction. Therefore, quitting is complicated by the fact that, over time, a genuine *physiological addiction* develops. The body comes to need and crave nicotine; it becomes physically dependent (McMorrow & Foxx, 1983). Consequently, unless carefully planned, attempts at stopping will be accompanied by unpleasant withdrawal symptoms, which can tempt even the most determined to give up half way.

Causes, Signs, and Symptoms

Environmental. As with eating, certain times, situations, and people become associated with smoking (e.g., after a meal, when under stress, at a party, while out for a beer; see Shiffman, 1982). Other smokers can also exert pressure: "Come on; don't be so sensible."

Physiological. Nicotine effects people differently. For some, the main reason for smoking is stimulation; they feel that cigarettes wake them up, give them energy, and keep them going. This "charge" is a natural result of nicotine in the body; but it also encourages people to continue smoking (Pomerleau & Pomerleau, 1984). Others experience a craving, due to addiction. For these people, attempts to quit are usually accompanied by withdrawal.

Behavioral. How and why people *develop* the habit of smoking has already been outlined—by association, reinforcement and observation. However, handling and manipulating cigarettes is also an integral part of *maintaining* the habit for many people. The ritual of taking a cigarette out of the pack, lighting it, inhaling, sighing gloriously, and placing it at a particular angle on the ashtray is constantly self-reinforcing. Cigarettes also frequently serve to keep shy persons' shaky hands busy when feeling uncomfortable in company, and dieters' hands off of food. For others, the behavior involved in smoking is simply habitual. Many cigarettes are lit and smoked automatically and with very little conscious awareness.

Cognitive. Two out of three smokers say that smoking actually makes them feel good. Cigarettes also provide support in times of stress; they help some people to unwind when they are under pressure. Ironically, they are used in *coping* with life's pressures on a day-to-day basis. Therefore, as well as physical addiction, psychological addiction and dependence must also be taken into consideration. In fact, for some, the psychological craving for the next cigarette begins the very minute the lighted one is put out.

Most people smoke for a variety of reasons—habit, immediate buzz, physical and psychological need. Therefore, as with obesity, it is extremely important to analyze the dynamics of the *individual* smoker's habit in order to plan the most effective strategy for quitting.

TREATMENT

One ingredient (probably the main one) in endeavours to lose weight or quit smoking is *motivation*. This is especially important if the problem habit is of long standing or if there have been several previous attempts that were either abandoned or followed by relapse. Unlike the other areas discussed in this book, people *enjoy* these problem behaviors. Consequently, it is imperative for the therapist to start with an assessment of the person's motivation to change and to emphasize to the client the long-term consequences—particularly to health—of remaining as they are (Appendix I: Motivation Analysis). Ironically, at this point, the client must also be helped to anticipate the consequences, and possible problems, that may result from a *successful* intervention. For example, a significant weight loss might leave a dieter with much more energy and a renewed desire to socialize and buy new clothes—both of which require extra time and money. The ex-smoker may have to develop ways, other than smoking, of coping in times of stress or when under job pressure. Such potential outcomes must be considered, discussed, and built into the treatment plan from the start.

The next step is for clients to keep a detailed diary, for at least 3 weeks, to establish the dynamics of their problem—the situations, people, or places that *trigger* the bad habit. Problems of overindulgence are particularly likely to be linked to times of emotional arousal, both positive and negative—anger, boredom, loneliness, frustration, excitement, and enjoyment. When the triggers have been identified, the therapist then helps the client to understand how the problem is *maintained* (e.g., by association with certain faces, activities, times, or moods). It is essential for clients to continue self-monitoring their progress throughout the program (Appendix I: Self-

Monitoring Behavior). Useful information can also be obtained from questionnaires, such as the Smoking Questionnaire reproduced in Table 10.1. In planning the changes, a realistic time span is essential, so that the mind, as well as the body, has time to adjust (Appendix I: Change Plan).

Because the intervention essentially involves changing patterns of behavior and lifestyle, clients are first supplied with basic facts (e.g., about nutrition and healthy eating, or the effects of nicotine). They then need to learn how to utilize environmental resources, to identify *problem prime times,* and to plan ahead and diffuse potentially problematic situations (Appendix II: Problem Prime Time; Temporary Avoidance; Stimulus Control). They are taught how to make their environment work for them—for example, by making a list of essential purchases *before* going to the store, or by not taking enough money for cigarettes when meeting friends for a beer or to go to a movie. Many people find it extremely useful to enlist the support of friends (Appendix II: Enlisting Friends) or to reward themselves along the way for effort (Appendix II: Behavioral Programming). At a later stage, they are encouraged to explore their environment for health-inducing activities and recreations. Sports, which are genuinely appealing and are incompatible with the habit they are trying to break, are ideal (Appendix II: Utilizing Environmental Resources).

The cognitive component is also extremely important in problems of overindulgence. Along with self-monitoring behavior, clients are taught to monitor their cognitions (Appendix I: Self-Monitoring Thinking) and to identify what goes through their minds in situations defined as problematic. They learn to dispute maladaptive self-statements, such as "I've got to have a cigarette to calm me down," "I can't refuse her apple pie—she'll be offended," "Next week I'll quit," or "Ice cream is not *really* fattening"; and then to apply their new objective self-evaluations in real life (Appendix V: Self-Disputation). Counterproductive visual images can be replaced with more appropriate ones; for example, visions of the family happily gathering around to enjoy another wickedly rich chocolate-fudge cake can be replaced with images of them savoring a colorful and creative salad and admiring the client's new clothes and figure. Images of sending irresistible smoke signals to a sexy woman across the bar can be replaced by imagining the same beauty blowing them back in the client's face. Those who have a natural ability to generate visual images can also use this facility as a motivator—by imagining themselves mingling comfortably and confidently at an upcoming party or wedding, for example. *Negative* images (e.g., of cancerous lungs, or of slowly suffocating in a hospital bed surrounded by helpless medical personnel) can be equally effective (Appendix V: Developing Coping Imagery).

On a deeper level, many clients benefit from exploring underlying beliefs in relation to their problem. A long-term weight problem, for example, might

TABLE 10.1 Smoking Questionnaire

Here are some statements made by people to describe what they get out of smoking cigarettes. How often do you feel this way when smoking? Circle one number for each statement. Important: ANSWER EVERY QUESTION.

	always	fre-quently	occa-sionally	seldom	never
A. I smoke cigarettes in order to keep myself from slowing down.	5	4	3	2	1
B. Handling a cigarette is part of the enjoyment of smoking it.	5	4	3	2	1
C. Smoking cigarettes is pleasant and relaxing.	5	4	3	2	1
D. I light up a cigarette when I feel angry about something.	5	4	3	2	1
E. When I have run out of cigarettes I find it almost unbearable until I can get them.	5	4	3	2	1
F. I smoke cigarettes automatically without even being aware of it.	5	4	3	2	1
G. I smoke cigarettes to stimulate me, to perk myself up.	5	4	3	2	1
H. Part of the enjoyment of smoking a cigarette comes from the steps I take to light up.	5	4	3	2	1
I. I find cigarettes pleasurable.	5	4	3	2	1
J. When I feel uncomfortable or upset about something, I light up a cigarette.	5	4	3	2	1
K. I am very much aware of the fact when I am not smoking a cigarette.	5	4	3	2	1
L. I light up a cigarette without realizing I still have one burning in the ashtray.	5	4	3	2	1
M. I smoke cigarettes to give me a 'lift'.	5	4	3	2	1
N. When I smoke a cigarette, part of the enjoyment is watching the smoke as I exhale it.	5	4	3	2	1
O. I want a cigarette most when I am comfortable and relaxed.	5	4	3	2	1
P. When I feel 'blue' or want to take my mind off cares and worries, I smoke cigarettes.	5	4	3	2	1
Q. I get a real gnawing hunger for a cigarette when I haven't smoked for a while.	5	4	3	2	1
R. I've found a cigarette in my mouth and didn't remember putting it there.	5	4	3	2	1

1. Enter the number you have circled for each question in the spaces below, putting the number you have circled to question A over line A, to question B over line B, etc.

2. Add the 3 scores on each line to get your totals. For example, the sum of your scores over lines A, G, and M gives you your score on Stimulation—lines B, H, and N give the score on Handling, etc.

				Totals
A ___	+ G ___	+ M ___	= ___	Stimulation
B ___	+ H ___	+ N ___	= ___	Handling
C ___	+ I ___	+ O ___	= ___	Pleasurable Relaxation
D ___	+ J ___	+ P ___	= ___	Crutch: Tension Reduction
E ___	+ K ___	+ Q ___	= ___	Craving: Psychological Addiction
F ___	+ L ___	+ R ___	= ___	Habit

Scores can vary from 3 to 15. Any score 11 and above is high; any score 7 and below is low.

turn out to be related to an erroneous belief, such as "I'll never be able to lose weight—its impossible for me," or "If I slim down, I might be asked out on a date—and I just couldn't handle *that*," or "I have to smoke—otherwise I'll gain weight" (Appendix V: Vertical Arrow). If it becomes apparent that the main reason for overeating or smoking in company stems from an inability to say "no," then maladaptive underlying beliefs about needs for approval are examined (Appendix V: Uncovering the Shoulds). Problematic situations are then practiced, or role-played, with the therapist (Appendix IV: Behavioral Rehearsal). If general assertion skills are needed, the client may be referred to an assertiveness training course, such as that described in chapter 8 and Appendix VI (see Assertion).

Less essential but also useful techniques are to get the clients to make a *graph* of the course of their weight loss, or of the decreasing frequency of cigarettes consumed. Many also find it useful to write positive or negative self-statements to themselves, like "Do I want to dig my grave with my teeth?" and to place these strategically—in the cookie jar or refrigerator, for example. These tactics may sound too simple to be effective, or to be taken seriously; in fact, their simplicity and concreteness is their strength (Appendix II: Portable Motivators).

Finally, relapse is currently recognized as one of the major challenges in designing effective programs for overindulgence and substance abuse, and for personal change in general. Guidelines for preventing, as well as for dealing with the reality of, relapse must be included in any comprehensive program. The problems of attrition, adherence, *and* relapse are dealt with in the next chapter.

SUGGESTED FURTHER READING

Theory and Research

Ashton, H., & Stepney, R. (1982). *Smoking: Psychology and pharmacology.* London: Tavistock.

Baer, J. S., & Lichtenstein, E. (1988). Classification and prediction of smoking related episodes: An exploration of individual differences. *Journal of Consulting and Clinical Psychology, 56,* 104–110.

Best, J. A., Wainwright, P. E., Mills, D. E., & Kirkland, S. A. (1988). Biobehavioral approaches to smoking control. In W. Linden (Ed.), *Biological barriers in behavioral medicine* (pp. 63–99). NY: Plenum Press.

Brownell, K. D., Cohen, R. Y., Stunkard, A. J., Felix, M. J., & Cooley, N. B. (1984). Weight loss competitions at the work site: Impact on weight, morale and cost-effectiveness. *American Journal of Public Health, 74,* 1283–1285.

Brownell, K. D., & Foreyt, J. P. (Eds.). (1986). *The physiology, psychology and treatment of the eating disorders.* NY: Basic Books.

Brownell, K. D., Marlatt, G. A., Lichtenstein, E., & Wilson, G. T. (1986). Understanding and preventing relapse. *American Psychologist, 41:7,* 765–782.

Colletti, G. & Brownell, K. D. (1982). The physical and emotional benefits of social support: Applications to obesity, smoking and alcoholism. In M. Hersen, R. M. Eisler, & P. M. Miller (Eds.), *Progress in behavior modification (Vol. 13, pp. 110–179)*. NY: Academic Press.

Condiotti, M. M. & Lichtenstein, E. (1981). Self-efficacy and relapse in smoking cessation programs. *Journal of Consulting and Clinical Psychology, 49,* 648–658.

Curry, S. G. & Marlatt, G. A. (1985). Unaided quitter's strategies for coping with temptations to smoke. In S. Shiffman & T. A. Wills (Eds.), *Coping and substance abuse* (pp. 367–386). Orlando, FL: Academic Press.

Davidson, P. O. & Davidson, S. M. (Eds.). (1980). *Behavioral medicine: Changing health lifestyles.* NY: Brunner Mazel.

Glasgow, R. E., Klesges, R. C. Klesges, L. M., & Somes, G. R. (1988). Variables associated with participation and outcome in a worksite smoking control program. *Journal of Consulting and Clinical Psychology, 56,* 617–620.

Hall, S. M., Rugg, D., Tunstal, C., & Jones, R. T. (1984). Preventing relapse to cigarette smoking by behavioral skill training. *Journal of Consulting and Clinical Psychology, 52,* 372–382.

Jeffrey, R. W. & Wing, R. R. (1983). Recidivism and self-cure of smoking and obesity: Data from population studies. *American Psychologist, 37,* 852.

Kirschenbaum, D. S. (1987). Self-regulatory failure: A review with clinical implications. *Clinical Psychology Review, 7,* 77–104.

Marlatt, G. A., Curry, S., & Gordon, J. R. (1988). A longitudinal analysis of unaided smoking cessation. *Journal of Consulting and Clinical Psychology, 56 (5),* 715–720.

Marlatt, G. A. & Gordon, J. K. (Eds.). (1985). *Relapse prevention: Maintenance strategies in addictive behavior change.* NY: Guilford.

Miller, W. R. (Ed.). (1980). *The addictive behaviors: Treatment of alcoholism, drug abuse, smoking and obesity.* NY: Pergamon Press.

Murray, A. L. & Lawrence, P. S. (1984). Sequelae to smoking cessation: A review. *Clinical Psychology Review, 4,* 143–157.

Orford, J. (1985). *Excessive appetites: A psychological view of addictions.* Chichester: John Wiley and Sons.

Perri, M. G. (1985). Self-change strategies for the control of smoking, obesity and problem-drinking. In S. Shiffman & T. A. Wills (Eds.), *Coping and substance abuse* (pp. 295–315). Orlando, FL: Academic Press.

Perri, M. G. (1987). Maintenance strategies for the management of obesity. In W. G. Johnson (Ed.), *Advances in eating disorders* (pp. 177–194). Greenwich, CT: JAI Press.

Perri, M. G., McAllister, D. A., Gange, J. J., Jordan, R. C., McAdoo, W. G., & Nezu, A. M. (1988). Effects of four maintenance programs on the long-term management of obesity. *Journal of Consulting and Clinical Psychology, 56,* 529–534.

Shiffman, S. (1984). Coping with temptations to smoke. *Journal of Consulting and Clinical Psychology, 52,* 261–267.

Stuart, R. B. (1980). Weight loss and beyond: Are they taking it off and keeping it off? In P. O. Davidson & S. M. Davidson (Eds.), *Behavioral medicine: Changing health lifestyles* (pp. 151–194). NY: Brunner Mazel.

Supnick, J. A. & Colletti, G. (1984). Relapse, coping and problem-solving training following treatment for smoking. *Addictive Behaviors, 9,* 401–403.

U.S. Dept. of Health and Human Services. (1983). *The health consequences of smoking: Cardiovascular disease. A report of the Surgeon General.* Washington, DC: Author.

Popular and Self-Help

Brownell, K. D. (1985). *The LEARN program for weight control.* Unpublished treatment manual: University of Pennsylvania.

Gartner, A. & Reissman, F. (Eds.). (1984). *The self-help revolution.* NY: Human Sciences Press.

Glasgow, R. E., Schafer, L. & O'Neill, H. K. (1981). Self-help books and amount of therapist contact in smoking cessation programs. *Journal of Consulting and Clinical Psychology, 49,* 659–667.

Hodgson, R. & Miller, P. (1982). *Selfwatching: Addictions, habits, compulsions: What to do about them* (Chapters 8 and 9). London: Century Publishing Company.

Ossip-Klein, D. J., Shapiro, R. M., & Stiggins, J. (1984). Freedom line: Increasing utilization of a telephone support service for ex-smokers. *Addictive Behaviors, 9,* 227–230.

Stuart, R. B. & Davis, B. (1972). *Slim chance in a fat world.* Champaign, IL: Research Press.

ALCOHOL: THEORY, RESEARCH, AND SELF-HELP

Bratter, T. E., & Forrest, G. G. (1985). *Alcoholism and substance abuse: Strategies for clinical intervention.* NY: Free Press.

Brown, S. (1985). *Treating the alcoholic: A developmental model of recovery.* NY: John Wiley and Sons.

Burk, J. B., & Sher, J. K. (1988). The "forgotten children" revisited: Neglected areas of COA research. *Clinical Psychology Review, 8,* 285–302.

Cox, W. M. (Ed.). (1987). *Treatment and prevention of alcohol problems: A resource manual.* Orlando, FL: Academic Press.

Hodgson, R., & Miller, P. (1982). *Selfwatching: Addictions, habits, compulsions: What to do about them* (Chapter 12). London: Century Publishing Company.

Marlatt, G. A. (1983). The controlled-drinking controversy: A commentary. *American Psychologist, 38,* 1097–1110.

Miller, W., & Munoz, R. (1976). *How to control your drinking.* Engelwood Cliffs, NJ: Prentice-Hall.

Miller, W. R., & Hester, R. K. (1980). Treating the problem drinker: Modern approaches. In W. R. Miller (Ed.), *The addictive behaviors: Treatment of alcoholism, drug abuse, smoking and obesity.* NY: Pergamon Press.

Moos, R. H., & Finney, J. W. (1983). The expanding scope of alcoholism treatment evaluation. *American Psychologist, 38,* 1036–1044.

Nathan, P. E. (1983). Failures in prevention: Why can't we prevent the devastating effects of alcoholism and drug abuse? *American Psychologist, 38,* 450–467.

Nathan, P. E., & Wiens, A. N. (1983). Alcoholism: Introduction and overview. *American Psychologist, 38,* 1035.

Neidigh, L. W., Gesten, E. L., & Shiffman, S. (1988). Coping with temptations to drink. *Addictive Behaviors, 13,* 1–9.

Sobell, L. C., Sobell, M. B., & Nirenberg, T. D. (1988). Behavioral assessment and treatment planning with alcohol and drug abusers: A review with an emphasis on clinical applications. *Clinical Psychology Review, 8,* 19–54.

Vaillant, G. E. (1983). *The natural history of alcoholism: Causes, patterns and paths to recovery.* Cambridge, MA: Harvard University Press.

11

Attrition, Adherence, and Relapse

Three of the major problems in health and mental-health care today are attrition, adherence, and relapse. In other words, too often people do not go back after their first visit. If they *do* continue to attend for treatment, therapy, or counseling, they do not necessarily follow the guidelines offered. Finally, *even* if they do take the professional advice on how to overcome their problems, too often they are not equipped to prevent a relapse.

PATHS INTO CARE

Accepting the need for specialist help is very difficult for many people. Generally speaking, people like to feel that, with a little time, understanding, or luck, things will somehow work out. Many also, wrongly, view being referred to a specialist, such as a psychotherapist, as a sign of impending doom. There is fear of the unknown, of being told that something awful is wrong. There is also apprehension about having to go through the whole process of telling their story yet again, and to a stranger—another unknown quantity. Finally, there is the question of pride—feelings of inadequacy about not being able to cope and of not being in control.

Consulting health professionals, particularly mental-health professionals, is more complex than consulting other professionals; it reflects more directly on intimate and personal aspects of people's private lives. There are significant sex differences here, both in respect of patterns of care seeking, or pathways into care, as well as in how men and women behave when they are actually with the professional. In other words, the "sick" role means different things for men and women (Horowitz, 1977).

In the area of *general health*, it is assumed that women are the weaker sex overall. Medical statistics reinforce the idea that women are sicker than men; health and morbidity figures show repeatedly that American females have higher illness rates. The same statistics, however, show that, although illness rates are higher for women, death rates are lower (Verbrugge, 1976). The most comprehensive explanation is that excess female illness statistics are due primarily to social and psychological factors, rather than to acquired or inherited health risks.

In other words, due to socialization, it is more acceptable for women to be ill. They are, therefore, more willing to report their symptoms than men, and to take care of themselves. Men try to continue on as if there is nothing wrong. Women are also more likely to consult professionals; and, at interview, are more cooperative, have better recall of their symptoms, and verbalize their ailments (Mechanic, 1962; Nathanson, 1975). Men, on the other hand, consult at a later stage, when the condition is often already chronic and therefore more serious. When they are *with* the professional, they do not report their symptoms; consequently, the diagnosis that is made, unless very obvious, may be less serious than for a woman with the *same* condition who has done more talking. Misdiagnosis is therefore more likely to occur with men. Time inevitably reveals the true gravity of the situation; but this can be time lost in terms of chronicity and treatment.

In attempting to understand these trends and differences, it is necessary to take into account that, statistically, men form a larger part of the work force; they literally cannot afford to be sick as much as women. The fact remains however, that women's "illness behavior" and "interview behavior" are very different from men's; and it is likely that these differences inflate the illness statistics in relation to women. Ironically, women may, in fact, be healthier than men.

The pattern is the same for *mental health* and psychological problems. There are more women on the psychiatric statistics than men, and it is generally assumed that women are more susceptible and vulnerable to psychological problems. However, one would be ill advised to draw any firm conclusions from these trends either, for the same reasons. Studies indicate that it is culturally more acceptable for women to be expressive of their difficulties. They are therefore more likely than men to disclose intimate information about themselves, especially unpleasant feelings, such as anxieties and fears. This greater distress-reporting leads to more help-seeking on the part of women (Padesky & Hammen, 1981). Men, in contrast, are socialized to bear their problems with greater self-control and not to admit to symptoms of distress (David & Brannon, 1976). Even the most recent reports (e.g., Farina, 1981; Warren 1983) show that the stigma of mental illness and psychological problems continues to be greater for men.

In conclusion, women are more likely to seek help—both informal advice from friends, and professional guidance. Women enter treatment through two major pathways: They either define their problem as a psychological or psychiatric one and seek referral for help from a member of their informal network (e.g., general practitioner or priest) or they discuss their problems with others and accept the need for specialist help when it is proposed. Men are resistant to seeking psychological help until circumstances allow no alternative. They then usually enter "care" by a process of social control (e.g., boss). Finally, as with general health complaints, by the time they seek help, or are brought to help, they are often a lot sicker.

When actually in care, women see therapy as offering a way to solve their problems, to resolve interpersonal conflicts, or to overcome depression or anxiety. Men usually enter treatment only when they can no longer conceal their symptoms, and others coerce them into getting help. Consequently, they see themselves in a weak position of power when they enter care, and are therefore often much less open, or even actively resistant, to accepting help (Phillips & Segal, 1969). All of this suggests an active role in the future for both health and mental-health socialization and education, as the current situation is differentially disadvantageous to both sexes. Men, in particular, need support and help in construing psychotherapy, not as a sign of failure, but as a step in the direction of self-help, which will, in time, put them fully back in control of their lives.

PATHS OUT OF CARE

Attrition

Of those who attend mental health clinics, 20% to 50% fail to return after their first visit; and roughly 31% to 56% attend no more than four times. Attrition for general medical treatments can be as high as 80%, and drop-out rates for self-help groups is also in the range of 50% to 80%. Twenty percent to 80% of people drop out of various lifestyle change programs designed to deal with problems such as obesity, smoking, and stress management (see Meichenbaum & Turk, 1987). What do these figures mean? Much as one would like to believe that simply visiting a clinic produces some kind of magic, this is not the case. Visiting does make some people feel better; this is a placebo effect (Shapiro, 1971). It brings temporary relief, but it does not make problems disappear.

What are the reasons for these large drop-out, or attrition, rates? Two sets of interrelated factors seem to be responsible: the characteristics of the client and the characteristics of the therapist.

Client Characteristics.   Sex differences have already been discussed in the context of paths into care; but, other factors are important in understanding why so many people drop out of treatment (Baekeland & Lundwall, 1975). Severity of diagnosis is highly relevant: schizophrenic and manic-depressive patients, for example, can be inconsistent and erratic attenders. When people are very depressed, motivation to attend can present a major obstacle. Agoraphobic clients sometimes find it hard to get themselves out of the house, for fear of having a panic attack. Forgetfulness, especially in the elderly, can be a problem in itself. Individuals who are socially isolated, or who do not belong in any social group, frequently drop out. Likewise, lack of resources (e.g., money for transport or fee payment, lack of social supports, familial or residential instability) and—in minority groups—competing sociocultural and ethnic concepts of disease and treatment, can *all* increase the likelihood of attrition.

Clients *expectations* are also very significant. Unknown to themselves, people generally have pre-conceptions of what a new situation will be like— in this case, an idea of the place, and an impression or image of what the therapist will look like or sound like. If the setting is drab or noisy, or the personnel very unfriendly, people will not be encouraged to return. If the therapist does not tally with expectations (is younger or older, more casual or formal, or the opposite sex to them), clients can find this disconcerting to the extent that they switch off and do not come back.

Therapist Characteristics.   The therapist's attitudes and behaviors are equally important (see Stein & Lambert, 1984). Most professionals are busy people. They are often forced to form an overall impression, as well as getting as much information as possible, in a very short time. Often, they are working under pressure; and it can be difficult for them to establish a balance between optimal use of time in gathering information, and being personable. However, looking and acting very busy—by consistently glancing at a clock or watch, for example—will obviously make clients feel that they do not have the therapist's interest or attention. Therapists are human too; and, irrespective of time pressures, their manner of relating sometimes genuinely leaves a lot to be desired. Therapist behaviors that interfere with patient communication and facilitate attrition are: acting unfriendly, distant, disinterested, unapproachable, very formal, or cold. Likewise, if he or she mumbles or uses a lot of jargon, ignores the client's questions, interrupts their statements, does not allow them to express their ideas, expectations, or concerns, *or* if the client feels that his or her *problem*—rather than he or she as a person—is being treated, these will all be very discouraging, especially to an already anxious, apprehensive, or depressed person.

Characteristics of the therapist's immediate surroundings are also important. If the office is chaotically untidy or dirty, or there are constant interruptions by the staff or the telephone, communication will be affected. Likewise, things as basic as the therapist failing to make eye contact, sitting behind a large, formal desk or at a different level to the client, *or* abruptly terminating the session, all, understandably, lead to people dropping out (Baekeland & Lundwall, 1975).

Therapists also frequently have expectations of what a new client will, or ideally might, be like. A study carried out by Goldstein and Simonson (1971) sums up the characteristics of desirable and undesirable clients as follows. Clients of the YAVIS variety—young, attractive, verbal, intelligent, and successful—stand in stark contrast to the HOUNDs, who are homely, old, unattractive, nonverbal, and dumb. In short, therapists would like every client to stroll confidently into their office, and to entertain them with humorously delivered, crystal clear facts about their problem. These clients would also have thought carefully about their difficulties in advance; and provide succinct, written summaries of detailed and dedicated self-monitoring.

Unfortunately, the reality is somewhat different. Just visiting a therapist is a major event for many people. Frequently, they are so eager to find out what is wrong, or so worried about what they will be told, that they do not do themselves justice. Normally intelligent people can come across as confused and scattered, or find it hard to concentrate on what is being said or to answer questions with any degree of clarity or accuracy. Depressed clients can be very unresponsive and unrewarding to deal with; sometimes, they will have taken little or no care with their dress or personal hygiene. Anxious people can come across as superficial (e.g., giggling frequently) or unfriendly and distant. It can be hard to establish rapport with the socially unskilled. Couples with marital or sexual problems can be uncooperative, defensive, or aggressive. This is the real world.

All of these problems point to one thing—the importance of *communication*. A lack of congruity between the characteristics and expectations of the client and the therapist will result in a lack of communication; and communication is vital in determining the duration, quality, and effectiveness of any therapeutic relationship.

Adherence

Current estimates of the magnitude of the adherence problem suggest that, following consultation, 20% to 80% of patients do not follow the professional advice or guidelines offered—be it a change of diet, cutting down on alcohol or cigarette consumption, increasing exercise or relaxation, reducing commitments, or taking prescribed medication. Nonadherence for long-term or life-term medication regimes and for general life-change programs is in the region of 50% *and* the incidence of nonadherence increases over the course of therapy (Haynes, Taylor, & Sackett, 1979). In other words, a lot of time, money, and words are being wasted on both sides of the desk. There are two main reasons for this: inadequate communication and the nature of the treatment itself.

Communication. The importance of adequate communication has been elucidated in relation to the problem of attrition. In sum, the greater the communication, the greater the compliance. There have been many attempts, over the years, to establish the most effective *components* of various therapies. Interestingly, what consistently asserts itself as an essential ingredient in any therapeutic intervention is the quality of the therapeutic relationship (Luborsky, Singer & Luborsky, 1977). All of the traditional, classically quoted therapist qualities of empathy, warmth, caring, and trust repeatedly emerge as integral to therapeutic effectiveness (Frank, 1971; Paul, 1966).

In other words, the client's perceptions of the approachability and friendliness of the therapist are vitally important. Clients need to feel that they are held in some esteem and treated with respect, and that the therapist is considerate of their concerns and feelings. The degree to which the therapist succeeds in conveying such a caring attitude, nonverbally, and in establishing an atmosphere of trust, will greatly effect the quality and level of verbal rapport. Only when the client feels relaxed and unthreatened can the therapist hope to elicit relevant personal information. In other words, establishing a trusting, supportive relationship and demonstrating interest in the client is all-important in the process of acquiring information about the difficulties that he or she is experiencing.

The client must *then* be helped to understand his or her problem; and here again, communication is the essential tool. Unfortunately, at this stage also, professional–client communication is often inadequate (Ley, 1975). Professionals are sometimes so used to using technical jargon that they genuinely forget that the people they are talking to will not understand. If clients are anxious, shy, or depressed, they may not have the courage, energy, or assertion skills to ask the therapist to explain. Even though it is imperative for the client to get as clear a picture as possible while still at the consultation, too often people go away worrying about what was meant by some big words or phrases that they cannot even remember clearly but that sounded like bad news. *One* very effective way of delivering information and overcoming this type of problem is for therapists to provide clients with short, simply written *handouts,* containing the essential facts about their problem. Depending on the individual client's level of literacy and motivation, self-educational *books* and *tapes* (on anxiety, agoraphobia, depression, high blood pressure, etc.) are often also recommended.

Regarding the treatment regime itself, in order to motivate clients to cooperate, the therapist must convey competence, confidence, and knowledge concerning the chosen therapy. This will also *only* be achieved if the treatment regime and its rationale are clearly explained and understood. Clients must understand what they have to do and why, as this makes it easier for them to accept the changes and the necessity for them. Therapists must be selective in the information they deliver. The fewer the instructions, the greater the recall. Giving too much, as well as too little, information can contribute to treatment nonadherence. Ideally, therapists should provide clear, specific, concrete, instructions and use short words and short sentences. Down-to-earth language helps enormously. Instructions should be detailed; but small amounts of information only should be supplied at each visit (Meichenbaum & Turk, 1987).

The program should always be individually tailored and paced. Therapists must also repeat the information as often as possible, and use concrete illustrations. They should constantly check their clients' comprehension and ask them to repeat any key points, in their own words. If clients want to make notes of basic information or of instructions, this is encouraged. Clients are also encouraged to express their concerns, fears, or apprehensions regarding details of the treatment plan, and to ask questions. Finally, by continuing to self-monitor, they can greatly facilitate communication regarding their own progress (Appendix I: Self-Monitoring Behavior).

In the context of progress, the necessity of *completing* courses of treatment, in order to avoid relapse, is also emphasized. Clients are encouraged not to stop the very minute they begin to feel better (e.g., half-way through a course of psychotherapy, relaxation training, social skills training, or medication). Courses of treatment or therapy are the length they are because precisely *that* amount of practice, exposure, or time, is required to deal with the particular problem. Clients are also requested to resist the urge to *not* go back because they do *not* feel better—all the more reason to return. People need to understand that treatment—particularly of long-standing habits—takes time and effort, but that the long-term benefits of treatment *will* far outweigh short-term inconvenience and discomfort. Problems will not go away of their own accord. Clients are informed that, if they decide to drop out, it is likely that they will have to return in a couple of weeks anyway, and in a more chronic state of anxiety, insomnia, high blood pressure, or whatever their particular problem is. If they stay in treatment, the skills that they acquire will serve them for life.

Details of the Treatment Program. Some treatment plans are more difficult to follow and stick to than others—particularly if they involve changing long-standing habits or ingesting unpleasant substances. Clients, as explained, are first equipped with all the relevant information about their particular problem. Ideally, they then get involved in the planning and implementation of their own therapy program. They learn to set realistic goals that can be broken down into easily attainable steps (Appendix I: Planning Changes). If they do not have the skills required to follow the plan, these are taught and then elaborated on in a gradual, incremental fashion (see Treatment Section of chapters 4 through 10). Feedback, praise, and reinforcement for effort are essential throughout.

The regime is made as simple as possible and clients are helped to overcome any barriers caused by the program itself. For example, guidance may be needed on how to avoid making the prescribed changes too much of a penance, that unnecessarily interfere with other areas of their lives *and* affect other people. With a little imagination, changes *can* usually be tailored to fit comfortably into an existing routine, rather than changing everything else and resenting it in the process. For example, cutting out caffeine need *not* mean also cutting out the coffee break with colleagues; a client might be advised to bring his or her own decaffeinated coffee or orange juice. People are also advised to avail of social supports—colleagues, spouse, friends, family—when appropriate, both in the planning and the implementation of their treatment program (see Pomerleau, 1979).

PATHS BACK INTO CARE

It is extraordinary how people will toil away effortfully for months on end, sometimes at considerable personal inconvenience, and admit to feeling "wonderful" on reaching their goal—only to let things slide back to exactly where they started from. How often do people set out to be more positive, less irritable, or more independent? How many times do people *successfully* quit smoking, alcohol, or junk food? In the treatment of addictive behaviors, such as smoking or excessive alcohol assumption, 60% of successfully treated clients revert to their old behavior patters and bad habits within 3 months of concluding therapy. This figure increases to 70% after 6 months, and to 75% after 12 months (see Marlatt & Gordon, 1985). Relapse can be attributed to three sets of factors: inadequate planning, inadequate maintenance, and inadequate coping-skills training.

Planning

One of the main reasons why people relapse is that things just do not seem as great as they had anticipated, on or after arrival. Consequently, it is imperative to think things through with clients, very thoroughly, in the *planning* stages of a change program (Appendix I: Change Plan). This has been emphasized consistently in the Treatment sections of chapters 4 through 11. A number of examples will illustrate.

Other people are usually very enthusiastic and congratulatory when clients first reach their goal; but, after a few days, life goes on. If a change plan is motivated primarily by a need to please *others* or gain their respect, approval, or love, then the arrival will not be as rewarding as expected. The planned changes *must* be for the clients themselves; so that they can continue to reward themselves for their maintenance efforts and achievements. This is what "owning one's own life" is all about; friends or partners have their own lives to lead. Clients must be helped to plan changes that they want for *themselves*. Sometimes, they need reassurance that this is not selfish; they need help in understanding that, on the contrary, it will render them more independent, less demanding, and less needy of others' time and attention.

Another common reason for relapse is the mistaken belief that, with the planned changes, their entire life will somehow be magically transformed— that with a weight loss, for example, a bad marriage or an unsatisfactory sex life will suddenly improve also. When planning changes, the therapist must carefully examine the client's perceptions of their difficulties. If one problem is labelled "it"—the root of all evil—and this is *not* detected and discussed in advance, then the arrival will almost certainly be disappointing. Clients must realize, in advance, that solving one problem or resolving one difficulty will *not* change everything. In many cases, it is just the first stage in a long change process, or in creating a new life. In the course of making changes, the client may rediscover pleasant, forgotten assets; but, he or she may also uncover other areas that are in need of modification or improvement.

On the other hand, once they gain control of their lives, clients sometimes find that they have more time on their hands—time that was hitherto spent worrying, checking, cleaning, drinking, eating, working, or arguing. Using this newfound time constructively necessitates building other activities into their schedule, and these activities can also create difficulties. Widening their social life and contacts can create financial demands—more money may be needed for gasoline, clothes, or meals out. On the other hand, people sometimes discover, or rediscover, *problems*, such as shyness or a dislike of crowded places, for example, that were masked in their more sedentary days. These kinds of difficulties must be anticipated and prepared for in the planning stages.

Furthermore, adventures into new pastures can make those who were used to the client as he or she was before—the quiet person who was perfectly content to stay at home all the time, for example—feel uncomfortable. Sometimes they do not like the changes. They wonder and worry about what will happen next. They feel threatened that they will lose the person's friendship or intimacy; that the client will start to see them differently or will try to change them also. In fact, many of these apprehensions and worries *are* justified. When clients start living a more active and satisfying life—which usually involves meeting new people—old faithfuls *can* be seen in a new, less flattering light. Clients often need to be reminded of these people's good points, which were appreciated when they were more dependent. Likewise, the therapist sometimes has to spend time with a client's spouse or family to help them understand and accept the changes and to construe them as the positive development they are.

Occasionally, clients also experience anger towards a partner or friend who is, in retrospect, suspected of having let their former problem remain untackled because, in some way, it suited them. The explanation is usually very simple and much less devious; frequently, the other person just got used to the client being depressed or overweight, and did not want to add to the situation by hassling them further. On thinking back, clients often remember that "Yes, there was a time" when the other party did try to get them to change. They then realize that, over time, and with little cooperation, they just gave up.

Thoughtful planning greatly reduces the likelihood of such problems developing; but, no matter how carefully things are planned, these kinds of revelations, discoveries, and demands can still arise. Whatever stage they occur at, they have to be faced, and sorted out, to minimize the likelihood of relapse.

Problems can even arise in situations where clients are feeling wonderful, super-confident, and things are, in every way, as good as expected. Here, they must caution against taking on too much too soon. All changes require some getting used to. Horizons must be broadened gradually, the environment explored little by little. Clients are helped to carefully sample and slowly choose the activities they *really* want to commit themselves to, and to gradually introduce themselves to new interests and people. It is easy for people to become prematurely overcommitted to things they are not genuinely interested in. Lots of new friends and acquaintances, and their diverse involvements, can be seductive; but they are also time-consuming and often not very rewarding once the novelty wears off. Like all the changes discussed so far, new interests, friendships, and commitments must be carefully planned and monitored, so that clients do not become over-tired and over-stretched (Appendix II: Knowing and Utilizing Environmental Resources).

As a final word, many problems, however unhealthy, are rewarding in some way. This is why they persist for so long. It is therefore *normal* for clients to miss the buzz of their old bad habits. Even if they are now slim and trim, there will be times when they will miss the nocturnal raids on the refrigerator, or secret chocolate binges. Although they may now be working more effectively, there will be times when they will miss just wasting time, putting things off until tomorrow, or doing nothing. It was not *all* bad. They need to be reminded that the reason they invested so much time and effort in changing was that, basically, they were not happy with the way things were (see Colvin & Olson, 1983; Stuart, 1980a).

Maintenance

We are creatures of habit, and habits die hard. So, unless a consistent eye is kept on things—at least until the new habits are firmly established—things slide. For about 3 months after reaching their goal, I advise clients to continue keeping their daily diary, and to sit down once a week to evaluate it (Appendix I: Self-Monitoring Behavior). Daily activities are scanned, and they remind themselves of the things, situations, or people that used to trigger, and maintain, their problem. They remind themselves of "low spots"— *prime times* of the day or week—when they used to get angry, lonely, or depressed. It is very important for clients to remain aware of these habits and patterns, in order to prevent such circumstances from arising again (see Kirschenbaum, 1987; Krantz, 1987).

After a few months, when they feel that their new habits are well established and automatic in their own right, they continue to self-monitor on a *weekly* basis. In other words, once a week they sit down and write out a summary of how the last 7 days have gone. This quick exercise allows them to keep an eye on things, and to identify any build-ups. If they feel *in any way* under pressure, they are advised to stop and ask themselves: "Why?". They must try to stop at the earliest possible time, to nip things in the bud, and *not* to wait until the following week to acknowledge that there is a problem. By then, they are likely to feel that much *more* hassled, anxious, depressed, or pressured, and be that much *less* able to give themselves the time they need to stop and think. For these reasons, many clients find it invaluable to monitor and reward themselves weekly for self-maintenance (Appendix II: Behavioral Programming). As well as providing a positive experience, it also keeps them in tune with themselves.

There are occasional setbacks in *everybody's* life. So, with this in mind, client and therapist frequently construct a definite plan, in advance, of what the person should do at such times, of how lapses or relapses should be handled. Many clients find that making a list of people who they know they can call on at such times—therapist, M.D., best friend, priest, tutor, counsellor—acts as a buffer in itself. Another useful strategy is to keep a book—for example, a self-help manual or handout that has been helpful in the past—close at hand. This often gets people started again, by reminding them of all the things they have learned and achieved. Others find it useful to ask themselves what they would say to *someone else* in their situation, that is, to pretend they are advising a friend who has relapsed. Finally, and above all, clients must develop the cognitive skill of not *catastrophizing* a lapse, of not mislabeling the situation "back to square one." They must learn to retain their objectivity, to dispute any exaggerated thinking, and to "psych" themselves back into their program again (Appendix V: Self-Disputation).

Coping Skills

It has been increasingly realized in recent years that the dynamics of overcoming a problem, and those of maintaining the gains, are two different stages in self-knowledge, and are governed by partially different psychological processes (Wilson, 1985). Research indicates that when people relapse it is frequently due to negative emotional states, social pressures, or interpersonal conflicts (Cummings et al., 1980). If there is resistance or disappointment when their goal is reached, this will exacerbate a general tendency to return to baseline. But, even if there is no letdown or disappointment, life itself is problematic and challenging, and there will be times when things go anything but smoothly.

There has been a particular focus on the problem of relapse in the last few years (Brownell, Marlatt, Lichtenstein & Wilson, 1986b; Marlatt & Gordon, 1985); and increasingly, relapse prevention skills are being integrated into comprehensive treatment packages from the very start. The ingredients of relapse prevention, by and large, are *general coping skills* for dealing with the unpredictables of everyday living, and, in particular, with social pressures and conflicts. These include problem-solving and decision-making skills (Appendix V: Indecision; Appendix VI: Problem Solving), cognitive skills for dealing with feelings of anger, self-blame, and "catastrophe" (Appendix V: Self-Disputation; Uncovering The Shoulds), and assertion skills (Appendix VI: Assertion).

Clients must be taught that successful long-term maintenance is all about getting to know their own strengths and weaknesses, assets and deficits. It is about getting to know their own life space—their professional and social environment, colleagues, friends, and family. It is about tuning in to their body, and knowing their own bad habits and vulnerabilities. It is about getting to know their own mind, and to recognize its familiar tricks. Above all, successful maintenance is about generating feelings of self-efficacy, feelings of being on top, and in control—which come only from knowing that one knows oneself.

SUGGESTED FURTHER READING

Baum, A., Taylor, S. E., & Singer, J. E. (Eds.). (1984). *Handbook of psychology and health (Vol. 4): Social psychological aspects of health*. Hillsdale, NJ: Lawrence Erlbaum Associates.
Beck, A. T., & Emery, G. (1985). *Anxiety disorders and phobias: A clinical perspective* (Chapter 10: Principles Of Cognitive Therapy). NY: Basic Books.

Brownell, K. D., Marlatt, G. A., Lichtenstein, E., & Wilson, G. T. (1986). Understanding and preventing relapse. *American Psychologist, 41:7*, 765–782.

Frank, J. D. (1985). Therapeutic components shared by all psychotherapies. In M. J. Mahoney & A. Freeman (Eds.), *Cognition and psychotherapy* (pp. 49–79). NY: Plenum Press.

Goldfried, M. R. (1981). Psychotherapy as coping skills training. In M. J. Mahoney (Ed.), *Psychotherapy process: Current issues and future directions* (pp. 89–119). NY: Plenum Press.

Goldfried, M. R. & Davison, G. C. (1976). *Clinical behavior therapy* (Chapter 2: Behavioral Assessment; Chapter 3: Methods Of Behavioral Assessment; Chapter 4: The Therapeutic Relationship). NY: Holt, Rinehart, and Winston.

Kessler, R. C., Brown, R. L., & Broman, C. L. (1981). Sex-differences in psychiatric help-seeking: Evidence from four large-scale surveys. *Journal of Health and Social Behavior, 22*, 49–64.

Mahoney, M. J. (1988). The cognitive sciences and psychotherapy: Patterns in a developing relationship. In K. Dobson (Ed.), *Handbook of cognitive-behavioral therapies* (pp. 357–386). NY: Guilford.

Marlatt, G. A. & Gordon, J. R. (Eds.). (1985). *Relapse prevention: Maintenance strategies in addictive behavior change*. NY: Guilford.

Meichenbaum, D. & Turk, D. (1987). *Facilitating treatment adherence: A practitioner's guidebook*. NY: Plenum Press.

Ross, S. & Buckalew, L. W. (1983). The placebo as an agent in behavioral manipulation: A review of problems, issues and affected measures. *Clinical Psychology Review, 3*, 457–471.

Sweet, H. A. (1984). The therapeutic relationship in behavior therapy. *Clinical Psychology Review, 4*, 253–273.

White, L., Tursky, B. & Schwartz, G. E. (Eds.). (1985). *Placebo: Theory, research and mechanisms*. NY: Guilford.

Wilson, G. T. (1980). Towards specifying the "non-specific" factors in behavior therapy: A social-learning analysis. In M. J. Mahoney (Ed.), *Psychotherapy process: Current issues and future directions* (pp. 283–307). NY: Plenum Press.

Appendix I
Identifying Problems
and Planning Changes

IDENTIFYING THE PROBLEMS

Very often, when clients are first referred, they are acutely aware that all is not as it should be, but they cannot put their finger on the cause of their unease. Frequently, people complain that they feel nervous, confused, or under pressure. These vague phrases indicate that the source of the discomfort and unhappiness has not been identified; and this ambiguity adds to their distress. The cause of a problem can lie in a person's environment, body, behavior, or thinking. Moreover, frequently what starts off as one problem quickly breeds problems in other areas. The initial problem often gets lost in a web of confusion and increasing stress.

On the other hand, even when people *are* sure of what their problem is (e.g., "I smoke too much"), they can rarely report the times, places, and context within which the problem occurs, or why. In other words, correctly *identifying* problems does not mean that the dynamics are also understood. For example, people smoke for a variety of reasons: for the taste of the tobacco, for a food substitute or a tranquilizer under pressure, or simply for something to do with their hands when feeling uncomfortable in company. Most smokers, if asked *why* they smoke, would probably answer something like: "I just do—I suppose I like it." People are generally unaware of the many factors that influence their behavior; and furthermore, as explained in chapter 1, verbal self-report and introspection are also surprisingly unreliable.

People are bad observers, both of their own behavior and of the world in general (see chapter 1). For this reason, it is essential to provide clients with a way of establishing a degree of objectivity on themselves. Only in this way can problems be identified and understood and the necessary changes be planned. The solution is a simple, effective technique that does not require any great expenditure of time or financial resources. It is called *self-monitoring,* which means keeping a diary. People can learn to monitor both their behavior and their thinking.

Self-Monitoring Behavior

The idea behind self-monitoring is quite simple. Clients keep a systematic daily record of their behavior, over a number of weeks, and sometimes months. With the guidance of the therapist, they learn to identify patterns and trends in their behavior—how they react and respond at different times and in different situations. These patterns elucidate and clarify where their problems lie, and why. The idea is not dissimilar to that of a cardiac monitor, where visual information is provided on sudden changes, as well as systematic patterns and irregularities over a period of time. Self-monitoring is a very flexible technique. As well as its usefulness in *identifying* problem areas, it can also be used to obtain more *detailed information* on specific, recognized problems, such as smoking, fears and phobias, feelings of depression, panic attacks, overeating, shyness, lack of assertion, relationship difficulties, or compulsive rituals.

The procedure is as follows. The client buys a small notebook and allots a page to each day. I restrict people to *one* page per day, as writing too much defeats the whole purpose of the exercise, which is to clarify things. The date and the day of the week are put at the top of each page. They then keep a systematic daily record of their behavior—the "whens, wheres, whys, with whoms, and how muches" of what they did and how they felt. This can be done by making short notes at intervals during the day, if they are trying to monitor the frequency of a *particular* behavior; but, I generally advice people to write a resume of their day *in the evening,* when they have a perspective on how the day, overall, has gone. This also establishes a habit. The importance of writing their notes *every day* is consistently repeated. Memory is fallible; but, more importantly, the very days people do not feel like keeping their diary usually turn out to be the most informative. Overall, diary-keeping only takes a few minutes, and even less as one gets used to it. Hours can be wasted going over things in one's mind.

After a minimum of 2 but preferably 3 weeks, the diary is reviewed with the therapist. It may have to be read through several times before any trends become obvious. Days of the week are compared with other days, weekends with the rest of the week, times of the day with other times, situations with other situations. Certain days of the week, times of the day, or people often

Monday 10th

Got up 7.30 am; felt bad. Went to work; panic when Boss came in. Met Bob for lunch - made me feel much better. Didn't want to go back to the office. Bad afternoon. Too many things to do. Drank coffee continuously. Felt really anxious. Home 7pm. Didn't feel like eating dinner; had a few beers instead. Couldn't stop thinking of the office, and all I had to do. Stomach ache. Bed early to be in good shape for work; couldn't sleep.

TUESDAY 28TH.

UP EARLY. FELT GREAT. ORANGE JUICE, ONE SLICE WHEAT BREAD, AND COFFEE (DECAF.) FOR BREAKFAST. DID HOUSEWORK. MET SUSAN IN CITY - SHE LOOKED GREAT, FULL OF ENERGY. FELT FAT AND UGLY. WENT HOME INSTEAD OF SHOPPING FOR NEW DRESS. BINGED ON THE KIDS' COOKIES AND CANDY. FELT WORSE. CANCELLED EVENING CARD GAME WITH JOE AND GAIL. ARGUMENT WHEN HUSBAND CAME HOME. MY FAULT. WATCHED T.V. ALL NIGHT. POOR FORM. FEEL I'LL NEVER LOSE WEIGHT.

Thursday 30th

Woke at 8 am - couldn't get up till ten. House in mess. No energy to tidy up. Day just passed doing nothing. Kept thinking of when Harry was alive - things we so different then. I was so different. Sent the kids for a take-out dinner again. Feel guilty. They're not eating right. Don't have the energy to cook. Bed at 9. Didn't sleep well.

Figure I.1   Typical Diaries

emerge as consistent stressors. It might become apparent, for example, that a client regularly feels ill on Saturday mornings. Why? Because he or she frequently eats shellfish, fast food, skips dinner altogether, or drinks too much on Friday nights. People are often quite surprised by the reality that unfolds. Clients who had initially reported feeling anxious "all the time" or "out of the blue" come to see that, in fact, they only get anxious when they are alone, or when in crowded places, after an interpersonal upset, when something unexpected happens, when they have taken on too much, or when they have to speak in public, for example.

The dynamics of specific problem behaviors can also be highlighted. One client who wanted to quit smoking learned, after keeping his diary, that he was smoking far *more* than the 40 cigarettes that he bought daily; as many again were offered. He also noticed that he worked through his lunch break on several days, smoking ciagrettes instead of eating, and that these were the days that he just happened to have an argument with his wife when he got home. Usually, this was because he was very hungry, and overreacted angrily if the dinner was not ready. He improvised with ice cream, cookies, and *more* cigarettes, and remained wound up all evening.

The idea is to help clients identify the triggers—times, places, situations, or circumstances—that consistently spark off the behavior that they are trying to understand and change. Once these triggers have been identified, a chain of responses can usually be traced, and the problem can be put in context. This same client had been vaguely aware that pressure at work wound him up; but, looking closer, it became obvious that these were the times when he also doubled up on cigarettes *and* skipped lunch to get through the paperwork. Why was he under so much pressure, when his colleagues could go out to lunch? From his diary, it also became clear that every day he took on new projects, before the ones in hand were completed. Why? He admitted that he found it very hard to say "no." "It's important to be liked . . . to have a reputation for being cooperative. I like to do my share—it also increases my chances of promotion." But, he *also* agreed that he would like to be more assertive, and to feel less pressured. Furthermore, he began to see that his frustration was being taken out anyway—at home—and that it did not end there. When he was angry, he always binged on junkfood, and then he felt guilty, and even more frustrated and irritable, and all the more likely to snap at his wife and children again. People are often on such a wheel, without even realizing. What looks like a number of different problems is often simply *one* problem in different guises. Furthermore, the problem a client initially presents with, or is referred for, is not always the main difficulty at all. In this example, smoking and overeating were just offshoots of more basic difficulties: primarily, a lack of assertion and poor stress-management skills.

The idea of keeping records of their own behavior sometimes strikes people as overly simple, pointless, or artificial. Others have expressed a concern that they will become too introspective and go around scrutinizing their every move at the expense of concentrating on other matters. Another concern is that, by watching themselves in this way, they will *not* behave as they normally would, and thereby defeat the whole purpose of the exercise. All of these apprehensions are understandable, but they rarely, if ever, occur. After keeping a diary for a couple of days, it, like so many other behaviors, becomes a habit and fades from active consciousness, and therefore does not interfere.

The advantages of keeping a diary are many—mainly, that it provides the objectivity that people lack, by allowing them to unobtrusively observe their own behavior. The quality and quantity of information gathered would literally be impossible to obtain in any other way. It provides both client and therapist with a better insight into the problem. With this information, things become clearer and more manageable; and they can then go about planning the necessary changes. Furthermore, *continued* self-monitoring is being increasingly acknowledged as an essential ingredient in long-term self-maintenance and relapse prevention (e.g. Kirschenbaum, 1987; Krantz, 1987).

Self-Monitoring Thinking

In many cases, the problematic situations, triggers, and chains are not at all clear cut: Clients report feeling anxious or depressed at certain times, for no apparent reason; and nothing in their diary stands out as a trigger. In such circumstances, it is usually the person's *thinking* that is the problem, that is, the kinds of things they are saying to themselves in these situations. Learning to analyze thinking is, therefore, particularly helpful in identifying triggers for changes in mood; it also helps take the disconcerting mystery out of things.

Understanding one's thinking is more difficult than observing behavior, but it, too, begins with self-observation. Basically, clients are instructed in how to become more aware of what they are silently saying to themselves in multifarious problem situations. They continue to keep a daily record of their activities—what they did and how they felt, and the situations or times when they became anxious, upset, or angry, whatever their particular problem is. At the next consultation, the therapist takes any *one* such situation, and asks them to remember, as clearly as possible, what went through their mind at the time—before, during, and after the event.

If, for example, an upset was a spontaneous social gathering in the office, the client recreates the situation in his or her mind, getting as clear a picture as possible, and asks: "What went through my mind as I *entered* the situation, while I was *in* the situation, and *afterwards*?". It might go something like this:

1. *Entering the situation..*   "Oh no, I can't face this. I wish I had known in advance; I could have made some excuse not to come. What will I talk about? What if I go blank?".

2. *In the situation..*   "They all seem so confident and at ease. They all have their own little groups, too. I don't fit in. I'm sure they can sense my tension. Why doesn't somebody talk to me? I wish I didn't look so dull—even my clothes are dull. What if someone asks me something I don't know anything about? Oh no, please don't come over. . . . I'd better move . . . look as if I'm going to the restroom. Actually, that's an idea. I'll be alone there. I've got to get out of here anyhow."

3. *Afterwards..*   "I hate situations where I'm forced to make small talk. They are so artificial. Anyway, I had nothing in common with those people. They are not my *real* friends. . . . I can talk to *them* fine . . . most of the time anyway. People are so insincere."

Likewise, analyzing an anxious moment in the office might reveal a sequence of thoughts like the following:

1. Oh no, here comes Mr. Jones.
2. He always makes me feel as if he thinks I'm wasting time . . . and then I blush.
3. Oh please, don't let me go red.
4. I knew I would—now he'll think he was right . . . that I blushed because I had something to hide.
5. He's looking right at me. . . . please don't come over.
6. Phew. Thank God; he's been called away.
7. But I know he saw me blushing . . . maybe he thinks I fancy him. Oh no, that's even worse.
8. How will I face him the next time?

Hours, or even the rest of a day, can be wasted in anticipation of a Mr. Jones' reappearance. People can be left feeling totally drained and frustrated by such invisible personal dramas, by such apparently trivial events. It is usually *afterwards* when bad feelings or a change in mood are felt. In both of these examples, there is frustration, anger, and disappointment. Such feelings can last for hours, as well as making people more likely to overreact to minor problems, *and* to other people, in the course of the day. They can also trigger *other* problem behaviors, such as overeating, smoking, spending, or withdrawal, generating a spiral of stress responses.

Understanding one's thinking is a very powerful tool. After a number of practice sessions with the therapist, clients are asked to start doing the exercise alone, at home. They take problem situations from their diary, and write their thoughts down along the *left hand side* of a page—as many as they can remember, and the order in which they occurred. This only takes a couple of minutes, and it allows them to understand how and why their mood did, and can, change over the course of the day. Even if it were feasible and ethical to hire a cameraman to follow people around 24 hours a day, making videos of their less dignified moments, the camera and its owner would still not be able to record what was going on in the client's mind; people can only do this for themselves.

In addition to analyzing thinking by using a diary in this way, clients are also encouraged to become more aware of their thinking during the day, when they are actually *in* their problem situations. Any time they feel that their mood has changed—that they are beginning to feel tense, unhappy or angry, for example—they are asked to stop and examine the thoughts or images that are going through their mind. One client discovered, for example, that although she was sitting by a homey, welcoming hearth, she was thinking: "I wish my husband and children would come home, or that *someone* would call. I always seem to be sitting here alone. What's wrong with me? The house feels so empty, and I feel so full. I've eaten so much junk today again. I feel so guilty."

Another client found that every time he caught himself daydreaming, he was, in fact, ruminating over a recent loss—a bereavement that he had not yet come to terms with. In the same way, people can discover that they do a lot of exaggerated "What if-ing"; they live in constant dread of even minor changes or problems, because they do not feel equipped to cope. A warm and comfortable external environment does *not* mean that people's internal one is the same.

PLANNING CHANGES

Motivation Analysis

Change is not easy, and it does not happen overnight. Consequently, motivation is essential. Even the most highly motivated clients sometimes tire or lose sight of their goals. For these reasons, both client and therapist must be quite clear, from the start, as to what *exactly* needs to be changed and why, as well as the possible wide-ranging consequences of such changes on other areas of the client's life. The first step in most interventions, therefore, is to carry out a simple but essential *motivation analysis*; to establish whether, and why, the person *really* wants to make changes. Clients answer the following three questions as clearly and honestly as possible:

1. Why do I want to change?
2. What are the consequences of changing—positive and negative?
3. What are the consequences of not changing?

The answers are written down, and then discussed in detail with the therapist.

1. Why do I want to change?   Clients must ask themselves: "Do I honestly want things to be different?". Sometimes, problems can, in subtle ways, be convenient. Contemplating silent questions, such as: "Why am I a workaholic? Is it *possible* that it suits me? Does being so "busy" all the time excuse me from getting down to the gardening and repair jobs at home, or from taking a look at my marriage and my nonexistent social life?" can be very revealing. "My weight problem means that my husband has to leave the car for me to do the shopping and get around in. Is it *possible* that I just want to hold on to the car? If I get slim, I will lose it—is that what I *really* want?" Most problems are not convenient in these ways, or, at least, not obviously so. But, life is a subtle marketplace, so it is imperative for clients to acknowledge the possibility of such hidden cover-ups and pay-offs at this point—because when the problem goes, so do they.

2. What are the consequences of changing?   Sometimes a particular problem is identified as the "root of all evil." Everything would be wonderful—"if only I were 20 pounds lighter," or "more assertive," or "more sexy," or "less fussy around the house." Life is not that simple. If a change program is motivated by such a belief, and the magical transformation does not occur, disappointment follows. Losing weight will not transform a bad marriage. Becoming more assertive will not guarantee promotion. A better sex life will not automatically bring a long-tried-for baby.

Clients are asked to make a list of the *positive* consequences of overcoming their problem or bad habit. They then have to consider how such changes might effect other areas of their life, on a wider level. Would it leave them, for example, with time on their hands, hitherto spent worrying, fussing, eating, or drinking? Would it put extra demands on their time or resources? Would losing weight or being more assertive or less depressed bring a desire to socialize more and to spend more money on new clothes? Such consequences, both positive and negative, must be anticipated and, if necessary, built into the change plan.

3. *What are the consequences of not changing?* Answering this question frequently helps to launch people into their change program—even if it now seems more complicated and daunting than was initially envisaged. Clients are supplied with up-to-date, factual information on the long-term consequences—to both physical and psychological well-being—of remaining as they are. They then make a *personal* list of the long-term consequences to their relationships, career, and family life, of *not* changing. It is important that they hold on to these lists, because they are invariably used as reminders and motivators at a later stage.

What to Change

Clients are next helped to define exactly what they want *and* need to change, and what they can realistically *hope* to achieve, given their personal resources and circumstances. Again, the following questions are answered on paper and discussed:

1. What exactly do I want to change?
2. What can I work at changing, in myself and in my environment?

1. *What exactly do I want to change?* Everyone would like certain aspects of themselves or their environment to be different—to have a better figure, a better memory, a better way with people, or to have more money. But, it is important for people to keep in mind that nobody is perfect; and, like the pursuit of constant happiness, discussed in chapter 2, total perfection is not what one should realistically aim for. It would only bring disappointment and frustration. Using the information from their diaries, clients write out a short, *realistic* description of the way they would like to be—exactly what they think they need, or would like, to change. They are instructed to be as specific as possible, and not to use vague terms like *fulfilled, mature,* or *successful.* More concrete words allow them to define their goals. One client made the following list: "I would like to be able to assert myself at work, and with my boyfriend," "I would like to lose 15 pounds, and to get fit," "I would like to be able to cope on days when I feel down," and "I would like to be a world-famous model." These goals are then ranked, the most important at the top, and the rest following in order of priority. They can then be further subdivided, according to whether the desired changes relate to environment, body, behavior, or thinking (see Table I.1).

TABLE I.1.
Defining Goals

Where Do The Problems Lie?	Order of Priority	Specific Desired Changes
1. Environment		
2. Body	2	To lose 15 pounds; and to get fit.
3. Behavior	1	To be able to assert myself at work, and with my boyfriend.
	4	To be a world-famous model.
4. Thinking	3	To be able to cope better on days when I feel down.

2. What can I work at changing in myself and in my environment? The next step is to consider whether the client can realistically hope to effect these changes, and over what period of time. This means that, with the objective guidance of the therapist, the person must take a hard look at himself or herself and his or her personal resources, circumstances, and environment. There are always a number of things about oneself and others that people wish were different, but that cannot ever be. If someone is 5 feet tall, no amount of hoping or stretching will ever make them 5'9". Such things must be accepted. Likewise, clients frequently express regrets: "If only I had married earlier, or later, or furthered my education, or chosen a different career, everything would have turned out better." They need to be reminded that, for all they know, things might have gone a lot worse; and that there is no point in asking themselves the unanswerable or in dwelling on the past. They are encouraged to be "present" and "outer-oriented," to work at constructing the best change program, given the current ingredients. In the previous example, the client's fourth goal was to be a world-famous model. This was discussed with her, as to how realistic she felt it really was. She admitted that it was more a fantasy than anything else—considering she was only 5'2"—and she was quite happy to drop it from the list.

Change Plan

All changes require motivation, planning, and practice. Because people are such creatures of habit, they really must *want* to change before anything will happen. A goal can seem very far away in terms of weeks, words, or feelings; thus, the importance of keeping the list of long-term consequences of *not* changing. Even when people are really motivated, changes still have to be planned and must take place gradually. The areas that need working on and the exact changes the client wants to realize have to be identified and

TABLE I.2
Example of a Simple Change Plan

Assertion

Linda agrees to attend an assertion skills training program over the next 10 weeks. Typical problem situations, identified from her self-report and diary-keeping (e.g., being able to stand up to her boyfriend), will be incorporated into the role-plays at the group. Specific homework assignments will provide practice between sessions.

Weight

A *simultaneous* weight reduction program will span approximately the same 10 weeks. *Goal:* To lose 2 pounds per week. This will form the main topic of bi-weekly individual consultations. *Skills to be acquired:* Stimulus control, advance preparation, and behavioral programming; also healthy eating habits and regular exercise.

Cognitive

Cognitive component of assertion training course to be followed by individual cognitive work, aimed at alleviating negative thinking on down days. (Effective completion of the assertion course, and successful weight loss, may make this intervention unnecessary). Plan will be reviewed in 10 weeks time.

Note: Both the client and the therapist are supplied with a copy of the change plan.

discussed, as outlined. *Only then* can a detailed change plan, encompassing the areas, priorities, the steps, and the time span, be constructed. Change does not occur overnight; and it generally takes longer than expected. The steps toward change, therefore, must be small and concrete, and the time span realistic. Generally speaking, behavior changes more quickly than attitudes and feelings. So, therapists usually start off by focusing on some aspects of their clients' environment, body maintenance, or behavior, and, at a later stage, embark on cognitive intervention.

Appendix II
Making Changes
in the Environment

I once had a client who said that he felt like a cork, bobbing around on a sea of problems and pressures, being pulled this way and that way by bills, deadlines, commitments, and uncertainties. Most people occasionally feel like this, but things somehow seem to fall back into place. People under pressure, however, frequently complain that their time belongs to everyone but them, that even their leisure time is not their own. They feel that they are not free to plan their life or their future; that their environment and circumstances are controlling them. This feeling of being trapped then adds another link to the chain. As explained in chapter 1, feeling that one is in control and able to cope is psychologically very important. Among the negative consequences of *not* having this feeling of self-efficacy are helplessness and depression.

It would be unrealistic to suggest that, with a little effort, life can be perfect for everyone. Stress is inevitable. Life is challenging; and some people's circumstances are, by any standards, far from ideal. One man I treated was in a job that he found totally unfulfilling and monotonous; but he had a mortgage to pay, and a wife and small children to feed. He could not leave just to suit himself. Similarly, the mother of a young family cannot come and go as she pleases; her movements are genuinely restricted. These are realistic constraints. They will not disappear with a few beers or a good cry.

The first step in helping a person to establish a feeling of control over their life and environment is to evaluate what can and cannot be changed (Appendix I: Change Plan). They can then be helped to accept the currently unchangeables and to channel their mental and physical energies into doing what they can about the rest. People benefit from being reminded that their goal should not be to achieve a state of constant happiness; coping is all about making the best of one's unique situation and set of circumstances at any point in time.

People's lives consist of many different environments—domestic, professional, and social. Changes may be necessary in all, or in just some, of these. Environmental changes can be instituted in two main ways: (a) utilizing environmental resources, and (b) advance preparation.

UTILIZING ENVIRONMENTAL RESOURCES

Very often, people become so familiar with a particular place that they switch off, and effectively stop noticing what is going on around them. In other words, people can be quite blind to their own environment. By becoming aware of this, however, and acquainting themselves with what their environment has to offer, they can often make up for negative circumstances that cannot realistically be changed in the past, present, or immediate future. An unfulfilling job can be compensated for by building up interests in other areas. The confinement of young children can be lessened by identifying supportive resources—such as a local young mothers' group. The environment is a very powerful and pervasive part of people's existence, so it is essential for them to learn how to make it work in their favor.

I frequently suggest to clients who are trying to renew their acquaintance with their environment (e.g., a long-term agoraphobic client who has not been out much in recent years, or a couple in marital therapy who are trying to increase their shared interests) that they start off by pretending they are entirely new to the area. With this mind-set, they are asked to buy a detailed up-to-date map, and, if available, a publication of local activities and organizations. The first step is to identify *landmarks*. Libraries can be a vital source of information about local activities, as well as of both educational and leisure reading material. Other important landmarks are hospitals, police stations, banks, post offices, churches, schools, parks, health and fitness centers, and venues for social and civic events and public meetings.

Identifying landmarks is also very important for the person who *has* just moved to a new area, and is trying to adjust to the loss of familiar faces and places. Major shopping complexes should be identified, as well as the location of all-night stores, gasoline stations, and pharmacies. Knowledge of the local public transport system is also essential, even if they have a car. The location of art galleries, drama and movie theaters, and concert halls is also important; and, for those who are interested, popular singles' bars and restaurants.

When landmarks have been identified and clients have a feel for the area, they then ask themselves how they can best *utilize* these resources. Regarding *educational* facilities, if a person's job is not fulfilling, or if there is a possibility of redundancy, it makes sense to acquire skills in another area of expertise, for example. There are courses in almost everything: computer programming, languages, interior design, carpentry, cookery, antiques restoration, exercise, accounting, marketing, car maintenance, wine making, Greek mythology. They are encouraged to find out from local newspapers, magazines, notice boards, and radio about the availability of such classes.

If they cannot go to classes during the day, there are as many evening amenities to choose from. Other evening activities include clubs and discussion groups, such as film societies, debating groups, and photography clubs. Meeting other people on a repeated basis, at either a course or a club, carries the added advantage of informally increasing one's social contacts. For the housebound, reading is a wonderful method of self-education. Even scanning the newspapers and tuning in to certain radio and television stations can provide a constant source of information, stimulation, and company.

People's *social* contacts, and social life, often tie in with their preferred activities—be they of a sporting or academic nature. Depending on clients' interests, therefore, they are advised to find out about classes, social clubs, or sports centers in the area, as mentioned above. Sport, which is discussed in more detail in Appendix III, can provide a perfect combination of relaxation, body maintenance, fun, and socializing. By pursuing a *personal* interest that is genuinely appealing, rather than going to a more public venue where interests and backgrounds will be much more diverse, clients are more likely to meet people they will be comfortable with and have things in common with. The importance of friends and social supports cannot be overemphasized; social contacts are a vital part of good living.

ADVANCE PREPARATION

With just a little forethought, the impact of many life events and daily hassles, can be lessened dramatically. In other words, with some advance preparation, many life stresses can be avoided, or at least rendered less traumatic. For example, a lot of people go into marriage unprepared for the inevitable change in lifestyle that it brings, or without discussing obvious practical considerations, such as contraception or finance. Ironically, people do not plan ahead for retirement, even though it is the one thing for which they have had their whole life to prepare. Many could be more equipped for the possibility of redundancy by developing skills in other areas. Many people wait *until* an accident or illness to take out life or health insurance, or to think about making a will.

Likewise, accidents—whether at home or on the job—could often be prevented. Most are caused by momentary forgetfulness or by lack of preparation. People do not get into the habit of automatically assessing their environment for potential hazards. They do not know whether the necessary legal safety measures have been taken, or they do not follow them. They do not take the time to find out where emergency exits, fuse boxes, first-aid kits, hoses, alarm bells, or even telephones are located. At work, basic safety practices, such as wearing required uniform or protective equipment for eyes, ears, and skin are often just not respected. Machinery and equipment is not checked regularly enough to make sure it is working properly. In the same way, people do not ensure that *they* are working efficiently—that they are properly trained for the job they are doing or the equipment they are using. Certain tasks require a basic level of alertness, concentration, or fitness, and should not be attempted unless these requirements are met; but, all too often, they are not.

The promotion of occupational health is now an area of major concern, and a focus of active research (Glasgow & Terborg 1988; Paine, 1984; Quick & Quick, 1984). However, one of the most basic difficulties is proving to be that of getting individuals to *change* old habits—to learn to take the necessary, tiny precautions and to think ahead.

OCCUPATIONAL HAZARDS

Each year in the United States, thousands of people die because of work activities—both from injuries and from occupational diseases. The cost of compensation payments, insurance claims, damage to plants and equipment, and working time comes to millions of dollars. Work hazards include both the likelihood of accidents and the possibility of developing illnesses and disease. Some jobs are undoubtedly more hazardous than others, for example, shipping, coal mining, railway work, agriculture, and construction, as well as some kinds of factory work. Even places such as restaurants, dry-cleaners, and hairdressing salons carry their own, often unnoticed, hazards. Unlike accidents, work-related illnesses often take a long time to develop. These are the silent, hidden killers that can lead to various cancers and diseases of the skin and lungs. The main offenders are chemicals, dust, and radiation.

Advance preparation is also an essential ingredient in many formal intervention programs for dealing with problems of living, especially those that aim to increase the client's ability to exercise self-control. The dynamics of self-control and related training programs generated a lot of interest in the 1960s and early 1970s, raising not just theoretical questions for psychology, but also philosophical issues that have not yet been resolved (Catania, 1975; Kanfer & Karoly, 1972; Thoresen & Mahoney, 1974). It also heralded the start of the "cognitive revolution." Two self-control techniques are of particular relevance. These are environmental planning and behavioral programming.

Environmental Planning

People come to associate certain times, faces, and places with particular activities. Many people always have a cigarette with a drink or after a meal, for example. Others find that they spend, eat, or drink too much in the company of certain people, or when they are in certain moods. Situations trigger the same responses again and again, until the associations become automatic. These maladaptive behavior patterns can be modified by changing or rearranging the triggering stimuli that give rise to them. People can be helped to make their environment work for them by setting things up *in advance*, so that they can cope with difficult situations when they arise. By changing what are called the *setting conditions*, or antecedents, the problem behaviors can be prevented. This can be orchestrated in a number of ways, as discussed next.

Temporary Avoidance. Sometimes, it is better for a person to *temporarily* avoid a problem situation, until they are better equipped to cope with it. For example, in the early days of a weight-loss endeavor, it can be more advisable for a client to go to work past the fruit shop instead of the bakery. When feeling low, it is not a good idea for people to go to places that are guaranteed to remind them of happier times, or of a lover who is no longer part of their life. This *is* avoidance; but, as part of a graded intervention program, it makes sense in the early stages to "tread softly."

Stimulus Control. In many cases, it is not feasible to avoid the problem situations, even temporarily. Here, *stimulus control*, the principal environmental planning strategy, is very effective. Technically speaking, the client changes environmental and situational factors so as to modify the reinforcement contingencies that ordinarily occur *prior* to executing the target behavior. In other words, people prepare *in advance* for problem situations. For example, if a client is trying to lose weight, he or she would make a list of essential purchases before going to the store, and bring only enough money for these items. The smoker who is trying to quit would leave home without cigarettes, without money to buy them, and might enlist friends to discourage him or her from accepting cigarettes when they are offered during the day. If the problem is one of overspending—when alone or with certain people,— the person would simply not bring his or her checkbook or credit cards into these situations. Before attending a gathering where the guests share an area of interest—for example, politics, wine, or literature—clients are encouraged to acquaint themselves with basic up-to-date facts and vocabulary. By doing their homework, they can relax, and the people present will be impressed and complimented by the effort. Potentially problematic situations can be defused by just a little forethought and preparation.

Problem Prime Times.   Advance preparation can also help deal with what I call problem "prime times." These are times or situations that *always* generate problems; and yet, the same scenarios are played out again and again. For example, many well-suited professional couples consistently have a major argument on Friday nights. It is the end of the week. They are both tired. The apartment is untidy. The ice-box is empty, but neither partner has the energy to go to the store. Simply agreeing *in advance*, for example, to both eat a substantial lunch on Fridays, and to have a simple supper that does not require any preparation, can allow them to relax and unwind. Likewise, people often find themselves saying, on the way to the dinner party, for example, "I just *know* I'll eat too much . . . I always do when I go to Susan's." "*Just knowing*" is a decision in itself. The key to this strategy is to get the client to decide *in advance* exactly how they will behave (e.g., exactly how much they will eat or drink), leaving no room to maneuver. What can be viewed as not accepting other people's hospitality is another difficult situation for many people to handle. Hosts and hostesses, with the best will in the world, can insist that guests indulge in their gastronomic creations. Dealing with such conflict situations demands a lot of assertion— both with oneself and with other people. It is essential for clients, with the help of the therapist, to think out an alternative response to their usual one, and to decide in advance exactly what they will say and do. This is practiced repeatedly with the therapist, and then alone, until they feel comfortable that they are prepared for the real thing (Appendix IV: Behavior Rehearsal).

Enlisting Friends.   Another effective way of utilizing environmental re- sources by advance preparation is to enlist the support of other people— spouse, partner, colleagues, or friends. To be effective, I advise clients to proceed as follows. First, they explain to the person or persons concerned exactly what they are trying to achieve (i.e., their change plan). They also convey that they have *already* worked out their goals and the time span. In other words, the client makes it clear that he or she is in charge and in control. Advice on how to change behavior is not needed; but support is. Friends also need to be told exactly what they can do or say to help, and when. It is important that they do not get the idea that they have to monitor the person's progress or constantly check on them, as this can be irritating for all. It is also essential for clients to ensure that their supporters take the plan seriously, that they recognize it as a genuine effort to change, and realize that their support and encouragement are extremely important. They are also asked to be tolerant of occasional slips in control; change is not easy.

Portable Motivators.   In the early stages of effecting both cognitive and behavior change, *concrete* aids and reminders, in the shape of personal self- statements, are extremely effective. Clients simply identify a word or a phrase—something short and punchy—that they find particularly effective in helping them deal with their bad habit or problem behavior. It is essential that people choose their own self-statements, and that they are personally meaningful and motivating. Self-statements can be positive or negative, depending on the nature of the problem. For example, "Life is what *I* make it," or "I *can* do it" might come in useful when motivation or self-confidence is low. Alternatively, negative comments, such as: "Do I want to dig my grave with my teeth?" or "Smoking is choking," are more effective when tempted to succumb to habits of overindulgence.

The self-statement is then matched with an activity that the person does several times a day—drinking glasses of water or cans of soda, or making telephone calls, for example. Clients get into the habit of saying their personal self-statement silently to themselves every time the frequent activity is carried out. Some also find it useful to *write* their self-statement in some strategic places, were they will be confronted by it several times a day and thereby reminded of their good intentions. Written on a small card, it can be kept in a pocket, purse, wallet, beside the telephone, on the dashboard of the car, or in a cookie jar. Likewise, it can be written directly onto a shopping list, appointments diary, or inside the flip-top of a pack of cigarettes. People are frequently very skeptical about "portable motivators"—that they sound artificial, or too simple to be taken seriously. Their simplicity is, in fact, their strength.

Behavioral Programming

Often, even with the best will in the world, initial motivation to overcome bad habits—of overeating, smoking, or overdoing things—begins to dwindle. The end can seem very far away. Family or friends are not as supportive as had been hoped and expected. Things are not happening as quickly as one thought they would. This is where pay-offs, which are built into the change plan from the start, can help clients to persevere. They can learn to reward themselves, along the way, for their efforts. This type of personal contract system is called *behavioral programming*.

Inherent in the rationale of behavioral programming is the concept of self-reinforcement, that is, the self-delivery of reinforcers, contingent on performing certain responses. In other words, unlike environmental planning and stimulus control, behavioral programming involves the self-administration of consequences *after* the target behavior occurs. Clients modify the consequences that normally *follow* the target behavior, by rewarding themselves if they refrain or by punishing themselves if they give in.

At the beginning of the change program, specific, concrete, and realistic goals are agreed on. There can be a goal for each day, or one for the week or month. The important thing is to ensure that clients can judge clearly whether or not they have reached their goal, so that they can reward themselves accordingly. They must also decide, in advance, how frequently they will reward themselves. For example, on a weight reduction program, one could reward oneself for restraint at the end of every day, or for a certain weight loss at the end of the week, or when one's ideal weight is reached. This is very much a matter of personal choice; but, obviously, the more frequent the rewards, the smaller they will be.

It must also be decided, in advance, *what* the rewards will be. This is important, as it gives people something concrete to work toward. Rewards can be anything—an extra 15 minutes in bed, a new video cassette, a new dress, a night out—but should obviously not be counterproductive. When clients are dieting, they do not reward themselves for weight loss with a box of chocolates. Rewards should also be genuinely appealing to the person, something they will work to attain. There is no point in the therapist suggesting a night out at the theater if the person does not like live entertainment or if there is nothing good running. Clients should decide on their *own* rewards.

Perhaps most important of all, clients must accept and agree that if they do not reach their goal, they do *not* reward themselves—even for effort. This can be hard at times, especially if they have really been trying. However, if they know in their hearts that the reward will be delivered, whether the goal is reached or not, they will simply be less motivated to try. It also takes the value out of the reward as something they have worked toward and genuinely earned.

Appendix III
Making Changes in the Body

Recent research has shown that the morbidity and mortality rates of Americans are no longer related to the infectious diseases that were prevalent at the turn of the century, but to chronic disorders related to lifestyle (see Pomerleau, 1979). In other words, influenza, pneumonia, diphtheria, tuberculosis, and gastroenteritis have been replaced by heart, respiratory, and cerebrovascular diseases, obesity, and the various cancers—all of which are, in part, a product of how people live. These are ultimately not medical problems at all, but behavior problems, requiring the alteration of characteristic response patterns, bad habits, and attitudes. What and how much people eat and drink, whether or not they smoke, and how they deal with everyday stress, in effect, determines the quality and length of their lives.

As explained in chapter 2, a large number of physical illnesses and conditions are accompanied by psychological symptoms, such as anxiety and depression; and a significant number of clients who avail of mental health facilities turn out to be suffering from physical problems. The opposite situation also exists. It has been estimated that over a third of patients who seek medical help are experiencing symptoms arising, not from physical illness, but from psychological difficulties (Lader, 1975). Psychological stress, whatever it's source, can increase susceptibility to major and minor illnesses (Ader, 1980).

People vary greatly when it comes to body maintenance. Many treat their body with respect, feed it regularly and nourishingly, wash it, rest it, insure it, inspect it for wrinkles, pimples, lumps, and bumps, and go for regular physical examinations. Others go full speed ahead and ignore all warning signs—until something gives out. A certain minimum of rest, relaxation, and sleep is essential; as are adequate amounts of nourishing food, at regular intervals. As well as the obvious physical advantages in terms of energy level and robustness, how people maintain their body also has a large impact on their psychological well-being—on their alertness, irritability level, and "joie de vivre."

Body maintenance involves developing and sustaining healthy habits of: eating, exercise, relaxation, and sleep.

EATING

So much has been written about diet and nutrition that people should know themselves inside out. Yet, the fast food industry, the market for junk food, and the problem of obesity continue to grow. Also, surprisingly, the average person remains extremely ignorant of basic food facts. Clients whose problems relate to their eating habits usually need to start off with information.

Nutrition is a very complex area; but some facts are simple. We are what we eat. If people consistently eat more than they need (i.e., consume excessive calories), they put on weight. If, on the other hand, they do not eat enough (i.e., burn up more calories than they ingest), they lose weight. Even if a person's weight is steady, it does not necessarily mean that his or her body is being adequately nourished. Nutrition plays a very important role in overall feelings of physical and psychological well-being. Certain foods, drinks, additives, and drugs can compound feelings of anxiety and depression. As explained in chapter 10, *what* people eat and *how* they eat can also help or hinder efforts they may be making in other areas, to reduce their stress level, or to improve their lifestyle (Miller, 1981).

What to Eat

Foods can be divided into six nutrient classes: proteins, fats, carbohydrates, vitamins, minerals, and water. These interact to perform three basic functions. Proteins, minerals, and water facilitate growth and maintain body structures. Vitamins, proteins and water control and coordinate internal processes. Fats, carbohydrates, and proteins provide energy and maintain body temperature. A crucial balance exists between these nutrients. For example, if a person's carbohydrate intake is too low, their body will have to metabolize protein for energy. This places stress on the system—because it is more difficult to metabolize protein—and may also deplete protein resources needed for growth and maintenance of body structures.

It is vital for people to eat a balanced diet, one that contains adequate amounts of all nutrients. People vary significantly in their dietary requirements; but, by and large, every day everyone should eat some concentrated protein, fruit, potatoes, some vegetable oil or margarine, and wholemeal cereals or bread.

Fats. Modern man is not suited to metabolizing large quantities of fat. Too much fat in the diet can increase vulnerability to certain cancers. Accumulation of fat in the blood vessels increases susceptibility to heart attacks and strokes. People are, therefore, advised to eat less meat and processed meats and more fish and poultry, choose lean cuts of meat, trim off all visible fat, and grill rather than fry. Instead of butter, cheese, cream, and ice cream, they are encouraged to use low-fat dairy products, such as skimmed milk, cottage cheese, yogurt, soft margarine, and vegetable oil. Commercial cookies and cakes made with hard fats are discouraged. The current advice on eggs is not to eat more than three per week.

Sugar. Another major offender is sugar. Quite simply, people eat too much of it. Sugar causes tooth decay, and is also believed to be related to arterio-sclerosis, cancer, diverticulitis, and coronary thrombosis. There is, in fact, no physiological need for refined sugar; but, nonetheless, sugar is absorbed quickly and easily into the bloodstream, elevating blood sugar. In the stress response, the liver releases glycogen (i.e., stored body sugar) into the blood, preparing the body for "fight or flight." When people eat sugar, the body interprets the increased sugar level as a sign of stress, and the other characteristic physiological reactions are also triggered. The body's response to this quick "sugar rush" is to struggle for equilibrium; but sometimes it overreacts, and the blood-sugar level drops to below normal. This can make people feel suddenly depressed or lethargic. To restore equilibrium again, there can be a craving for sugar. Many people see-saw through life in this way.

Finally, many sweet things are "empty calories." In order to metabolize them, the body must use stored nutrients, that are not replaced by these empty calories. Consumption of overrefined and processed foods can also destroy people's appetite for more nutritious food. Again, the advice is to cut down on obviously sugar-rich foods, such as sweets and cookies, including sugar in tea and coffee. Sugar is concealed in many foods—cereals, canned foods, white bread, salad dressing, mayonnaise, and ketchup—so, clients are asked to read the list of ingredients on all foods before buying. All the sugar the body needs can be obtained from fruit, wholemeal bread, grains, potatoes, and other complex carbohydrates.

Roughage. Roughage is the indigestible fiber in vegetables and grains. Ironically, modern technology has reached such a "refined" level that people now eat too little roughage. The consequences are slow bowel movements and constipation, which can eventually cause piles and diverticular disease. There is also an association between a low-roughage diet and cancer of the bowel. The risk of developing these illnesses can be reduced by eating some fresh fruit everyday; and more vegetables, washed, preferably unpeeled, and raw or lightly cooked. Clients are also advised to eat wholemeal bread, wholemeal breakfast cereals, and brown rice. Some need to take extra bran, if their diet is very bland.

Salt.   Salt is an important cause of high blood pressure. Like sugar, it is concealed in many prepared foods, such as potato chips, popcorn, crackers, and peanuts. Other, less obvious, sources are canned vegetables and soups, pickles, smoked fish, and salted meats, such as corned beef and bacon. People's sense of taste adapts to different quantities of salt in their diet; but if they gradually reduce salt intake, the palate becomes more sensitive, and therefore better able to judge the seasoning in foods. People are therefore encouraged to taste their food before salting it; and, ideally, to remove salt from the table altogether, or to substitute with one of the commercially available low-salt or sodium-free products. It is advisable for women, at certain stages of their menstrual cycle, to reduce salt intake; salt can lead to fluid retention and increase the experience of premenstrual syndrome (PMS). On the other hand, when people lose fluid through perspiration—due to fever, change of climate, or active sport—both salt and water need to be replaced.

Beverages.   Caffeine is contained not only in coffee, but also in tea, cocoa, and cola drinks. Caffeine stimulates the nervous, cardiovascular, and respiratory systems. As with sugar, the entire stress response mechanism is triggered. Caffeine also acts as a diuretic and washes water soluble vitamins (C and B complex) out of the body, which further compounds the effects of stress by depleting nutrients. People are encouraged to change to decaffeinated coffee, grain beverages, herb teas, fruit juices, and mineral waters. I also point out to clients that, although people are inclined to associate caffeine primarily with coffee, there is a substantial amount of caffeine in tea also. The longer it is brewed, the higher the caffeine concentration. Furthermore, tea bags have a higher concentration of caffeine than instant or leaf tea. Recent findings also indicate that the tannin in tea may be responsible for washing vitamin B out of the system.
    Alcohol is another stress-producing substance. It is high in calories but is of little nutritional value. It places a burden on the detoxification system— the liver, kidneys, and the pancreas. Needless to say, it can be addictive, and excessive consumption is implicated in blood-sugar level imbalances. It is also a depressant; people feel temporarily relaxed, but the overall effects are stressful. It depletes the system of magnesium, cyamin, and other B vitamins.

It is also associated with high blood pressure. Finally, many clients are unaware that there are hidden calories in the mixers so liberally used to dilute alcoholic drinks.

Eating Habits

Eating habits determine the amount of nutrients that will be absorbed from food. When people are stressed, they can get out of tune with their body, not knowing whether they are hungry or not. Anxious people often eat at irregular times and do not know when they are full. When stressed or bored, some people eat more, as well as more often, than is necessary—for "comfort." People under pressure are also inclined to eat more quickly, and this disrupts the digestive process, as well as placing strain on the gastrointestinal tract.

Eating more, as well as more quickly, leads to weight increase—producing yet another stress on the body, as well as the mind. The body also adjusts to larger quantities of food; the more people eat, the more they can eat. Ironically, people on diets can also get into the bad habit of eating too quickly. Against medical advice, they frequently starve themselves during the day. When they finally give in, they can then eat more in 5 minutes than they would have eaten in the previous 5 hours by following a healthy weight-reduction plan.

Other people react to pressure and stress with *anorexia*, or loss of appetite. When people go for long periods without eating, their blood sugar drops, producing *hypoglycemia*; and they can find themselves irritable, shaky, and even *more* nervous. Furthermore, for those who respond to stress with increased gastric secretions, on an empty stomach, this can lead to ulcers. Finally, due to loss of appetite, depressed people also frequently lose weight, which further decreases their energy level.

Lifestyle can be another reason for unhealthy eating habits. *Type A*s, for example, are often "too busy to eat"; or they eat on the go, in transit between appointments, in the car, on the train, hurrying along the street, or while on the telephone. This puts enormous pressure on the digestive system; and furthermore, the quality of food gulped down under these conditions is usually far from ideal.

Lifestyle can also result in the bad habit of eating large meals late at night. This is very debilitating, as it does not allow the body to rest. Already tired, it tries to digest throughout the night. Sleep can also be disrupted. The soundest advice for people is to start at the other end; a good, balanced breakfast sets them up for the day.

People are very different. Some foods suit some people more than others. A high-protein diet might suit *A* but not *B*, depending on their metabolism and activity level. A hard-working manual laborer will need more calories, fluids, and salt than a sedentary business executive. People need less food, and more fluids and salt, in hot weather. Body build and size also determine the amount of food that people require. If I suspect that a client's eating habits need modification, I ask them to keep a diary for a couple of weeks (Appendix I: Self-Monitoring Behavior). This establishes, more quickly and clearly than anything else, whether or not they are eating a balanced and nutritious diet, as well as *how* they are eating—that is, their eating habits. Clients are asked to follow these simple guidelines:

- Start the day with a good breakfast.
- Eat enough to satisfy yourself, several times a day.
- Do not go for long periods without food.
- Do not eat late at night.
- Watch your consumption of fats, sugar, salt, and caffeine.
- Eat enough roughage.
- Avoid preprepared, processed, and canned foods, if at all possible.
- Examine the contents of foods before purchasing.
- Do not eat in transit, or while doing something else.
- Drink enough fluids, but drink alcohol only in moderation or not at all.

EXERCISE

As well as a balanced diet and healthy eating habits, exercise is also essential for good body maintenance. Exercise increases the efficiency of the heart and circulation, as well general muscular strength and endurance, coordination, and agility. Regular exercise also accrues wider benefits, such as decreasing mild hypertension, levels of blood fats, triglycerides, and, it is speculated, cholesterol. Exercise burns up calories; and therefore has a role to play in weight control (see chapter 10). For many people, it also helps to improve the quality of their sleep (see Haskell, 1984).

Recent research indicates that exercise may also play a significant role in psychological well-being. A number of investigations have concluded that physical fitness training leads to an improvement in mood and self-concept, as well as in work and cognitive performance. There is also increasing evidence that routine, vigorous aerobic activities, such as running, cycling, or swimming, may be an effective strategy for moderating the intensity and duration of depression and anxiety (Doyne, Chambless, & Beutler, 1983; Sime, 1984).

Unfortunately, many people have the wrong idea about exercise. Common

---

ALLERGIC REACTIONS

There are many kinds of allergies to foods and drugs, as well as to substances in the environment. Sometimes it is sufficient for a client to simply monitor their diet to identify the offenders: "Every time I eat shellfish I feel really nauseous." By and large, however, allergies are difficult to detect. This is because, firstly, the allergic response to food is often delayed; and it can therefore be hard to spot the relationship and make the link. Secondly, many people with such delayed reactions are allergic to *several* commonly eaten foods, and therefore reactions can overlap. Some people are "pan-allergic."

The best way for people to identify a food allergy is to go on an "exclusion diet"; this is a diet least likely to cause allergic reactions. Then, by reintroducing various groups of foods, one by one, they endeavor to identify the substances they cannot tolerate. In other words, the allergens must be completely removed from the diet, and then reintroduced in pure form. this is the most effective way; but it is a lengthy process, and it requires patience and expertise. For these reasons, if I suspect a serious food allergy, I refer the client on to an allergist or nutritionist for expert advice. A number of simple prick tests can usually identify specific allergic reactions.

---

erroneous beliefs are that exercise necessarily involves large expenditure on expensive equipment and sports gear; or, that getting fit means climbing out of a warm bed at dawn to go hobbling into the early morning mists, or bouncing up and down at every opportunity.

There are two main kinds of exercise: *dynamic* and *isometric*. Dynamic exercise, the one I am concerned with here, involves movement of the *whole* body, and therefore repeated contraction of many muscle groups. It improves general fitness and health. Isometric exercise—like weight lifting—involves contraction of particular muscles, without moving the rest of the body. The main kinds of *dynamic* exercise are (a) sports, (b) indoor exercise, and (c) aerobic exercise.

Sports

There are many different kinds of sports, ranging from archery to kayaking to wrestling. Different sports require different levels of muscular strength, mobility, and endurance. They also have different effects on the body. People who are unfit must build up gradually. Some sports—even hill walking—require a certain basic level of fitness before people can even begin. It is important, too, for people to choose a sport that appeals to them, and that they will enjoy. In other words, the right psychological approach is essential. One client proudly reported that he had taken my advice about sport, and had started playing squash, for relaxation. In the next breath, he added: "Yeah, and I'll beat my partner yet, if it kills me." As I informed him, he would be better off to just stay at home and drink strong, sugary coffee.

Indoor Exercise

For some people, indoor exercise is more feasible—due to work or domestic commitments—or more appealing. An obvious advantage of indoor exercise is that it can be done alone, and in any weather. Over the last 10 years in particular, fitness centers have become a popular venue for indoor exercise and socializing. They are usually well equipped, and they cater to diverse requirements. Indoor exercise can be done on machines, such as exercise bicycles, or through calisthenic exercises and some forms of yoga. Another increasingly popular form of indoor exercise is dance, which is flexible in the amount of energy that needs to be expended.

Aerobic Exercise

The term *aerobic*, coined by Dr. Kenneth Cooper, was so called because it requires a lot of air, or oxygen, to be used. It is also, and perhaps more appropriately, called *cardiovascular* exercise. Aerobic exercise involves large muscle groups and must be vigorous enough to engage the whole body. It is neither gentle nor intense; it is exercise that is *sustained* at a steady, vigorous level for a certain period of time. Opinions vary on the length of time required for exercise to be considered aerobic. The crucial factor is not the exact *number* of minutes; but that the heart rate should be elevated to between 60% and 80% of its maximum. Below 60%, exercise will not have an aerobic effect; but only very fit people can gain aerobic benefit from exercise above 80%. Therefore, the general advice that people should exercise for about 20 minutes minimum makes sense, in that it often takes 10 minutes or so to build up to an aerobic level (Cannon & Einzig, 1983).

What is aerobic will depend very much on general fitness level. The exercises most likely to be aerobic are jogging, swimming, aerobic dancing, cycling, and brisk walking in hilly countryside. Stop–start exercises, like squash and judo, are less likely to be aerobic, because it is very hard to keep going at these unless one is extremely fit. On the other hand, golf, although it is a stop–start exercise, can be aerobic for older people—not while actually *playing*, but while walking between shots. Clients are advised to start exercising slowly; and to build up gradually. A combination of walking and jogging, for the unfit person, will put quite enough pressure on the heart, and will probably be aerobic.

In sum, when planning an exercise program with clients, it is important to remember that it should not, and need not, be very time-consuming, space-occupying, or expensive, as these precious commodities are usually in short supply. It is also very important for people to choose an exercise that is genuinely appealing, whether it is conducted indoors or outdoors, with others or alone. Perhaps the most important message for people to digest is that they must build up *gradually* and not expect miracles or steady progress. Advice as basic as not exercising vigorously until 2 hours after a meal or not eating until 20 minutes after exercising also has to be consistently repeated until such habits are formed.

RELAXATION

There are many methods of relaxation, some more formal than others. Relaxation is any activity that helps people calm down, physically and mentally. Some people are genuinely more easygoing than others. They remain unruffled through any crisis; they can fall asleep at will. They seem to be always relaxed. Others wind up more easily and frequently, and therefore have to make a conscious effort to remain calm. It is worth keeping in mind, however, that appearances can be deceptive; the apparently placid individual can be churning inside.

There are many informal ways of relaxing, and, here again, people vary enormously in what appeals—relaxation is a very personal thing. Some people find that a couple of hours painting, reading, cooking, listening to music, or watching television helps them unwind. Others put their feet up, take a hot bath, nap, jog, do some gentle gardening, go for a stroll, knit, or chat with friends.

There are also a number of formal methods of relaxation (see Walker, 1975). As explained, stress involves both increased mental and physical arousal. So, formal relaxation techniques aim at decreasing the level of arousal in these different areas. Methods of relaxation have been around for a long time, but they came into the mainstream of psychology in the 1930s. The influx of Eastern culture in the 1960s also revitalized interest in body–mind dynamics.

There are many methods of relaxation, some more complicated than others. The most common is *formal muscular relaxation*. When under pressure, the body automatically reacts by tensing muscles. Sometimes, people under chronic pressure can literally be tense all over. Others unknowingly get into the habit of tensing *particular* muscle groups. This is why some people get headaches, others diarrhea or constipation; others feel wobbly in their legs, or their hands shake. Other reactions to stress are "butterflies" in the stomach, difficulty breathing, and feeling stiff and achey. *Progressive relaxation* was originated by Edmond Jacobson in the late 1920s (Jacobson, 1929). He demonstrated that, by relaxing muscles, anxiety and stress are also markedly reduced. In other words, if people can learn to control muscular tension, they can learn to relax. If the body is totally relaxed, the mind becomes more calm also. Relaxation was later integrated into the technique of *systematic desensitization* by Wolpe and Salter in the 1950s (Appendix IV: Systematic Desensitization).

Following Jacobson, most methods of relaxation involve tensing muscles and then "letting go". The idea is that, with practice, people gradually become more familiar with their own musculature and learn to identify the various muscle groups. Once they have gained a sense of what tension in these muscles feels like, and of which muscles *they* are inclined to tense, they can learn to relax these muscles. Initially, this is done for each muscle group separately, but gradually, and with practice, various muscle groups can be coordinated, and relaxation can be more rapidly achieved. In time, people can also learn to *differentially relax*, that is, to relax particular muscle groups at will, and in real-life situations (see Goldfried & Davison, 1976, chapter 5). For example, one client, a travelling salesman, realized in the course of acquiring relaxation skills, that he always tensed the back of his neck when driving. This, in turn, gave him severe headaches. With practice, he learned to relax these particular muscles; and to apply his new skills even when driving long distances.

Learning to relax is learning a skill; so, like learning to type, the more people practice, the better they get. The regularity of *practice* is constantly emphasized, and clients are strongly encouraged to get into the habit of including a period of relaxation in their daily schedule. This means choosing a suitable time, when they are unlikely to be disturbed by the telephone, or by a partner or children, *or* when they are not hungry, cold, or overtired. Ideally, relaxation should take place in a quiet, warm room—on a bed or in a big, comfortable armchair—and away from disturbances. The head should be slightly raised, and all tight belts, buttons or zippers opened. Shoes should be removed. With regular practice, people quickly begin to feel the benefits. In fact, it is often only *in retrospect*, that people realize how tense they *were*, that is, when the muscle groups that had been automatically tensed in particular situations begin to relax again.

Correct breathing is also a very important part of learning to relax. When people are very tense, they sometimes *hyperventilate;* that is, they take in too much air too quickly, and in large gulps, and consequently feel dizzy and more panicky. The other side of the coin is when the muscles of the chest become so tense and tight that people cannot take a deep breath, and "air hunger" is experienced. It is important, therefore, for clients to learn how to "deep breathe." This involves inhaling down into the diaphragm; and can be practiced by lying on the floor and taking a deep breath. The stomach should rise. Breathing in and out to a phrase like "easy and slow" ("easy" on the inhale, and "slow" on the exhale) creates a soothing rhythm.

RELAXATION INDUCTION

There are many different relaxation inductions, some more lengthy and flowery than others. Many clients find the following useful, in that it covers all the major muscle groups, but is not long or tedious.

Find a quiet place where you will not be disturbed for 30 minutes. Lie on a bed or sit in a big comfortable armchair. To block out distractions, close your eyes. Take a deep breath, and let it out slowly. Then, in an easy, rhythmical way, tighten and relax the following muscle groups: right hand and forearm, by making a fist; left hand and forearm, in the same way; both biceps, by bringing fists to shoulders; forehead and scalp, by frowning hard; middle face, by squeezing eyes tightly shut; jaw and lower face, by clenching jaw; neck, by bringing chin towards chest; neck, by pressing the head back against the chair or pillow; shoulders and upper back, by raising the shoulders up toward the ears; back, by arching it gently; stomach, by tightening the stomach; both thighs, by stretching the legs out; both calves, by pointing toes toward the head.

Each muscle group is tensed for about 5 seconds and relaxed for about 10 to 15 seconds. This is done twice for each group. These exercises are much easier if the client is talked through in this sort of way:

"Settle down comfortably. Take a deep breath and let it out slowly . . . Now clench your right fist quite tightly and notice the tension as you do so . . . hold this for a few seconds . . . and relax . . . let your fingers spread out and become loose. Now clench your right fist again, and hold it . . . and let go . . . relax. Now turn your attention to your left hand, and make a tight fist . . ." and so on, for each muscle group. After practicing a few times with the therapist, the client can be given a tape of recorded instructions. They can then continue to practice at home, to a familiar voice (i.e., the therapist's). Many prerecorded cassette tapes of relaxation instructions are also commercially available. To gain maximal benefit from these procedures, *practice* is essential. Many people find it useful to do these exercises once a day, even after they have learned how to relax or have overcome a problem of excessive tension.

When exhaling, clients are asked to exhale *more* air than they normally would, by blowing out gently. This empties the lungs, and ensures that they take a good, deep breath on the next inhalation. People occasionally experience slight dizziness or tingling sensations when they start learning to relax. This is no cause for alarm, and can be fed back to them as a positive indication that they are beginning to "let go." In fact, one of the things people frequently find hardest to do *is* to "let go." This is related to a general fear of losing control. People, by and large, like to remain self-vigilant "just in case." The paradoxical thing about learning to relax is that it involves

---

MEDITATION

Meditation involves mental, as well as physical, relaxation. Since the influence of Eastern culture in the 1960s, meditation has become very popular in the West. There are several different forms of meditation, but all have three features in common. The meditator assumes a comfortable posture, stays physically still, and concentrates on some object. The focus of concentration varies from one type of meditation to another. In one system, the meditator concentrates on a physical process, like breathing; in another, on an external object, like a flower or a candle; and, in another, on a meaningless word, called a *mantra*. The last of these is the best known in the West. Thus, the actual technique of meditation is quite straightforward. The meditator finds a quiet place, assumes a comfortable posture, and concentrates exclusively on one thing for a period of time.

---

what sounds like a contradiction—*gaining control by losing control*. In other words, by letting go of their body tensions, people get to know their body better. Ultimately, they have even more control; by letting go, they gain ultimate control.

SLEEP

Considering that people spend, on average, one third of their life asleep, it is surprising how little is known about the whys and wherefores of this mysterious silent period. Sleep is a universal phenomenon, and obviously, therefore, a basic need. People cannot get by without it. One reason for switching off for 7 to 8 hours every day is to allow the body to rest and repair itself. During sleep, growth hormones pour into the blood and stimulate various tissues and organs. A good night's sleep leaves people rested and rejuvenated. Likewise, on a psychological level, people feel alert, receptive, and able to concentrate after sleeping well. However, the cognitive dynamics of sleep are complex and less well understood. Electroencephalic studies have identified four stages of sleep, each characterized by a particular EEG pattern and behavioral changes. These stages are also related to depth of sleep and to dream activity. Beyond these tentative conclusions, things become hazy. The meaning of dreams and the role of both sleep and dreaming in overall psychological well-being remain a mystery (Foulkes, 1985).

Problems in sleeping greatly affect people's lives—both physically and mentally. The term *insomnia* means an inability to sleep and includes problems of not being able to fall asleep, of waking repeatedly during the night, waking early unable to go back to sleep, or a combination of all. It is not possible to say with any degree of accuracy how common the problem of insomnia is, for a number of reasons. Firstly, problems of sleep are uniquely difficult to study objectively—precisely because one cannot rely on self-report. Consequently, people are often brought into laboratories to be observed, but being in unfamiliar surroundings or in a strange bed can affect sleep and, therefore, confound the behavior under study. Secondly, there is the problem of determining whether the physical and psychological signs of stress are a *cause* of the sleep problem or a *consequence*. Finally, people's sleep needs vary enormously; some people go through life surviving comfortably on 4 to 5 hours sleep, whereas others genuinely and consistently need 9 to 10 hours per night to function. As a general rule, the need for sleep declines with age (see Pressman, 1986).

Given these difficulties in acquiring accurate figures on the prevalence of insomnia, a number of recent surveys suggest that, for many, life is not a dream. In one American survey, between 30% and 50% of the sample complained of current or past sleep disorders (Bixler, Kales, Soldatos, Kales, & Healey, 1979), and 7% to 10% of an English sample reported taking sleeping pills.

Causes

Environmental. There are large individual differences in people's sensitivity to their external environment. Consequently, for many, sleep can be interrupted or totally disrupted by external factors such as unusual or loud noises, or by sleeping in a room that is too warm, too cold, or too bright. Clients sometimes do not realize that a habit as simple as leaving the electric blanket switched on, or a clock that ticks too loudly, a lumpy mattress, a new house, or a change in weather—all fairly obvious aspects of their immediate environment—can greatly affect sleep.

Physiological. Illness and its entourage of symptoms—nausea, pains, aches, fever, or dyspnea—can all affect sleep. Depression, manic depression, and chronic anxiety can also result in changes in sleep pattern, such as inability to go to sleep, broken sleep, or early-morning wakening. Likewise, periods of hormonal change, such as menopause and pregnancy, can witness sleep disturbances. As already mentioned, sleep is lighter and the body also appears to require less as age advances. Drugs, such as caffeine and alcohol, can also cause insomnia. Certain foods (for example, cheese) are more difficult than others to digest; they can tax the system, sometimes inducing breathlessness and sweating. A hungry stomach will also interfere with a good night's sleep, as will the body's efforts to metabolize large amounts of food eaten late at night. Exercising vigorously at night can induce sleep in many, but in others it can have the opposite effect.

Behavioral.   Sometimes people develop work, social, or recreational habits that prevent the maintenance of regular sleeping patterns—for example, working very long hours, eating late at night, or smoking in the bedroom. Using the bedroom for activities other than sleep—for example, to study, watch television, eat, read, or listen to the radio—may be necessary, but sometimes the association of sleep with the bedroom is lost. Another bad habit, and one of which older people are particularly guilty, is that of napping during the day; "forty winks" several times a day add up.

Cognitive.   A very common complaint is that of being unable to "switch off." Although tired, some people's minds race, going over and over things that happened during the day or that might happen in the future. Many people routinely relive the events of the day in bed, and worry about what other people thought of them or how their actions were interpreted. Efforts to solve problems or come to terms with life events or external stressors (a bereavement, job pressures, forthcoming deadlines and financial commitments, for instance) can also keep the mind from resting. Unfortunately, an inability to go to sleep, for whatever reason, can result in anxious preoccupation *about* the insomnia. This, in turn, can lead to excessive worry about the anticipated, adverse effects of sleep loss—which usually creates a self-fulfilling prophecy.

What To Do

First and foremost, it is necessary for the therapist to establish as clear a picture as possible of the dynamics of the individual client's sleep difficulties. The client is asked to start off by keeping a diary for several weeks. As explained, there are unique difficulties in self-monitoring sleep problems; so, they are asked to make notes *in the morning* of how well they slept, overall. Problems in getting to sleep, how often they woke up during the night, if they woke up very early and were unable to go back to sleep, and if anything in particular was on their mind when they awoke or when they were trying to sleep, are all noted. A partner is sometimes kind enough to validate these observations, as far as it is possible. Clients are also asked to keep a *daily* diary, recording every evening what they did during the day, and how they felt, including the foods and drinks consumed on different days, and any interpersonal upsets or problems at work (Appendix I: Self-Monitoring Behavior). These two sets of records are kept for a minimum of 2 weeks. They are then examined by the therapist for patterns—days of the weeks when the person slept badly, particular foods, drinks, people, or situations that seemed to lead to upset or excitement. Sometimes work stress, health problems, or a change in lifestyle or habits, stand out as related to the recent onset of insomnia. More often, it is a combination of things. Once the causes have been identified, the necessary changes can be planned.

Environmental. It is important that the surroundings in which people sleep are as conducive as possible. If the bedroom or bed, is too hot or too cold or the atmosphere is too stuffy or smoky, it can interfere with sleep. If there is unavoidable noise, some find the solution in leaving gentle music playing in the background; or, if light is seeping through the curtains, to face the bed away from the light source. The impact of such small, concrete changes can be quite dramatic; and people are often surprisingly blind to the blatantly obvious aspects of their environment that are causing problems. Seemingly complex problems sometimes require very simple solutions—like opening a window or turning up the central heating.

Physiological. Taking drugs and stimulants—caffeine, nicotine, or alcohol—near bedtime, is not sensible. It is also counterproductive to assault the body with rich or spicy foods *or* large meals, late at night. On the other hand, it is important to ensure that clients are not hungry going to bed; if so, a hot, milky drink or a light snack is recommended. Some clients find that an airy walk helps them to sleep. Others do formal relaxation exercises. If the therapist is unhappy about the general state of a client's health— particularly if the insomnia is accompanied by symptoms such as sweating and palpitations, which cannot be attributed to diet, climate, or time of life—a physical examination is arranged. Likewise, if sleep patterns have changed, and the client is also feeling depressed, overly energetic, or experiencing changes of mood, it is likely that a biochemical depression or elation is the cause, and a psychiatrist needs to be consulted.

Behavioral. Sometimes, social, recreational, or work habits need to be modified in the direction of increasing sleep time. Napping during the day, for example, can be counter-effective. Also, using the bedroom for activities other than rest and sleep is not ideal. Sometimes this is unavoidable—for example, if it has to be used as a study also. It is essential, in these circumstances, for the client to develop the habit of making a clean break, of at least half an hour, between finishing these activities and returning to the room to sleep. I advise people, if at all possible, to get some fresh air into themselves *and* into the room during this time also.

Cognitive. If a client has a specific worry that is interfering with sleep and is on his or her mind during the day also, this must be tackled first. For example, one client's sleep difficulties were related to anticipatory anxiety concerning an upcoming exam, for which he was, in fact, well prepared. He found it extremely effective, when in bed, to rehearse the scene in his imagination, seeing himself calmly and confidently coping, and answering the questions in a systematic fashion (Appendix V: Cognitive Rehearsal). He could then relax, and sleep. Other people, whose minds are very active, and especially so when under pressure, have to learn to set aside a definite period of time for relaxation, before going to bed. Many find formal relaxation exercises induce sleep, especially if accompanied by deep, rhythmic breathing, or pleasant visualizations. Finally, some people find that in the period just prior to sleep, they remember all sorts of things that must be done, *or* that solutions to problems appear from nowhere. Keeping a notebook and pen by the bed is a simple and effective solution. It only takes a minute to write these things down; a whole night can be wasted in trying not to forget. (See also *Clinical Psychology Review, Vol. 6, No. I,* [1986]: Special Issue on Sleep Disorders.)

Appendix IV
Making Changes in Behavior

Attitudes and feelings change more slowly than behaviors, so, it is advisable to start any intervention by helping clients to make changes in their environment or body maintenance, *or* to modify behaviors and bad habits. Behavior change has an immediate impact; actions do speak louder than words. Furthermore, it frequently also paves the way for changes in attitudes and feelings. Having said this, changing behavior is not easy; we are creatures of habit. Behavior change programs, therefore, have to be carefully planned and take place slowly. Old habits must be gradually replaced by new ones. It is also essential that the time span for change is realistic and that the steps are small and concrete. In this way, every small success, every piece of positive feedback, gives clients confidence and motivation to go on to the next step. Finally, the importance of practice cannot be overemphasized. These are the simple but powerful ingredients of change.

This appendix describes a number of recognized behavioral treatment techniques for dealing with some of the major problems of living—fears and phobias, depressive inactivity, compulsiveness, obsessional slowness, procrastination, and time management. (See also Goldfried & Davison, 1976, chapter 1; Yates, 1981.)

FACING FEARS

The most effective way of helping people overcome fears is by *exposure* to the objects, persons, or situations that generate anxiety. Clients must learn to confront their fear *and* to remain in their feared situations for long enough for their anxiety to diminish. Exposure consists of a flexible family of techniques. It can be carried out with or without prior relaxation training, in graded or in large steps, and in imagination or in real life. Exposure can be used creatively to deal with different kinds of problems: with fears and phobias, systematic desensitization is used; with skills deficits, behavioral rehearsal is preferred; and with obsessional compulsions, response prevention is particularly effective.

Systematic Desensitization

People tend to avoid things that generate anxiety. Avoidance serves to provide temporary relief, but it leaves the person as apprehensive as ever, if not more so. As explained in chapter 4, people can develop incapacitating fears and phobias that interfere with their working and social lives.

Exposure that is carried out in graded steps and with prior relaxation training is called *systematic desensitization*. The technique was developed by Salter (1949) and Wolpe (1958), and is the treatment of choice for fears and phobias. The rationale is to systematically expose, or desensitize, clients to the objects of their fear while they are in a state, or responding in a way, that is incompatible with the fear response (i.e., when relaxed). There are numerous theoretical explanations for the efficacy of the technique (see Kazdin & Wilcoxon, 1976; McGlynn, Mealiea, & Landau, 1981; Smith & Glass, 1977), which is carried out as follows.

From the client's self-monitoring and self-report, their feared objects, persons, or situations are clearly identified. A list of these is made, and the items are ranked in order of difficulty, with the *most anxiety-provoking* at the top. If the list has only 5 or 6 items, it can be "beefed up" to about 10 by introducing items of intermediate difficulty between the ones already identified. This ranked list is called the *fear hierarchy*. The items are then rated, usually on a 1 to 100 scale, according to the amount of anxiety the client feels each one would induce.

The therapist then systematically exposes the person to larger and larger amounts of the object of their fear by working up through the hierarchy, one item at a time. Systematic desensitization programs must be very carefully planned, with attention to minute detail and the personal significance of the items to the client. The therapist moves slowly through the hierarchy, ensuring that the client is relaxed and able to cope with each situation *before* going on to the next. Feeling comfortable and in control at each step gives the person confidence to go on to the next—like climbing stairs, one step at a time. The program, in other words, takes place very gradually.

Most therapists now practice live, or *in vivo*, exposure. Clients must remain in their feared situations for long enough for their anxiety to decrease, in order to break the avoidance spiral. This takes time, depending on the

TABLE IV.1
Typical Fear Hierarchies

(I) Heights	Fear Rating (Max. 100).
1. First floor window.	10
2. First floor balcony.	20
3. Second floor window.	30
4. Second floor balcony.	50
5. Third floor window.	50
6. Third floor balcony.	60
7. Fourth floor window.	70
8. Fourth floor balcony.	80
9. Fifth floor window.	90
10. Fifth floor balcony.	100
(II) Panic and Anxiety Attacks	
1. Walk to end of street accompanied.	10
2. Walk to end of street alone.	19
3. Walk to local shop, enter, walk back accompanied.	28
4. Walk to local shop accompanied, enter, walk back alone.	32
5. Walk to local shop alone, enter, walk back.	39
6. Lodge check in bank, alone at a quiet time.	45
7. Purchase a few items in supermarket, alone at a quiet time.	50
8. Lodge check in bank during rush-hour, accompanied.	57
9. Meet friend in supermarket during rush-hour.	62
10. Go to bank at a relatively busy time, alone.	70
11. Go to supermarket alone at a busy time.	77
12. Meet friend inside door of crowded bar; stay ten minutes.	80
13. Go to relatively busy bar alone, and wait five minutes to be joined by friend.	86
14. Sit in middle of a crowded bar for ten minutes, accompanied.	94
15. Sit in middle of a crowded bar alone, while awaiting a friend.	100

problem and the number of opportunities for practice. It is very important that clients do not feel under pressure to perform; but, at the same time, the more practice, the more progress. Every time a feared situation is faced, it gets a little easier; and, also prepares them for something just a little more difficult (see also Goldfried & Davison, 1976, chapter 6).

Traditionally, clients were desensitized first *in imagination*, and only at a later stage were exposed *in vivo*. Imaginal exposure is described in Appendix V. Basically, when clients were in a relaxed state, the therapist introduced the items by asking them to *imagine* themselves in the feared situations. If they experienced anxiety, they indicated this to the therapist, who automatically switched them to a pleasant, relaxing visual image. In recent years, imaginal exposure has been used progressively less, in favor of live exposure. There are a number of reasons for this. Many people find it difficult to generate clear images. There is also the theoretical assumption that an imaginary scene is the functional equivalent of the real thing. Finally, and perhaps most important, is the fact that clients eventually have to face the real world, alone.

Behavioral Rehearsal

Behavioral skills are required in many areas, the most obvious example being in the area of interpersonal interactions. As described in chapter 7, deficits in social skills can range from simply lacking the verbal and nonverbal ability to carry on brief conversations to more complex skills such as assertion and anger management. Sex is another area where skills are required (see chapter 9). Lovers gradually become more familiar with what pleases each other and what turns each other on and off. A good sex life is very much a matter of understanding and meeting the needs and appetites of one's partner, and of learning to relax. Relaxing is also a skill (Appendix III: Relaxation), as are managing time and resources effectively (see Managing Time). The phrase *coping skills* is currently very much in vogue, and it covers the whole range of general survival skills that help people deal with the inevitable problems and challenges of life. Skills acquisition involves two major components: information and practice.

Information.   Ignorance is not bliss. Information can go a long way toward reducing unnecessary anxieties and performance fears. People can acquire formal, factual information in various ways—by attending courses, by going to lectures, or by acquainting themselves with relevant literature. They can also glean information by asking other people and by observation. Sexual anxieties often arise out of ignorance; simply supplying clients with basic facts about sexual anatomy or dispelling some of the many myths about sexual performance and standards is often enough to put their minds at ease. Likewise, people who are afraid of illness and worry endlessly about contracting various diseases are frequently greatly relieved to be told that they do not have *any* of the symptoms of the illnesses they fear. Ignorance can be a major factor in maintaining anxieties.

Practice.   Reading the Highway Code can make people *feel* more confident about learning to drive, but it will not enable them to sit into a car and rally. This is where practice comes in. Practicing the mini-behaviors that together constitute a skill is called *behavioral rehearsal.* Children play freely, assuming many parts, with the utmost ease and flexibility. Adults are more self-conscious; they spend a lot of time worrying about what others think of them and trying to avoid looking foolish. This is often why people fail to develop necessary skills in the first place. The idea of live practice is very disturbing to many clients; but, once they get started, they find that behavioral rehearsal can be real fun. In the context of social skills training, it is often referred to as *role-playing*; and it forms an integral component of therapy programs for overcoming interpersonal difficulties (see chapter 7). Just as actors practice a script over and over again until the part is perfected, behavioral rehearsal requires repeated practice of certain behaviors (see Goldfried & Davison, 1976, chapter 7).

From clients' diary-keeping and self-report, the situations in which they feel uncomfortable, or for which they feel unprepared, are identified. A list of these *target situations* is made, and the items are ordered according to the *degree of complexity of the behavioral skills* required, rather than the degree of anxiety experienced, as in systematic desensitization. If clients are not sure of the behaviors that make up a skill, rather than just telling them, I instruct them to observe other people in everyday situations relevant to their problem: in trains, buses, stores, restaurants, banks, or cafes. Target situations can also be studied as they are played out on television. In other words, they are encouraged to use other people as *models*.

Then, beginning with the least difficult, or least complex, situation—something as simple as saying "good morning" to the postman—the client practices repeatedly with the therapist. When the first item or situation has been adequately mastered, clients progress to *in vivo* rehearsal. They try out their new skill in real life. Each item is rehearsed with the therapist in this way, until the person feels comfortable—as many times as it takes until the behavior begins to come naturally and flow easily. It is then practiced in the

TABLE IV.2
Behavioral Hierarchy: Social Interaction

	Degree of Complexity (Max 100).
1. Say "hello" to the postman or a neighbor.	10
2. Exchange a few words with the man in the paper shop.	19
3. Short conversation with a colleague or neighbor.	27
4. Longer conversation with same.	37
5. Exchange a few words with a stranger while waiting for a bus or train, or in a supermarket.	46
6. Strike up conversation with a stranger in a cafe, shop, or bar.	55
7. Arrange to meet an acquaintance for coffee.	64
8. Arrange to meet an acquaintance for lunch.	72
9. Arrange to meet a member of the opposite sex for coffee or a drink.	80
10. Invite a person of the opposite sex out for the evening.	90
11. Invite a new friend to dinner in home.	95
12. Give a small dinner party.	100

real world. Clients keep ongoing, daily records of their attempts—what they did, how others responded, situations or aspects of situations they felt they could have handled better. Problems are discussed in detail with the therapist, and situations are role-played *again*, until the behavior is perfected and does not generate anxiety. Using each newly acquired skill as a base, client and therapist gradually work through the skills hierarchy. The importance of the eventual feeling of being in control, of *self-efficacy,* cannot be overemphasized; and it is always worth the effort and persistence.

Response Prevention

Wolpe's contribution to the treatment of phobias by systematic desensitization in the 1950s was *not* matched by similar progress in the alleviation of obsessive-compulsive disorders. It was not until the 1970s that effective programs began to be developed. The factors that facilitated this were: increasing realization of the importance of live exposure (as opposed to exposure in imagination), recognition of the effectiveness of "flooding" (i.e., a form of rapid, upgraded exposure), and finally, acknowledgment of the clinical implications, and application, of Bandura's modeling theory of learning (see Rachman & Hodgson, 1980).

The treatment approach developed by Rachman & Hodgson is, in my opinion, among the most effective to date (see Hodgson & Rachman, 1976; Rachman, 1976). It comprises two major elements: exposure to the provoking stimulus and response prevention. Exposure is preceded, where possible, by the therapist modeling the feared behavior (e.g., handling a dirty cloth). In essence, the client is *exposed* to the stimulus, or the thing that triggers the compulsion (e.g., dirt), and then *prevented* from carrying out the neutralizing ritual (e.g., hand washing). The procedure is effected as rapidly as the client can tolerate, without generating too much discomfort. Effectively, it involves going to the pinnacle of the fear hierarchy, without prior relaxation. For example, one client was terrified of getting cancer from any kind of dirty household cleaning cloths or rags. So, during one session, she was repeatedly required to handle such cloths, over a period of 30 minutes or so, and prevented from carrying out her compulsive washing ritual.

The rationale, as explained in chapter 6, is to prevent the client from giving in to the compulsion, in order to prove that the feared consequence does *not* occur, and thereby defusing the anxiety. Clients must be prevented from carrying out the ritual for as long as it takes for their anxiety to decrease. Depending on the degree of belief in the possibility of the feared consequence *actually* occurring, and its gravity (e.g., death or cancer), preventing clients from carrying out their compulsive rituals can obviously

generate high levels of anxiety. For this reason, clients are particularly required to take an active part in the planning and timing of each stage of their
program.

Ideally, a large part of the intervention should take place in the client's
home. Occasionally however, clients with severe problems are treated in a
responses prevention ward of a hospital; where a high ratio of specially
trained nursing staff supervise the response prevention programs (to ensure
that the patients do not somehow manage to carry out their appeasing
rituals). Response prevention, if carefully planned and executed, can have
surprisingly speedy and effective results (see Rachman & Hodgson, 1980,
chapter 23).

GETTING STARTED

Sometimes, getting started is the biggest problem. This can occur for a variety
of reasons—depression, procrastination, or bad time management—all of
which must be approached differently.

The Daily Activity Schedule

Activity generates activity; inertia leads to more inertia. As explained in
chapter 5, when people are feeling low or depressed, they lack energy; they
have no motivation to do things or interest in what is going on around
them. Well-meaning prods to get moving or to "do something" are totally
counterproductive. Furthermore, the more things pile up, the more helpless
and depressed people feel about *ever* being able to catch up. Finally, the
longer this goes on, the more guilty they become about their own inertia.

The Daily Activity Schedule is very useful and effective in helping depressed people get started. Every day, they simply take a page of a notebook,
divide it lengthwise into two columns, labelling the left column "Prospective"
and the right column "Retrospective." The page is then subdivided into
rows, each row representing an hour, as illustrated in Figure IV.1.

Each morning, the client fills in the Prospective column with an hour-by-
hour plan of how they will spend the day and the things they would like to
achieve. The activities do not have to be mind-boggling or complex, especially if they have not been bothering recently to even get dressed or tidy
their home. They are encouraged to just include the basic things that they
have not been doing (e.g., washing, eating, shopping). Planning the day like
this should not take any longer than 5 minutes and should include as many
pleasant or "P" activities as possible.

Then, in the evening, they fill in the Retrospective column, itemizing what
they actually *did* that day. It does not matter if it is very different from what

Daily Activity Schedule

PROSPECTIVE:	RETROSPECTIVE:
Plan your activities on an hour-by-hour basis at the start of the day.	At the end of the day, record what you actually did and rate each activity with an M for Mastery or a P for Pleasure

Date _____

TIME

8–9	
9–10	
10–11	
11–12	
12–1	
1–2	
2–3	
3–4	
4–5	
5–6	
6–7	
7–8	
8–9	
9–12	

*Mastery and pleasure activities must be rated from 0 to 5: the higher the number, the greater the sense of satisfaction.

Figure IV.1

was planned in the morning, or if they did not get very much done. Even if it turns out that several periods were spent daydreaming or brooding, they are asked to write these in. Then, where it applies, they label some of the things they *did* with either an "M," for mastery, or a "P," for pleasure. In other words, they note the things they did not think they could do, but *did*, *and* the things they enjoyed doing.

Over even a few days, clients generally rediscover that any activity is better than none, and that activity generates activity. Motivation also increases, as they begin to see that there are things they can achieve and enjoy. They also become aware of how they spend their time. It does not matter if they are not getting very much done; the important thing is that it is usually more than the previous day. Gradually, the Retrospective column fills up. They can use this information—on how they spend their time and what they enjoy doing—to plan the subsequent days.

Low periods also become more obvious, and can then also be planned for. Many people, particularly those who live alone, find evenings, weekends, and leisure time particularly barren and depressing. Clients need help in planning ahead for these times. I usually suggest that, once they are feeling even a little more sociable and more able to face life, they should start investigating their environment's resources and scheduling in "P" activities for these low periods (Appendix I: Utilizing Environmental Resources). Appointments or arrangements that cannot be broken or cancelled without incurring monetary loss or social embarrassment are ideal. One courageous client of mine used to book tickets for a show several days ahead, and arrange to go with a friend who could not be contacted in the interim, so that she *could not* cancel (see also Burns, 1981, chapter 5).

Procrastination

Some people constantly do only the things they like to do. They put off the unpleasant, less interesting chores of life. Others just like to do as little as possible. No-one can afford to fall consistently into either category. Such people lose opportunities and generally miss out, as well as frequently inconveniencing others. The consequences in business and friendships can be disastrous (Bird, 1986; McKenzie & Kay 1986). Most procrastinating occurs in relation to things that people really do not *want* to do, things that are not intrinsically reinforcing. One client could not understand how she had no energy to clean the house or prepare dinner, yet an invitation to a party would magically co-incide with a rush of enthusiasm and drive. She had come to me when her husband threatened to leave.

The solution is quite simple; it involves helping clients develop the habit of getting things done. They start off by making a list, however long, of all the things they have been putting off. The items are then rank-ordered in terms of unpleasantness, putting the most *unpleasant* at the top. The next morning, they start with the most unpleasant thing on their "to do" list— for example, returning something borrowed a long time before from a neighbor or paying a long-overdue account. This is done *first thing* in the day, because completion of the most unpleasant thing on the list, and early in the morning, gives a great feeling of achievement. Tackling one item per day is sufficient; as long as no days are missed. After a week or so, a new habit has developed. Clients usually also find that their *general* activity level has increased, and that they are getting more done all around.

For more severe problems, where people with serious deadlines, like exams, are still not getting anything done, a different strategy is necessary. Here, clients make a long list of all the things they need to do and have been putting off. These are then rank-ordered in terms of *importance*, the most important, or urgent, at the top. Then, starting with the first item, this is broken down into as many small and instantly do-able tasks as possible. Depending on the complexity of the task, there may be a large number of mini-tasks. The key is to make each incremental task so simple and quick that, in itself, it does not amount to very much—if possible, something that can be finished in a couple of minutes. Then, each mini-task is taken as an entity in it's own right, forgetting about the project as a whole. Some clients find it helpful to reward themselves for completion of the large task; although, more often, people find that the process itself is very reinforcing and self-perpetuating.

Another way of prodding clients into action is by helping them to *set themselves up*. Here, the person goes to the *end point* of the mini-activities that constitute a task, and does the last thing *first*, thereby necessitating completion of the rest. One client, after her husband's sudden death, had just let things go—her house badly needed to be cleaned, her hair needed to be cut, she had gotten out of the habit of cooking and was living on takeouts, and she had not bothered to return calls from friends and had, therefore, not seen them in a long time. So, she decided to hold a dinner party 2 days later. She set a time and invited her guests. She then *had to* get to it. A businessman who needed to get certain tedious files in order arranged a meeting to discuss them—which necessitated a detailed perusal of them in advance. He came into my office the following week, delighted with himself; he had thoroughly enjoyed the race. The key is to give oneself just enough time to get everything done, *provided* that one starts right away.

Managing Time

A basic skill that many people fail to develop, and that generates endless problems and frustrations, is time management (Adair, 1987; Sullivan, 1987). Here, I refer to the type of person who is constantly on the go, apparently doing countless things, but has nothing to show for it at the end of the day. These people seem to be perpetually scattered and are not very reliable where arrangements and deadlines are concerned. It is as frustrating to be like this as it is to be at the receiving end—to know that one has put in a good day's work without concrete results, and to always feel that there are hundreds of things half-done. One hard-working secretary came to my office in tears; she had been fired, although, ironically, she had voluntarily stayed late most evenings to "tie up loose ends."

Again, the answer lies in *starting* on the right foot. The remedy is very simple and effective, and it only requires a pen, a notebook, and some planning. The client takes a blank page at the beginning of each day and writes down all the things that have to be done. These are then arranged in order or priority, putting an asterisk beside the most immediate concerns. The items are then taken in order of urgency, and the person works through the list in the course of the day. The secret is to *complete each task before moving on to the next*. On finishing a job, many people give themselves the satisfaction of ticking it off with a bright pen.

When people learn to work systematically in this way, by the end of the day they have quite a number of things actually done *and* concrete evidence of how they spent their time. I advise clients that it is counterproductive to write out an unrealistically long list at the beginning of the day; they cannot expect to catch up on the backlog of 6 months in 24 hours. On the other hand, if they do have everything completed ahead of time, it makes sense for them to have a *reserve list* of long-term chores, such as returning correspondence or phone calls (see Bliss, 1984).

GETTING FINISHED

Routines ensure that things get done, and done on time. They also provide a feeling of being in control; they make people feel secure. However, as described in chapter 6, for obsessional people routines can become totally self-defeating, and can end up controlling *them*. Frequently, such people would *like* to be able to just leave things at a certain point without feeling compelled to finish them, but cannot. They would *like* to be able to get things done more quickly, but again, they feel compelled to go into things in minute detail and to follow rigid sequences in the execution of tasks. Getting started is a problem for some, but for obsessional people, getting finished can also present major difficulties.

People who are very particular about things being "done well" usually take much longer than those who are less fussy—sometimes much longer than is necessary, by any standards. Consequently perfectionistic and obsessional people are often seen (correctly) as slow workers (Rachman & Hodgson, 1980, chapter 15). Jobs are broken down into numerous mini-tasks, each of which has to be done well, or several times. Hours can be spent washing dishes, because every dish or cup has to be washed separately and then rinsed several times. One client used to spend over 2 hours getting dressed every morning, because each small part of her dressing routine had become a ritual in itself. For another client, a simple domestic chore like cleaning his car meant a crusade involving a whole day's scrubbing, rinsing, polishing, waxing, and vacuuming. By the time I first saw him, he was so overwhelmed by the mere *prospect* of such tasks that he was not even getting started. Perfectionistic people also find it hard to delegate, because things have to be done *their* way, and because they feel that only they will do it *right*. As a consequence, they often end up doing far more than their share.

Speeding Up

With clients who are excessively slow and fussy but whose rituals are *not* linked to feared consequences (see Response Prevention), the following steps are taken. First, they identify, by self-monitoring, the tasks that are taking up their time, *or* that are being totally avoided for the same reason. Having made a list of these, the client and the therapist then try to establish where exactly the time is going. Are they working very slowly? Are they going into too much detail? Are they daydreaming? Are they going over and over things? When feasible, I ask clients to model the behavior, that is, to carry out the task *for me*, so that I can observe the rituals and the expenditure of time. However, I also find it effective to get them to establish this *for themselves*, if possible, as it provides them with greater insight into their difficulty.

They are then asked to decide on a reasonable amount of time for completion of the task. If they are unsure, I suggest that they ask friends how long it takes *them* to, say, wash the kitchen floor or put away files. If they do not want to ask directly, they can learn from observing others doing the same *target behavior*. Acceptable times of completion are then negotiated with the therapist; and, beginning with the smallest, or theoretically least time-consuming item on the list, they gradually speed up. One client cut down by 10 minutes every time she cut the grass in her small front garden, until she reached the agreed-on normal range of 20 minutes. It had been taking her 90 minutes. It is essential that clients are strict with themselves in this respect, that is, that they set clear deadlines and stick to them, because *most* of their live practice inevitably takes place at home, or in their workplace, and *not* in the presence of the therapist.

Frequently, such people also need to learn how to delegate tasks to others. I advise clients to give their delegates *specific* instructions. In so doing, they very often realize where they are being excessively fussy (or, the people receiving the instructions often tell them in no uncertain terms). What they have to find out, for themselves, is that other people will not do a job in exactly the same way as they would; but, that this does not necessarily mean that they are not doing it right, or thoroughly.

Cutting Down On Checking

Routines also frequently incorporate excessive *checking* rituals. One elderly gentleman religiously checked that all the electrical appliances in his home were unplugged at night—not once, but 10 times. When going to the local store, he would feel compelled to go back again and again into his house, having locked the front door, to make sure that he had switched off the stove or unplugged the heater. His checking rituals had become gradually more extensive and time-consuming over the 25 years before he came into therapy; they took up enormous amounts of time—hours of every day. The same type of checking rituals can also take place, and take over, in people's workplace or office—in relation to accounts, files, addressing envelopes, or locking the safe, for example.

People who check excessively in this way can be helped by gradually cutting down (from ten times to nine, to eight, and so on). This is a more gentle and effective way to proceed than to prevent them from checking at all—which would generate high levels of anxiety and with *this* kind of problem, would be totally counterproductive. Having reduced the frequency of checking to once, I follow up with the cognitive attention-focusing technique described in Appendix V (see Fading).

Delaying and Disrupting

Delaying involves allowing clients to carry out their routines or rituals, but only after a reasonable period of time has elapsed. For example, one client who used to jump up and clear the table while her family was still eating was asked to delay the pleasure for 5, then 10, and finally 15 minutes. She gradually extended this delay period even longer, until she and her family were satisfied that their meals could be enjoyed and digested at a normal pace.

Disrupting is another strategy for helping people change maladaptive, rigid rituals and habits. Most people have a particular way of making their bed, of arranging their desk, or of washing themselves, for example; but, it is not a major catastrophe if the routine has to be changed or is interrupted. For obsessional people, this can be very difficult and upsetting. So, many such people find it useful, and even fun, to learn how to disrupt their own routines—by doing them, for example, backwards, or in *no* order at all. One client came into my office totally exhilarated to report that she had begun her shower by washing her feet first and working *up*, instead of working her way down, as usual. Likewise, having pasta on Tuesday instead of Thursday or trying out a new brand of soda after 10 years can bestow a great feeling of liberation. Again, the positive psychological impact of small, even seemingly trivial, changes in behavior can be surprising.

Role-Characterization

George Kelly, whose theoretical contributions and clinical insights are being increasingly recognized (Landfield, 1980; Neimeyer, 1985), introduced a technique called *fixed-role therapy* in the 1950s (Kelly, 1955). This technique, in fact, dates back to the 1930s and, in many ways, is closely related to both *behavioral rehearsal* and a technique called *exaggerated role-taking*, which was developed by Lazarus (1971). It is based on the general assumption that individuals can change their behavior by tentatively "trying out" certain behavior patterns. I use a modification of this procedure with obsessional clients who express a need to loosen up, to feel more free and flexible within themselves, or who would like to be less rigid about certain aspects of their behavior or social image but do not know how deep a plunge to take.

Firstly, clients write out a description, or *role-characterization*, of someone totally different, or the exact opposite, to themselves—in dress, habits, or interests. They then "become" that person for an hour, or an evening. One client who normally wore a pin-striped suit, drank one small gin and tonic per night, and listened only to classical music, tried out a new role. He dressed up in an old pair of blue jeans (which he borrowed from his astonished son) and went down to the local rock bar to have a couple of beers and hang out. After some initial self-consciousness, he felt terrific, "as if I were on vacation."

In the same way, clients can write out a description of someone with characteristics they would *like* to have—an acquaintance who dresses more flamboyantly, or someone they secretly admire for his or her directness or assertiveness, for example. Again, they put themselves, metaphorically, in the other person's shoes for an hour or an evening.

The idea is to help people loosen excessive controls and explore new avenues of experience. *Behaving* differently makes people *feel* different. It also facilitates *seeing* things differently. Many clients are surprised at how pleasant it is to do things that they had formerly scorned. Behaving differently—or perhaps opposite—to one's norm can also help people to understand and appreciate facets of other people's behavior or outlook that had hitherto seemed pointless or off-putting. Behaving like those whom one wishes to be like also often helps clients to realize that other people's lives are not as glamorous or as perfect as they had thought—"faraway hills." The overall goal is to shed some of the old and retain some of the new.

An extreme example of self-loosening is portrayed in a book by Luke Rhinehart, called *The Diceman* (1972). As the title suggests, the hero allows his actions to be determined *entirely* by throwing dice (1, Go to a movie; 2, Have a beer; 3, Go to bed; etc.). Eventually, the dice rule his life and, in so doing, totally defeat the purpose of the exercise, which was to experience real freedom.

Type A

A basic coping skill is to be able to allot adequate and proportionate amounts of time to the different areas of one's life—work, leisure, colleagues, friends, and family. Truly efficient people know when to switch off and when to recharge themselves. Unfortunately, for some compulsive people, work takes by far the biggest slice of the pie. It takes over. *Type As* are summed up as "aggressive, ambitious, competitive, self-demanding, and time-urgent" (Friedman & Rosenman, 1974). Not only are these people particularly vulnerable to heart disease, but those who try to share a life with a Type A also suffer.

One successful young businessman phoned to make an appointment with me; he was feeling stressed. In his efforts not to be late for his first consultation, *and* to answer his car phone, *and* to update his appointment book along the way, he drove into a wall. The appointment was rescheduled, and when he arrived, he was carrying a Year Planner that looked like a Christmas tree, and a daily appointments diary crammed with engagements and commitments. The planning, meant to be an aid, had become totally self-defeating; his diary was controlling *him*. In reviewing his diary for the previous weeks, I asked him to ask himself the following questions:

1. If someone else were reading this, would they think I was trying to do too much? *Or*, if this were someone else's diary, would I say "too much"?

2. Were any cancellations, on my part, social or personal things that gave way to business commitments or efforts to meet deadlines?

3. Am I constantly transporting a fixed number of things from one day, or week, to the next—things I just never get around to doing?

4. Am I always planning to take it a bit easier, starting "next week"?

Needless to say, he answered yes to all four questions. He was simply trying to squeeze in too much. He was advised to slow down while he still had the chance. I take this example because he was typical. Cutting down is never easy, because of ongoing commitments, but also, because such people *enjoy* working under pressure. They *like* having a lot of "balls on the hop." The adrenalin flow becomes internally self-reinforcing, so the time to slow down is never the present.

Basically, I supply such people with a gloomy list of the long-term consequences, to their health and relationships, of continuing as they are. I then suggest that they put their multifarious organizational skills into carrying out the following: They must agree not to take on any new projects, however tempting or challenging, until the ones in hand have been finished. Every day, they must allot a realistic number of hours to work, and the rest to leisure. Likewise, they set themselves a realistic number of things to do each day and tick them off as they are completed. What is "realistic" usually has to be negotiated. If they finish early, they are instructed not to succumb to the temptation of starting into the next day's work. If they feel they must sit it out, they may start into the mobile backlog, but only *until* the agreed-on time to leave the office. They do *not* take work home, either in their briefcase or in their head. They do not cancel, or borrow time from, social arrangements. If they absolutely have to, it absolutely has to be paid back.

"All work and no play" can be self-defeating in other ways too. What one tries to do when bleary-eyed and hungry at 10:00 pm will be slow and unsatisfactory. It could be done in half the time the next morning, after a nourishing dinner, some relaxation with friends, and a good night's sleep. I constantly remind such clients that all the money in the world cannot buy back lost time, repair a diseased heart, or buy back the hearts of those who used to care (see Freudenberger & Richelson, 1980; Haaga, 1987).

Appendix V
Making Changes in Thinking

The initial boost to the emergence of the cognitive movement started in the late 1950s and early 1960s, with the writings of George Kelly (1955), Julian Rotter (1954), Aaron Beck (1963), Albert Ellis (1962), and Albert Bandura (1969). Whereas behaviorists had focused on external influences on people's actions, cognitive theorists invoked central, cognitive, and symbolic mechanisms as necessary for change. Over the intervening 30 years, a large number of "cognitive therapies" have developed, witnessing a growing alliance between the cognitive and clinical sciences. Mahoney (1988), has identified at least 17 cognitive perspectives that claim to be distinct approaches (see also Dobson, 1988, chapters 1 and 10; Schwartz, 1982). In this appendix, I describe a number of recognized and effective cognitive techniques for dealing with specific problems, under the broad headings of: cognitive restructuring, visual imagery, and attention focusing.

COGNITIVE RESTRUCTURING

Techniques that can collectively be described as *cognitive restructuring* aim to help clients identify maladaptive cognitions and beliefs, recognize their adverse impact, and replace them with more adaptive thought patterns. The therapist usually starts off by examining clients' self-talk. If it is found to be faulty, they are taught how to dispute their problematic self-statements. Depending on the nature of the difficulties, a deeper analysis of underlying beliefs may also be carried out (See Beck & Emery, 1985, chapters 11,15; Dryden, 1984).

Self-Disputation

Self-disputation is one of the basic techniques of cognitive therapy. Clients learn to evaluate and dispute the truth of what they are saying to themselves in problematic situations, and to supply themselves with a more realistic and objective appraisal. In time, this new perspective replaces the older, maladaptive one. The more positive outlook so generated, in turn, influences feelings, attitudes, and behavior on a more general level.

The therapist first examines the client's diary of behaviors and thoughts (Appendix I: Self-Monitoring Behavior; Self-Monitoring Thinking). Generally speaking, certain thoughts, or sequences of thoughts, *recur* in situations identified as problematic. The last, or most recent, problem situation, *or a* situation that stands out as having been particularly upsetting and is, therefore, still vivid in the client's mind, is taken and examined as follows. A line is drawn lengthwise down the middle of a wide sheet of paper, dividing it into two columns. The left-hand column is labeled "Self-Talk," and the right-hand column is labeled "Self-Disputation." On the left-hand side of the page, the client writes down all the thoughts that accompanied him or her through the situation—before, during, and after—as many as they can remember, and the order in which they occurred.

Then, each of these self-statements is taken *in order,* starting with the first, and the therapist helps the person dispute it's validity. In other words, client and therapist work their way down along the page, answering each thought with an alternative, more realistic, appraisal. Ideally, the client should supply the answers, but it takes time to see things from a different perspective, so the therapist initially helps by suggesting alternative responses and self-statements until the client gets the idea. As each thought is disputed, the answer is written in the corresponding space in the right-hand column. It is important that clients get into the habit, from the very start, of writing out the *entire sequence* of thoughts, that is, 1, 2, 3 . . . *before* going on to dispute them; that they do *not* go 1–1, 2–2, and so on.

Initially, this exercise takes time, effort, and practice. Once clients have grasped the rationale and acquired the basic technique, they are encouraged to practice at home by working through incidents that upset them, or put them down, in the course of the day. They are also advised, when starting out, to ask other people (e.g., spouse) how *they* would answer a negative or upsetting thought, if they cannot think of an appropriate response themselves. With practice, clients quickly become more expert at tuning in on their thinking in various situations and at being able to dispute their negative thinking both on paper *and,* eventually, on the spot, in real-life situations.

Take the example that was described in chapter 2. (p. 39). A friend passes by and does not say hello. The thoughts at the time of the occurrence would be written, in order, down the left-hand side of the page. Then, each thought would be systematically disputed in turn, and the answer written opposite it on the right-hand side of the page. In this example, the first thought was: "She can't not have seen me." The therapist would ask the client (or, when doing the exercise alone, the client would ask himself or herself): *Where is the evidence?* How do I know that she *did* see me? Opposite this thought, the client could then write: "I have often passed by people and genuinely not seen them." The second thought, "Why did she snub me?", would be similarly examined for evidence; again, there is none. "I have no evidence that she *did* snub me. It would not be like her. She probably just did not see me, or had something on her mind at the time."

The third thought, "Maybe she has heard some gossip about me," (no evidence) could be answered "It's very unlikely that she's heard gossip about me. I have not done anything out of the ordinary." The fourth thought, "Why didn't I go after her, and question her?", was answered at the time with "Oh yes, I was in line," but then followed by a further doubt: "Maybe I was just afraid to go after her . . . come to think of it, I am not very assertive with people." Here, there *is* some evidence for why the client did not go after her, but nonetheless, the reaction is extreme. This thought could then reasonably be answered: "I am really letting things get out of proportion. I would have gone after her to say *hello,* not to start an argument. I *am* assertive when I have to be; and I'm working on the situations that I find difficult."

When the exercise is finished, the client reads down through all of the answers on the right hand side of the page:

1. I have often passed by people and genuinely not seen them.
2. I have no evidence that she did snub me. It would not be like her. She probably just did not see me, or had something on her mind at the time.
3. It's (also) very unlikely that she's heard any gossip about me. I have not done anything out of the ordinary. (See Table V.1.)

This column always paints a very different picture of the *same* situation—one that is kinder to everyone concerned. It also helps clients to understand the degree to which thinking effects behavior and mood. This kind of self-disputation can be carried out on *any* isolated problem situation, or on particular situations that have been identified as consistently upsetting. By calmly answering each of one's problematic self-statements with a more objective and realistic evaluation, a new perspective is created.

The idea, as with many cognitive techniques, is that by working things out on paper, the next time the person is in that or a similar situation, instead of automatically switching on the negative, self-defeating "tape," the more

TABLE V.1.
Double-Column Technique

SELF-TALK	SELF-DISPUTATION
1. She can't not have seen me.	1. I have often passed by people and genuinely not seen them.
2. Why did she snub me?	2. I have no evidence that she *did* snub me. It would not be like her. She probably just did not see me, or had something on her mind at the time.
3. Maybe she's heard some gossip about me.	3. It's very unlikely that she's heard any gossip about me. I have not done anything out of the ordinary.
4. Why didn't I go after her and question her . . . Oh, yes, I was in line.	
5. Maybe I was just afraid to go after her . . . come to think of it, I am not very assertive with people.	5. I am really letting things get out of proportion. I would have gone after her to say *hello,* not to start an argument. I *am* assertive when I have to be, and I'm working on the situations I find difficult.

rational alternative thoughts will interrupt and come to mind. When this happens on a number of occasions, and the outcome is more pleasant and rewarding, the new internal dialogue takes over from the old. In effect, a new habit is formed, and the psychological consequences are very different.

Due, in particular, to the pioneering work of Aaron Beck, the father of cognitive therapy, self-disputation has proven to be a valuable technique in the treatment of depression (Beck, 1976; Beck et al., 1979). More recently, it has also become integral to the comprehensive treatment of the whole range of anxiety-related disorders, as well as having applications with marital and sexual problems, social difficulties, and problems of overindulgence (see Dobson, 1988).

Changing Beliefs

As well as their transitory thoughts, people also hold a set of ongoing beliefs, or basic assumptions, about themselves and about life in general. These beliefs are the result of accumulated learning experiences, observations, and self-talk over a number of years. Everyone has personal beliefs about what is fair and unfair, just and unjust, for example, and these beliefs determine their approach to life and their behavior in everyday situations, as well as structuring their lives. Sometimes, however, as explained in chapter 2, beliefs can be too rigidly held, *or* can be downright erroneous.

As with self-talk, people are generally unaware of their underlying assumptions, and are often surprised at how extreme or unreasonable they are, when identified. Changing beliefs is a more challenging undertaking than improving self-talk. It involves, firstly, *uncovering* the client's basic beliefs by digging down through the layers of protective thoughts; and then, if necessary, *challenging* and thereby helping the person to change them (see Burns, 1980; Ellis & Harper, 1975).

Changing self-talk, as described, involves substituting unreasonable thoughts with more rational ones. The thought, "Why did she snub me?" was answered with, "I have no evidence that she *did* snub me. It would not be like her." This technique helps to change thinking patterns in the *here and now;* so that the client can view life more objectively, and feel more in control. Examining beliefs is more complex and wide-ranging. There are a number of techniques for examining and modifying basic beliefs. Two of these are (a) vertical arrow and (b) uncovering the shoulds.

Vertical Arrow. In this technique, unlike self-disputation, clients are asked to imagine that their negative thoughts are perfectly *valid.* This enables the therapist to penetrate to the core of a problem, and to examine any basic irrational thinking. I generally proceed by taking a *typical negative thought* that a client has identified, and repeat these questions over and over: "If that negative were *true,* what would it mean to you? Why would it upset you?"

By asking these questions repeatedly, a chain of automatic thoughts is generated. It is important to ensure that the client supplies the negative thoughts that *caused* the upset. To illustrate, I will take the example of a situation where a respected superior has advanced some negative comment or criticism:

Client:	"Mr. Brown has criticized me; he probably thinks I'm a bad student."
Therapist:	"And if that were *true,* what would it mean to you? Why would it upset you?"
Client:	"That would mean that I *was* a bad student—because he is an expert.
Therapist:	"And if that were *true,* what would it mean . . ."
Client:	"That would mean that I was no good, that I was a failure."
Therapist:	"And if that were *true* . . .
Client:	"That would mean that I would not be able to continue my studies. I would have to leave."
Therapist:	"And if that were *true* . . .

Client: "That would mean that everyone would know I had failed.
               They would not respect me any more."
Therapist: "And if that were *true* . . .
Client: "That would mean I was a total failure. There would be
               no point in pursuing other courses or trying to make new
               friends.

Leaving it there and reviewing the chain of thoughts, what are the underlying
assumptions? There are several, even at a glance:

1. If someone criticizes me, they must be right.
2. My self worth is determined by my accomplishments.
3. One mistake and the whole world falls apart. I must be successful at
   everything; otherwise, I am useless.
4. Others will not accept my faults. I must be perfect for other people
   to respect me.
5. I must have everyone's respect at all times; otherwise, I am a failure.
6. If I fail at one thing, I am bound to fail at everything else as well.

When the therapist digs down like this, clients begin to understand the
subtle reasons for their extreme reactions to seemingly innocuous situations—why little things upset them so much. The therapist can then show
them how their reasoning was exaggerated, or their expectations unrealistic.
It is a real learning experience. This type of analysis is particularly useful for
clients who are prone to depression or are low in self-confidence, because
these people are particularly susceptible to putting themselves down.

Uncovering the "Shoulds".   Another technique for getting at maladaptive, underlying assumptions and beliefs is to simply get the client to ask
himself or herself "Why?" This technique is used to identify "shouldy"
thinking—the type of thinking that can force socially anxious and unassertive
people into doing things they do not really want to do, or can leave obsessional people feeling guilty that they did not do something more carefully or
differently (see Lazarus & Fay, 1975). An example will illustrate.
    The thought "I couldn't say no to his request, even though I wanted to"
is very typical. I have explored the underlying cognitions with many clients.
What underlies the thought is usually something like this:

"I couldn't say no to his request, even though I wanted to."
"Why?"
"Because I would have felt guilty."
"Why?"

"Because people should be as obliging as possible."

"Why?"

"Because everyone should try to make everyone else as happy as possible."

"Why?"

"Because everyone should be as happy as possible all the time."

"Why?"

"Because when you are sad you waste time going over things, and you also bring others down, and these are both wrong."

"Why?"

"Because you shouldn't waste time. You should be on the go all the time, doing things that are useful and productive. You shouldn't bring others down, because it is wrong, and then you feel guilty."

"Why?"

"Because you should be in good spirits all the time."

Again, even at a glance, these statements clearly highlight many unreasonable assumptions, involving unrealistic expectations of self and others. The further one probes, the more extreme the thinking becomes. I could have continued asking "Why?"; but, even brought as far as it was here, the final statement, "Because you should be in good spirits all the time," is, by any standards, unreasonable.

When such a chain of thoughts has been generated, the client is then asked to read down through them and pick out all the "shoulds," "musts," "guiltys," and "wrongs," and underline them. They then pick out all the pronouns *other than "I"* (i.e., "you," "people," "everyone") and change them to "I." The sequence of thoughts generated in the preceding example becomes:

"*I should* be as obliging as possible."

"*I should* be as happy as possible all the time."

"When I am sad I waste time, and this is *wrong*."

"*I should* be on the go all the time."

"*I should* be in good humor all the time," and so on.

After practicing a few times with the therapist, clients can start doing this exercise themselves, using it as a quick way of discovering why, if they are feeling angry, annoyed, frustrated, or guilty about something they did or did not do. Little by little, people come to recognize and understand the rigid, impossible rules and restrictions that they are unconsciously imposing on themselves.

VISUAL IMAGERY

Some people are more "visual" than others (Richardson, 1977). Without any conscious effort, they make detailed mental records of faces, places, or telephone numbers—like carrying around an internal camera that takes nonstop photographs throughout the day. Natural visualizers can also open their "life album" at any page and recall clearly what Susan wore to the wedding party in 1979, for example. The majority of people do not have such a photographic memory but can, nonethless, bring familiar people and places to mind without great difficulty. Visual imagery has been an integral component of numerous therapies—for example, traditional desensitiza-tion—for decades; but its therapeutic potential has been increasingly recog-nized in recent years, and continues to unfold (see Crits-Cristoph & Singer, 1981; Simonton, Simonton, & Creighton, 1978).

Developing Coping Imagery

Some clients can report vivid images that accompany them through their problem situations and exacerbate their difficulties. Others look blank if asked to form a mental picture of, or describe, things they see every day—even their boss's face, or their own bedroom. Because visual imagery is a prerequisite for traditional desensitization and cognitive rehearsal, *and* be-cause it can also be used as an effective coping tool on a day-to-day basis, it is frequently advantageous to train nonvisual clients to develop this facility (see Rossman, 1987).

I get clients to start off by trying to generate a clear mental picture of things that are *familiar* to them—their office, apartment, or best friend's face. It is sometimes necessary for them to first study these things in detail—to sit in front of them, or a photograph of them, and observe them over a period of time. They then close their eyes and try to "see" the object or person in their mind's eye. This may have to be repeated several times before a clear image is formed. When they are able to bring these objects, people, or places to mind without much difficulty, they progress to things that are *less* familiar—an acquaintance, or a place they have visited only a few times or a long time before. Finally, they are encouraged to *conjure up* visual images—to imagine, for example, their dream house or dream partner, green snow or white coal. These are personal creations—as opposed to *reconstructed* visual memories. At this stage, they can start to put their new cognitive facility into practice.

Once clients can generate clear visual images, this skill becomes immedi-ately useful as a coping tool. They can quickly learn to make their imagina-tion work for them when actually *in* problematic situations. This is particu-larly relevant for the socially anxious. For example, one client who used to tense up at even the thought of social gatherings learned to cope by taking herself *momentarily* out of the situation—by imagining herself at home, sitting by a big log fire with her cat sleeping peacefully at her feet. This was immediately effective, and settled her down enough to remain in the situation and, eventually, to mix and mingle. It is essential that the image generated is both pleasant *and* relaxing to the individual. An overstressed businessman learned to calm himself down at high-powered meetings by imagining himself strolling along his favorite beach at sunset, with tiny sparkling waves licking his feet and the breeze gently brushing his face. Such personal images can be conjured up in a split second, and can take the sting out of the most difficult situations.

Finally, if there are people present in a situation with whom clients feel shy or inadequate, I suggest that they remind themselves that these "monsters" are human too, by imagining them crawling out of bed in the morning, hair ruffled and eyes half-closed, burning the toast or spilling the milk. With a little imagination, there is no end to the ways in which people can learn to turn even the most anxiety-provoking situation to their advantage (see Beck & Emery, 1985, chapter 12).

Systematic Desensitization In Imagination

As explained in Appendix IV, the original technique of systematic desensitization was developed in the 1950s by Wolpe, and visual imagery was an integral component (Wolpe, 1958). Traditional desensitization involved training clients in deep muscular relaxation, constructing a hierarchy of increasingly anxiety-provoking situations, and then working through the hierarchy *in imagination*. It was only at a later stage that they progressed to *in vivo*, or live, exposure. It is increasingly argued that, because clients will have to confront their feared situations in reality sooner or later, that sooner is better, and that imaginal desensitization is unnecessarily time consuming. Another argument against imaginal exposure is that it requires clients to be able to generate clear visual images, and many find this very difficult. On the other hand, many therapists feel that imaginal exposure justifies the extra time and effort, by preparing their clients to face the objects of their fear (Wilkins, 1971).

It is essential that imaginal desensitization occurs in a quiet place, with a minimum likelihood of disturbance. Clients are induced into a state of deep relaxation, and advised to keep their eyes closed throughout the exercise. The therapist then introduces the first, or least anxiety-provoking, item on the fear hierarchy, by asking clients to form a clear image of it. Some therapists expose their clients to the image for a *fixed* number of seconds, and then ask them to switch to a pleasant image. More often, clients are asked to remain with the image in mind *until* it generates anxiety, at which time they indicate this to the therapist (e.g., by raising a finger), who switches them to a pleasant alternative image. The alternative image will have been carefully chosen in advance, and is immediately relaxing. More recently, a form of *self-control desensitization* has been developed by Goldfried, in which clients, instead of deflecting from the image once it becomes anxiety-provoking, are asked to "stay with it" and see themselves coping and in control, until their anxiety decreases (Goldfried, 1971).

Whichever procedure is used, clients are repeatedly exposed to the items on the hierarchy until they feel relaxed and in control. Each item is practiced until it ceases to generate anxiety; and *only* at this time does the therapist proceed to the next item. The hierarchy is gradually and systematically worked through in this way.

Cognitive Rehearsal

A second major area where imagery has traditionally been used in therapy is the cognitive parallel of behavioral rehearsal (Appendix IV); it is called *cognitive* or *imaginal rehearsal*. As in traditional desensitization, clients *mentally* rehearse the various aspects of feared situations, and imagine themselves coping. The therapist guides and coaches clients through all the behaviors and potential pitfalls, in imagination, thereby preparing them for the real thing.

In preparation for cognitive rehearsal, the hierarchy is very carefully and painstakingly constructed. Progressively more complex situations are devised, incorporating as much detail as possible. The items consist of real-life situations that have presented difficulties for the client in the past, and that will have to be faced, and dealt with, again in the near future. These items are discussed and planned; and the therapist tries to get a feel for the client's life space. The more familiar the items sound on presentation (i.e., details of the surroundings, the people present and how they are dressed and behave), the better, as this makes it easier for clients to *feel* as if they are really there. It also makes them feel more familiar and relaxed when they are eventually *in* the real situation.

Again, it is essential to conduct therapy in a place where client and therapist will not be disturbed. The therapist first induces the client into a deeply relaxed state, in preparation for rehearsal of the first item on the behavioral hierarchy. The item is then presented to the relaxed client, who keeps his or her eyes closed throughout. They are asked to get as clear a picture as possible—of the people, the decor, the furniture, familiar sounds and smells. When they are mentally *in* the situation, the therapist talks and guides them through the behavioral details of each skilled action. For example, a client might be instructed to start off by saying hello to Bob, who is standing up at the bar, as usual. He then approaches the bar, catches the

attention of Mike—the big bartender—and orders a beer in a nice clear voice
. . . and so on. The goal is for clients to *see* themselves coping, in a relaxed
and easy fashion. After a time, they should not just see, but *feel* themselves
there, moving around comfortably in the scene. The image is held in mind,
explored, and expanded, until they feel fully in control. The therapist can
continue adding familiar details until they would not mind staying there
longer—until their attention is more on aspects of the situation and experiencing themselves in control, than on their anxieties and what others might
be thinking of them.

Mastering the first item on the hierarchy can take several extended presen-
tations, followed by discussions with the therapist. Sometimes, when vividly
experiencing an image, clients suddenly remember important details that
had slipped their mind. These then have to be incorporated into the scene,
and the related behaviors must be rehearsed. For example, the client in the
previous example might remember that he has to pass by Sandy, who always
makes some smart remark, *before* he even gets as far as Bob at the bar. Only
when the client feels ready does the therapist move on to the next item on
the hierarchy. The procedure is the same; client and therapist together
gradually work through each item on the skills hierarchy in this way.

FOCUSING ATTENTION

Problems sometimes arise as a result of a client's inability to *focus* attention
on the relevant aspects of a situation or problem, or to keep these in mind.
On the other hand, some find it difficult to *shift* their attention; they become
obsessed with one aspect or detail of a situation, at the expense of retaining
their perspective on the whole scene. Cognitive inflexibility can also take the
shape of excessive daydreaming, that is, when an individual gets into the
habit of *tuning in* exclusively to their internal world instead of being outer-
oriented. Ideally, people should be able to scan the multiple components of
a situation and, at the same time, focus on the most relevant aspects and
keep these in mind (Gendlin, 1978). The ability to sift and sort, stop and
start, focus and scan is essential for flexible cognitive activity; it is what
cognitive control is all about (Rachman, 1978b; Rachman & Hodgson,
1980, chapters 18 and 20). Deficits in attention focusing or cognitive flexibility result in problems of indecision, compulsive ruminating and checking,
and excessive daydreaming. Cognitive techniques for overcoming these difficulties are described here.

Indecision

Indecision is something that everyone experiences. Some decisions, such
as whether to move house or change one's job, genuinely require careful
consideration and thinking through. These decisions should not be made

hastily. For some people, however, like Hamlet, decision making is a huge problem, and it can stop them from doing almost anything or from making any changes.

Why do some people find making decisions so difficult? Why do they dither agonizingly over which tie to wear, or what drink to order? There are many reasons, the most general explanations being related to insecurity, inability to handle change, fear of making a wrong decision, or fear of things going out of control. Obsessional people, as explained in chapter 6, find decision making particularly difficult. Because they are so perfectionistic, *all* aspects of an issue and *all* of the possible consequences are analyzed in detail and are gone over again and again (Beech, 1974). Likewise, when people are depressed (see chapter 5), decisions also become difficult, due to lethargy, fear of failure, lack of confidence, or sheer pessimism about possible outcomes.

The essence of decision making is to accumulate all the available and necessary information, objectively evaluate the pros and cons, choose the alternative that seems best, and then proceed confidently in that direction. I always reassure my clients that if things do *not* turn out exactly as they had anticipated or hoped, quite simply, another decision may be required.

As explained in chapter 1, people are limited in the amount of information they can keep in mind at any time. This is why they can sometimes feel very confident when actually *making* a decision or taking a particular course of action, but later feel much less so, and even consider changing their mind. This usually happens because they think of, or remember, reasons against their decision and, at the time, cannot bring to mind the earlier reasons "for." Consequently, people for whom decision making is a problem must learn to attend to the relevant facts and details (rather than feelings), and to keep these firmly in mind. Clients have repeatedly found the following simple guidelines useful and effective, especially in making important decisions.

They are asked to take a sheet of paper and to divide it lengthwise into two columns, "Pros" and "Cons." They then fill in the respective columns with as many reasons for and against the decision as come to mind; *and* to add to these lists over the following hours or days. Making things concrete in this way helps to clarify which direction they should follow; in fact, it usually becomes obvious, quite quickly, which decision is the wisest. If the client wishes, things can be analyzed further, by weighting each reason along a 5-point scale, as illustrated in Table V.2.

It is essential that clients *keep their lists*—especially if the decision is a big one, and involves long-term financial or emotional commitments. At the very least, they should be kept until the decision realizes itself, and the immediate consequences begin to unfold. For example, after a decision to move house, people often become apprehensive as the day of moving approaches. Equally, people sometimes have regrets in the weeks immedi-

TABLE V.2.
Pros and Cons

Decision: Moving to a Bigger House?

PROs		CONs	
1. Good time to buy; investment in buyer's market.	(5)	1. Would lose wonderful neighbors.	(4)
2. Will need more space; larger family planned	(5)	2. Children would have to change school, lose friends	(5)
3. Present house too far from office	(3)	3. Financial commitment of bigger mortgage	(2)
4. Present house too far from city and facilities	(2)	4. Money invested in extension and house improvements would not be recovered	(3)
5. Area getting very built-up	(4)		
6. Need to do more entertaining: owe hospitality due to current space shortage.	(2)		
(Total:	21)	(Total:	17)

5—very important
4—quite important
3—average
2—not very important
1—not at all important

ately following a move to a new neighborhood, when all is new and strange and they are missing the security of familiar names and faces. It helps enormously, at such times, to be able to take out their original lists and remind themselves of the reasons why they decided to move, and of the disadvantages of remaining where they were.

Focusing On

Fading. In Appendix IV, I described a behavioral intervention technique for compulsive checking that involved gradually reducing the frequency of checking to *once*. I have developed a method for concluding such interventions, as follows. Clients first agree that they will check once, and only once. Then, when they are actually *checking*, they are asking to *focus their attention* exclusively on what they are doing—not on their next chore or commitment. They must attend fully to the object of the exercise and say to themselves *out loud:* "I have checked the heater (or plug, or stove)." On the following days, they proceed as before, but gradually lower their voice by speaking more and more quietly. After a few days, their voice will have reduced to a whisper; after a week it will be hardly audible. In other words, they gradually internalize their own speech, effectively self-regulating their behavior in the same way as it occurs in the normal course of development (as described in chapter 1). At this point, they are giving a thorough, quick, silent check, like most people do.

Exaggerating.   Another technique that facilitates people who are tempted to check excessively is that of exaggerating. If, for example, a client spends large amounts of time wondering whether he or she has unplugged the heater or locked the safe in the office, it can help to *focus* deliberately on the feared consequences *and* to exaggerate them. For example, clients with this kind of checking compulsion would ask themselves:

"What am I afraid might happen if I have *not* unplugged the heater?"
"There might be a fire."
"And, what might happen if a fire started?"
"The house might burn down."
"And what might happen then?"
"The neighbors' houses might also catch fire."
"And then?"
"Then the entire block."
"And then?"
"Then the whole neighborhood."
"And then?"
"Then the city . . ."

This kind of exaggerating can be brought to a logical or illogical conclusion, where, for example, the entire city or country is blazing away furiously because of one heater that the client thinks he or she *did* unplug. This technique is *not* intended to induce deep, structural change; but it does help people to realize when their concerns are excessive, and how easily any worry can be exaggerated to a ridiculous extent (see Mahoney, 1986, for a theoretical discussion of related issues.)

Focusing Out

Distraction.   Although there is no pleasure to be gained from worrying as such, obsessional people often feel compelled to keep going over things, to "get to the bottom of it," or "get it sorted out." On the other hand, worrisome, unpleasant thoughts or images sometimes just keep recurring, unbidden, time and time again. The cognitive dynamics of such persistent, intrusive thoughts and images are not well understood (Lang, 1977), but this kind of ruminating can be alleviated by helping clients develop the skill of *focusing out.* They learn to distract themselves with something that is equally if not more compelling than, and also incompatible with, the intrusive cognitive activity (see also Rachman & Hodgson, 1980, pg. 287). There are many things that can serve as useful distractors, such as making phone calls, meeting with friends, going to the local store, or doing some urgent work. Distractors should be either very *mentally absorbing*—like learning something new, having a stimulating conversation, doing a challenging crossword, or watching an action-packed movie—or *physically rigorous*—like playing squash, running, or strenuous work. Passive mental or physical activity such as knitting, listening to instrumental music, or solitary strolling, leaves the mind free to wander. In other words, clients must learn to distract themselves with things that require their full mental attention or all their physical resources, or *both,* over a period of time. Ideally, distractions should also be pleasant and satisfying, so that, as well as keeping attention focused out, they also reduce the overall anxiety level and help the client to relax. For a discussion of *thought-stopping,* a dismissal technique also used with obsessional clients, see Rachman (1976) and Stern, Lipsedge, and Marks (1973).

Daydreaming.   Many unhappy, depressed, or socially isolated people spend large portions of the day *and* night in "dreamland" (see Singer & Antrobus, 1972; Beck, 1971). For them, the world of daydreams—even when they are unpleasant—is a more secure place than reality. Such people can, and frequently do, get into the bad habit of "living in their head." This creates a vicious circle. The more they withdraw inside, the more difficult it becomes for them to get involved in living again, to make the effort to be "outer-oriented" and to break the habit of tuning into themselves and their private "movie."

Part of the problem is that, when these people *do* look out, their perceptions can be very selective (see chapter 1). They focus narrowly on aspects of their environment or types of people who have hurt them, brought them down, or frightened them in the past. So, what they see *reinforces* their idea of the world as a threatening place; they create and maintain a self-fulfilling prophecy. They therefore usually need a lot of help and encouragement to come out of their shell. Essentially, they must learn to broaden their perspective by sharpening all their senses to the richness of life. They must develop a habit of looking around and thereby experiencing things they would not otherwise even notice.

I start such clients off with some very simple exercises, like *looking* at people—their faces, expressions, lines of laughter or worry, dimples, the color of their hair or their style of dress. They are encouraged to *listen*—to bits of conversation from passers-by, to a voice on the radio, the sigh of the wind, the tapping of rain against the window pane, footsteps. Likewise, they can *feel* the softness of the rain, the heat of the sun, the texture of their clothes or food, the smoothness of their skin. So that they will not feel overwhelmed, I have found it effective to advise them to spend *one* day looking, the next listening, the next tasting, and so forth. Over a period of weeks—and sometimes months—they learn to experience different aspects and facets of the *same* situations, objects and people; and to gradually build up their awareness, and wealth of sensory experiences.

Once they break the habits of focusing in, or of focusing on aspects of their external environment that punished them in the past, these people really come alive. It is most gratifying to see; they want *more*. They wonder how they did not notice so many of the pleasant things that surround them: "I must have been in a dream." They see that not all people are out to use or hurt them; that there are sincere, helpful people out there also. They come to realize that things cannot be, and do not have to be, perfect all the time to be enjoyed. The real world is not a perfectly happy place, but it is more substantial and satisfying than the world of fantasy and daydreams, which disappear like cotton candy. Gradually, their old cognitive habits are replaced by new ones, and they see, hear, and in every way experience a very different world from the one they remember before they "switched off" (see also Singer, 1974; Singer & Pope, 1978).

Appendix VI
Making Changes in Relation to Others

Because such a very large part of people's lives involves contact with other people—at home, at work, and at leisure—it is essential to be able to relate. This means knowing what to do in company; what to say to others, and how to respond to them. Interaction skills constitute a basic tool for coping with life (Tisdelle & Lawrence, 1986). As explained in chapter 2, the consequences of *not* being able to relate in a meaningful and mutually rewarding way, and of *not* having an adequate and supportive social network, are enormous. Inadequate social skills, or a lack of social supports, can lead to loneliness, hopelessness, anxiety, and depression, as well as to perpetual misunderstandings and disappointments (Trower, Bryant, & Argyle, 1978).

Communication involves giving and receiving messages on both verbal and nonverbal levels. The most basic communication skill is making conversation, that is, knowing how to talk to people. Depending on the situation, or the purpose of the interaction, conversations can span a continuum from "small talk" to longer discussions that sometimes involve personal disclosures. The purpose can be either to express or communicate feelings, to solve a problem, or *both*. In this final Appendix, I look firstly at basic communication skills, and then, at the ways in which these skills can be acquired and used, both to solve problems in interpersonal relationships and to facilitate emotional expression.

MAKING CONVERSATION

Making conversation is one of the most universal and pervasive of human activities—something almost everyone has to do every day. Conversations can last a minute or go on for hours, can be trivial or serious in content and purpose, and can be successful or disastrous. Many people are skilled when relating facts and figures, or when carrying out a professional role (e.g., nurse, accountant, teacher, waitress) but dread the idea of interacting with others—even people they know well—on a more casual, personal level. "What will I say?" "I can't make small talk." This concern often stems from a lack of self-confidence, when the trappings of role or status are no longer relevant, or from an erroneous belief that the content of small talk has to be consistently interesting or witty.

Clients referred with *secondary social phobias,* or social skills deficits (see chapter 7), usually attend a social skills training course, which takes place in a group setting (Kelly, 1982). Over a number of consecutive weeks, they are taught the basics of communication, and especially the art of conversation. Making conversation can be broken down into four stages: introducing oneself, starting conversation, keeping conversation going, and closing (Gabor, 1983). Each of these stages is covered during a typical course; and clients are supplied with factual, written information on common mistakes and pitfalls. In learning how to *introduce* themselves, for example, they are informed of the disadvantages of being passive in social interaction and waiting for other people to speak or approach—that this puts a burden on *them,* and can wrongly convey a message that one is not interested. Furthermore, the longer they remain aloof and detached, the more they feel left out, thereby creating a self-fulfilling prophecy. Clients can usually identify with these bad habits and avoidance patterns, and begin to realize their own mistakes.

They are then given specific instructions on *how to do it.* Situations are first modeled by the therapist, and then practiced (i.e., role-played) during the sessions with the other members of the group. For example, *A* and *B* might pretend to be chatting at a cocktail party, and *C* would approach and try to join in. Constructive feedback is then provided by the therapist and the other participants. Sometimes, sessions are also video-taped and then played back; but, this usually takes place later in the course, when performance has improved and feedback will be encouraging, rather than depressing.

Handouts with written instructions, like on the next page, are distributed, because memory is fallible; but more importantly, because clients are required to carry out "homework assignments"—to practice the role-played skills—between sessions. Homework is reviewed at the beginning of each session, and any problems that arose during the week are discussed and role-played again. Certain messages are consistently repeated throughout the course: the importance of being active in conversation, giving adequate eye contact, observing aspects of the situation or person and using these observations for further conversation, balancing talking and listening, and timing self-disclosures. These things are also knitted into the handouts and

---

"HOW TO DO IT": STARTING CONVERSATION

1. Once the introductions have been made, do not just stand there and wait for someone else to say something.

2. Make an observation of your conversation partner, or of some aspect of the situation, and follow this up with an easy-to-answer question, like "There are a lot of strangers here—do you know many people?" or, "That drink looks interesting—what is it?" (Nothing too personal or direct, like "Your dress is lovely—how much did it cost?".)

3. Listen to the replies; and then ask some information-seeking questions based on what you have just heard.

4. If the other person reveals some personal information (e.g. marital status), you may do likewise; but, it is too early for any intimate self-disclosures.

5. Remember to look at the person you are speaking to, and to speak loudly enough to be heard—particularly if it is a noisy gathering.

---

role-plays. Finally, during the course, clients supplement their learning with required reading from a number of selected self-help books on the topics. A list of useful titles is supplied in the annotated bibliography at the end of chapter 7.

LISTENING

Whatever the situation or circumstances, or whoever the speaker—spouse, friend, client, or stranger—listening is imperative to good communication. Good listeners concentrate both mentally and physically on what the other person is saying, and on the message they are conveying, both verbally and non-verbally. The instructions I give to clients are quite simple. They should provide constant feedback to the speaker (e.g., nods or "hmmmms"), to show that they are listening and that they understand. They should also wait until the other person has finished speaking before they begin, that is, they should not interrupt or jump in, no matter how enthusiastically they agree *or* how strongly they disagree with what is being said. Finally, if they are very nervous, I emphasize the importance of *focusing* fully on what the other person is saying, rather than worrying ahead about keeping the conversation going. In other words, if they really *listen* to the speaker and what he or she is saying, it invariably provides ideas for further conversation, substance for the next question or comment.

These are general guidelines. What clients *also* need to learn and understand is that, depending on the purpose of the interaction and the type of feedback required, listening can be of two kinds. *Deliberate listening* takes place in a problem-solving situation, where the goal is to sort through the message, evaluate the components of the problem, and ideally, come up with a solution. *Empathic listening,* on the other hand, is nonevaluative. The purpose is more one of just sensing the other person's feelings, and tuning in to his or her message and emotional tone. Feedback, if necessary at all, may be simply one of validation, that is, that one has heard, understood, and is supportive.

It is very important for clients, and people in general, to be able to establish as early as possible in any situation, whether the *main* purpose of the communication is one of problem solving or emotional expression. Many misunderstandings, especially within relationships, occur when people label situations differently or incorrectly. If, for example, A bares her soul to B in anticipation of empathic validation, but is answered in a logical, objective fashion, she will undoubtedly feel disappointed and misunderstood; and B will probably feel that she is ungrateful of his efforts to solve her problem. On the other hand, if A has a problem and spells it out to B, looking for a solution or guidelines, and B, with the best of intentions, replies that he understands fully, has heard what was said, and proceeds to get very upset, but offers no concrete advice, A is left exactly where she started—but with another problem on her hands. Most situations involve *both* an element of empathy and evaluation.

PROBLEM SOLVING

Communication difficulties arise in many areas—between friends, work colleagues, family members, and perhaps most importantly, between spouses and partners (see chapter 8). In the early 1970s, D'Zurilla and Goldfried (1971) noted the need for clinical exploration of problem solving, and suggested that ineffective problem solving was linked to emotional disturbance. Since then, problem-solving methods have continued to develop as a form of cognitive learning therapy; and training in personal problem solving has been shown to be effective in various problem areas, such as marital discord. It has also been included in more integrated treatment packages (see D'Zurilla, 1988).

Problem solving in the area of facilitating communication involves analyzing the situation, identifying the elements that are causing confusion or disagreement, and breaking these down into smaller, workable units that can then be tackled more directly. Problem solving involves three main stages: (a) defining the problem, (b) discussion, and (c) planning and implementing the necessary changes.

Defining The Problem

When people are "not getting along," arguments and disagreements can be sparked off for almost any reason. Often, neither party is allowed to speak for very long, and comments are quickly defended or criticized. "Tit-for-tatting" often results in both parties going off the point, or jumping from one topic or incident to another. Time, as well as mental and emotional energy, is wasted. Little is solved, and often much is dissolved. Sometimes, even when both parties make a genuine effort to sit down and talk, they get quickly embroiled in the contents of old arguments. Consequently, people find the following, quick exercise very useful.

Both parties agree on a time that is mutually convenient, and on a topic, for example, "What I see as the problem." They proceed as follows. One party *(A)* speaks for 1 minute, *uninterrupted,* while the other listens. Then, the listener *(B)* "feeds back," or tells the speaker what they heard—*not* their views on the issue. This means that the listener really has to *listen.* In doing so, people frequently find themselves listening to, and realizing, the other's point of view, for the first time. Furthermore, their feedback lets the speaker understand that he or she has been listened to and understood. Then *B* talks, *uninterrupted,* for 1 minute—after which time *A* feeds back. Things can be left there, or can be followed by a further 2-minute discussion, conducted along the same lines.

Both parties then write down all of the problem areas identified from what they heard—difficult times or topics, situations or behaviors. These problems are then further defined, as specifically as possible, and form the basis of future discussion sessions; for example:

1. Sex
2. Money
3. Dual-career
4. Children
5. Alcohol
6. Social life
7. Friday nights
8. Aggression
9. Affairs

Clients are invariably surprised at how much can be said in just 1 minute when they know that they are not going to be interrupted, and at how much can be learned by really *listening* to the other party and trying to appreciate their point of view. This entire procedure takes less than 5 minutes; and a lot of ground can be covered. Hours can be wasted in arguing and getting nowhere.

This flexible technique can be used by spouses or business partners, to both define *and* discuss problems or issues that are causing concern or disagreement; for example, moving house or office, finances, lack of productivity or mutual support. It can also be used where *more* than two people wish to clarify areas of difficulty, such as a family discussion or a small professional gathering. The procedure is the same. *Each* person talks for 1 minute, uninterrupted, after which the others, in turn, feed back what they heard the speaker say. Several rounds may be necessary in order to clarify issues satisfactorily.

Discussing The Problem

Problems *can* be discussed in the same way as they were defined, that is, by each party speaking for 1 minute, uninterrupted. However, because what clients usually need to learn is to be able to discuss problems and opinions in an open and relaxed way, I encourage them to follow these guidelines for increasing open communication and exchange. Firstly, it is very important that only *one* problem or issue is discussed at a time; and that each party talks about the way *they* personally see things, rather than focusing on the other's faults. When talking about the other person, I recommend that they begin with something positive; this starts things off on a healthy footing, and minimizes defensiveness on the other's part: "You are very good at handling money, but there is one area . . ."

An essential ingredient in effective discussions is to be brief, and to get to the point. If the message is long, it helps if the speaker paraphrases (stops and summarizes) every so often. This keeps him or her to the point, as well as minimizing misunderstandings. As important as brevity is specificity. I constantly remind clients not to use unclear words, or to refer to vague impressions. Concrete examples—such as a *recent* instance of something that is causing difficulty—are a great help. Likewise, it serves all concerned to talk only about what can be observed. Inferences such as: "I think that you think that I think . . ." only create more misunderstandings.

Both parties are also encouraged to express their *feelings*—anger, disappointment, frustration, loneliness—whatever the case may be. Furthermore, they must learn to *listen,* with all of the skills already outlined. They must get into the habit of conveying to the other person—both at the time and afterwards—that they understood what was said, as well as the feeling tone with which their message was expressed. People are often adding to a situation, without even realizing; so they are also helped to identify and acknowledge their part in the problem.

Finally, in providing feedback, clients must understand that its value lies in its *feed-forward effect*. People often inadvertently give negative feedback when asked for an opinion, especially if they are already feeling negative; but this simply inhibits further exchange. Being as positive as possible, stressing desirable aspects of the other person's behavior—or, at the very least, being neutral, rather than negative—is always worth the effort. Feedback should also be brief and specific (Jacobson & Margolin, 1979; Stuart, 1980b).

Planning and Implementing Changes

Problems, once defined and discussed, are followed up with a plan of specific, concrete, behavioral changes. Otherwise, the exercise, so far, will have been a pointless and frustrating waste of time. At this point, the therapist again emphasizes the importance of motivation; and, that the changes will necessitate compromise on both parts. In planning changes, the couple must continue to focus on the present and the future, that is, on solutions, rather than harping on past grievances. This can be a surprisingly difficult habit to break. Finally, when the specific changes are agreed on, they are written out; and both parties keep a copy. These written plans serve to remind them of their original goals, especially if there are disagreements at a later stage.

Contracts. When things are going badly between people, it sometimes helps to set the ball rolling by using a simple contract system. Contracts are widely used in business transactions, to ensure that promises are kept and agreements are adhered to. Similarly, contracts can be used to induce and support desired changes between people—spouses, partners, colleagues, friends, and family members—when relationships are strained. Contracts are a way of *temporarily* structuring the environment to support the development of new or positive exchanges. Behavior change is more quickly and easily achieved than attitude change.

Most contracts are based on a *quid pro quo* (QPQ), or simple exchange, agreement. One person agrees to do something in exchange for a similar behavior change in the other. *A* promises to prepare dinner if *B* clears the table afterwards. The most effective type of QPQ contract is where the behaviors being exchanged are complimentary. The problem with this simple model, however, is that failure by *either* party to comply with the terms returns both parties to their initial position—but with the addition of resentment in the nonoffender. There may also be arguments as to "who goes first."

Looser, but more effective, are *good faith*, or *independent consequences*, contracts. Here, both parties exchange from a list of desired behaviors. Each party, furthermore, is free to choose how or when he or she will opt to do

Figure VI.1

QUID PRO QUO (QPQ) CONTRACT	
A . . . . . . on condition that . . . . . . *B*	
1. Will prepare dinner every evening.	1. Will tidy the house (while *A* prepares dinner).
2. Will stick to diet.	2. Will reduce alcohol intake to one beer per night.
3. Will allot two 1-hour periods per week for chat and shared recreation.	3. Will allot two 1-hour periods per week to take *A* grocery shopping.

Figure VI.2

INDEPENDENT CONSEQUENCES CONTRACT			
	A		*B*
Goal:	Twenty minutes' chat in the evening (about how the day went, any problems, news, etc.)	Goal:	Prepare the dinner *and* do the dishes (rather than leaving them until morning.
Reward:	One can of beer.	Reward:	Fifteen minutes sleep-in in the morning.
Punishment:	Forfeit jog.	Punishment:	Forfeit nightcap.
	Etc.		Etc.

things that please the other. Obviously, this depends on the existence of good faith to start off with.

Contracts are always made in writing, and they specify clearly the desired changes and the rules for compliance (Hops, 1976). Many clients find contracts too artificial, impersonal, or even embarrassing, that is, the idea that positive behaviors have to be induced by a rule-bound system. It is a personal choice. In their favor, it may be argued that when positive behaviors *are* increased—by whatever means—they generate good feelings. It may be the bottom line for cranking a relationship or partnership back into action again, but if it works, in my opinion, it is the improvement that counts.

Increasing Positive Exchanges. Based on research findings that distressed couples actually *do* exchange fewer rewards and a greater number of punishing behaviors than nondistressed couples, one initial goal of martial therapy is to increase the ratio of positive to negative behavior exchanges. This can be done in a number of ways.

Both parties can independently make a "gentlemen's agreement" to increase positive behaviors towards the other at certain times of the day or week. Stuart (1980b) introduced the idea of "caring days," where each spouse acts as if he or she cares for the other by engaging in behaviors designed to please. Wills, Weiss, & Patterson (1974) instruct their couples to hold "love days," where, without announcement to the partner, a spouse doubles or triples his or her rate of positive behaviors.

It is worth pointing out to the couple, however, *before* they start putting such magnanimous intentions into practice, that it is very easy to assume they know what their partner would like more or less of—based on "assumed similarity" or past observations. One can be very wrong in one's assumptions; also, people change over time. It therefore helps greatly if both parties write out, for the other, the behaviors they would like more, or less, of. These should be small, specific things that can be easily effected and observed. Asking a partner not to leave cigarettes burning in the ashtray or to talk more over dinner makes more sense than vague requests to be "tidier" or "more communicative." These goals are written down and listed in order of priority; and the list is made available to the partner.

A further option is for the couple to keep separate boxes containing all their wishes, written on separate pieces of paper. The other party is encouraged to spontaneously dip into this "dream box" and make one of the wishes come true. Another way of mellowing vibes is for the couple to do more things together, that is, more shared activities. People are very different; one party is often more independent, sporty, or intellectual than the other. Again, with compromise and discussion, it is usually possible to identify activities and interests that will allow the couple to relax in each other's company. These can be activities that they used to enjoy together and have just not made time for recently; or, it is often a good idea for people to take up something entirely new. Because increasing positive exchanges in these ways is looser than using a contract system, it is important that progress is reviewed on a weekly basis.

COMMUNICATING EMOTIONS

Just as listening can be either problem-solving or empathic in its goal, communication also has this dual function. I have dealt with problem-solving communication; but it is also imperative for both physical and psychological well-being for people to be able to express their emotions freely, and at the time they are experienced. Emotions also help *others* to make sense of one's reactions; and to understand how other people are feeling, and why. Emotional expression is therefore essential for meaningful communication. The error of assuming that "He must have known how bad I felt—although I tried not to show it," is all to common. Most people, understandably, go by what they see.

Expressing Emotions

Life does not always run smoothly, and emotions have not evolved at random. They serve an important function. It is *normal* to feel angry, frustrated, or disappointed (Novaco, 1978). Not being able to express emotions, or holding them in, is the problem. This can occur for a number of reasons—fear of rejection, fear of losing control, or fear of what other people might say or think. Some people do not know how to show their emotions at all, because they have allowed themselves so little practice. Frustrated emotions do not disappear. They can lead to depression and aggression, as well as a build-up of bad feelings against others, or against the world in general.

When it comes to expressing emotions, there are no rules. However, I do advise clients that, when they are trying to express their feelings—either to me or to somebody else—to just talk about themselves and how they are feeling at the time. They should try to forget about what their listener might be thinking, and just talk as simply and honestly as they can. I also encourage them to talk about *positive* emotions—happiness, excitement, relief. These are just as important as negatives ones, and sometimes just as difficult to express.

Accepting Emotions

Sometimes, as part of a structured intervention, a therapist will actively encourage a client to talk about an area of deep emotional conflict, such as a bereavement or separation, and to describe how they feel: "Tell me how you feel about X; I would like to understand. I want to help." Generally, people find it difficult to talk about painful aspects of their life, so it is essential that the therapist generates an atmosphere of acceptance, or *unconditional positive regard* (Rogers, 1958). In other words, the client should feel that he or she can talk freely, without fear of rejection, disapproval, or reprisal. Feelings and emotions are complex and delicate; if clients are not ready to talk, they should not be forced or pressured in any way.

On the other hand, when people feel safe and unthreatened, they often suddenly and spontaneously start to unfold. If this is unusual for a person, it is also likely to be difficult. It is important, therefore, that they are not stopped or discouraged—even if it means that the therapist has to extend the session, or to stay later than planned. The time may not be "right" for the person, the opportunity may not come again, for a long time, if ever. If they have been holding a lot in, for a long time, they should be granted the indulgence of talking—even if they repeat themselves, go on and on, or talk in circles. In a nonevaluative context, people feel secure enough to say things they have been bottling up. It is therapeutic for people to put words on their feelings, to hear themselves talking things out. As well as providing an enormous emotional outlet, it also helps them to put some shape on things, to define where their conflicts lie, and to start the problem-solving process.

In such situations of empathic listening, the emphasis of the therapist is on the *emotional tone* of what is being said, and on trying to understand how the client sees the world—rather than on evaluating the components of the message in order to come up with a solution. Often, the ideal response to someone who is upset or is expressing how they feel is simply to show eagerness to listen and to understand. More often than not, it is not necessary to *do* anything, or to *say* anything constructive. People, at such times, generally just need to feel accepted, listened to, and validated—to know that there is someone there who cares. If the therapist disagrees with what is being said, or the client contradicts himself or herself, it is not the time to say so. A lot of information is being freely given, and any issues that arise can be taken up at the appropriate time in later sessions, when both client and therapist are working on solutions.

Finally, sometimes after intimate disclosures—even in therapy—people regret their openness and become embarrassed, or feel vulnerable and threatened. At such times, a therapist will convey, as gently and subtly as possible, that he or she was really pleased and encouraged by the client's ability to talk about their feelings, that it has provided a deeper understanding of their difficulties, and that the therapeutic relationship has also benefited from their honesty and courage. The emerging *constructivist* movement within cognitive psychotherapy particularly emphasizes these empathic, caring aspects of the therapist–client relationship (Guidano & Liotti, 1985; Mahoney, 1988; Mahoney & Gabriel, 1987).

ASSERTION TRAINING

An integral part of the ability to express one's feelings and emotions is to be able to assert oneself (Alberti & Emmons, 1974). Assertion involves the expression and acceptance of both positive and negative feelings. Assertion has been defined as the ability to express one's rights without violating the rights of others. Aggression is when one expresses one's own rights, but at the expense, or by violating the rights, of others. Allowing one's rights to be violated defines passivity. Everyday situations in which assertion is required are: making and refusing requests, making and taking complaints, and giving and taking compliments.

Clients who need to develop assertion skills are usually catered to in the same way as people with social skills deficits, as outlined in chapter 7 and Appendix VI (Making Conversation). They participate in an assertion skills training course, over several weeks. Written information is provided in the shape of handouts, and participants are given specific instructions for handling various types of assertion situations. For example, they are taught to make requests by: always beginning with "I", and then getting to the point, by being simple and brief as well as open and direct. Similar instructions are provided for refusing requests, making and taking complaints, and for giving and taking compliments.

The therapist models assertive, aggressive, and passive versions of the behavior or skill that the group is endeavoring to acquire at any particular session. Participants then practice, by role-playing problem situations volunteered from their *own* ongoing experiences—skills like assertively refusing an unreasonable request to take on yet another project at work, complaining effectively to the neighbors about their dog's incessant barking, or giving a girlfriend a compliment without blushing or getting tongue-tied. Learning how to handle such situations can make a big difference to the quality of people's personal and professional lives.

The essential ingredients of effective assertion—eye contact, timing, objectivity, listening, clarification, remaining calm and focused on facts rather than feelings—are repeatedly emphasized throughout the sessions and integrated into the role-play demonstrations. As with social skills training, clients are required to carry out "homework assignments" between sessions, and to complete selected readings from recommended self-help books on the topic. A list of these titles is supplied in the annotated bibliography at the end of chapter 7 (see also Heimberg & Becker, 1981).

In essence, assertion involves knowing what one wants (i.e., defining one's goals), having the confidence to acknowledge this to oneself and to others, and then firing ahead and *doing* something about it. Obsessional or overly conscientious people sometimes worry that assertive behavior will be viewed as selfish, or that they will feel guilty about making a public demonstration of their wishes. I reassure them that it is *more* selfish to expect *others* to make up their minds, or to make their decisions for them. That is expecting too much of *them*. Everyone is responsible for their own, precious life; everyone must live and learn from their own success experiences and mistakes. This is the only way people can build up their own set of unique coping skills, their own identity, and their own sense of self-efficacy.

References

Adair, J. (1987). *How to manage your time*. U.K.: McGraw-Hill.

Ader, R. (1980). Psychosomatic and psychoimmunologic research. *Psychomatic Medicine, 42,* 307–321.

Alberti, E. R., & Emmons, M. L. (1974). *Your perfect right*. San Luis Obispo, CA: Impact, Inc.

Argyle, M. (1978). *The psychology of interpersonal behavior*. Harmondsworth: Penguin Books.

Baekeland, F., & Lundwall, L. (1975). Dropping out of treatment: A critical review. *Psychological Bulletin, Vol. 82, No. 5,* 738–783.

Bandura, A. (1969). *Principles of behavior modification*. NY: Holt, Rinehart, & Winston.

Bandura, A. (1977). Self-efficacy: Toward a unifying theory of behavior change. *Psychological Review, 84,* 191–215.

Beck, A. T. (1963). Thinking and depression: Ideosyncratic content and cognitive distortions. *Archives of General Psychiatry, 9,* 324–333.

Beck, A. T. (1971). Cognitive patterns in dreams and daydreams. In J. H. Maserman (Ed.), *Dream dynamics* (pp. 2–7). NY: Grune and Stratton.

Beck, A. T. (1976). *Cognitive therapy and the emotional disorders*. New York University International Press.

Beck, A. T., & Emery, G. (1985). *Anxiety disorders and phobias: A cognitive perspective*. NY: Basic Books, Inc.

Beck, A. T., Rush, A. J., Shaw, B. F., & Emery, G. (1979). *Cognitive therapy of depression*. NY: Guilford Press.

Beech, H. R. (1974). *Obessional states*. London: Methuen.

Benjaminsen, S. (1981). Stressful life events preceding the onset of neurotic depression. *Psychological Medicine, II,* 369–378.

Billings, A. G., & Moos, R. N. (1982). Psychosocial theory and research on depression: An integrative framework and review. *Clinical Psychology Review, 2,* 213–237.

Bird, M. (1986). *The effective time manager*. London: Ebury Press.

Bixler, E. O., Kales, A., Soldatos, C., Kales, J. D., & Healey, S. (1979). Prevalence of sleep disorders in the Los Angeles metropolitan area. *American Journal of Psychiatry, 136,* 1257–1262.

Blackman, D. (1974). *Operant conditioning: An experimental analysis of behavior*. London: Methuen.

Bliss, E. C. (1984). *Getting things done*. NY: Bantam Books.

Bowers, K. (1987). Revisioning the unconscious. *Canadian Psychology, 28(2)*, 93–104.

Bowers, K., & Meichenbaum, D. (Eds.). (1984). *The unconscious reconsidered*. NY: Wiley.

Brown, G. W., Bhrolchain, M. N., & Harris, T. (1975). Social class and psychiatric disturbances among women in an urban population. *Sociology, 9*, 225–254.

Brownell, K. D. (1984). The psychology and physiology of obesity: Implications for screening and treatment. *Journal of the American Dietetic Association, 84*, 406–414.

Brownell, K. D., Greenwood, M. R. C., Shrager, E. E., & Stellar, E. (1986a). *Dieting induced efficiency: Metabolic and behavioral adaptations to cycles of weight loss and regain*. Manuscript submitted for publication.

Brownell, K. D., Marlatt, G. A., Lichtenstein, E., & Wilson, G. T. (1986b). Understanding and preventing relapse. *American Psychologist, 41:7*, 765–782.

Bruner, J. S., Goodnow, J. J., & Austin, G. A. (1956). *A study of thinking*. NY: Wiley.

Burns, D. (1981). *Feeling good*. NY: New American Library.

Cannon, G., & Einzig, H. (1983). *Dieting makes you fat*. London: Century Publishing.

Catania, A. C. (1975). The myth of reinforcement. *Behaviorism, 3*, 192–199.

Cherry, E. C. (1953). Some experiments on the recognition of speech with one and two ears. *Journal of the Acoustical Society of America, 25*, 975–979.

Clarke, A. M., & Clarke, A. D. (Eds.). (1976). *Early experience: Myth and evidence*. London: Open Books.

Colvin, R. H., & Olson, S. B. (1983). A descriptive analysis of men and women who have lost significant weight, and are highly successful at maintaining weight loss. *Addictive Behaviors, 8*, 287–295.

Copeland, A. P. (1983). Children's talking to themselves: It's developmental significance, function, and therapeutic promise. In P. Kendall (Ed.), *Advances in cognitive-behavioral research and therapy* (Vol. 2., pp. 241–278). NY: Academic Press.

Crits-Cristoph, P., & Singer, J. L. (1981). Imagery in cognitive-behavior therapy: Research and applications. *Clinical Psychology Review, I*, 19–32.

Cummings, C., Gordon, J. R., & Marlatt, G. A. (1980). Relapse: Prevention and prediction. In W. R. Miller (Ed.), *The addictive disorders: Treatment of alcoholism, drug abuse, smoking and obesity* (pp. 291–322). NY: Pergamon Press.

David, D. S, & Brannon, R. (Eds.). (1976). *The forty-nine percent majority: The male sex role*. Reading, MA: Addison-Wesley.

De Longis, A., Coyne, J. C., Dahof, G., Folkman, S., & Lazarus, R. S. (1982). Relationship of daily hassles, uplifts and major life events to health status. *Health Psychology, I*, 119–136.

De Rubeis, R. J., & Beck A. T. (1988). Cognitive therapy. In K. S. Dobson (Ed.), *Handbook of cognitive-behavioral therapies* (pp. 273–306). NY: Guilford.

Dobson, K. (Ed.). (1988). *Handbook of cognitive-behavioral therapies*. NY: Guilford.

Doyne, E. J., Chambless, D. L., & Beutler, L. E. (1983). Aerobic exercise as a treatment for depression in women. *Behavior Therapy, 14*, 434–440.

Dryden, W. (1984). Rational-emotive therapy and cognitive therapy: A critical comparison. In M. A. Reda, & M. J. Mahoney (Eds.), *Cognitive psychotherapies: Recent developments in theory, research and practice* (pp. 81–99). Cambridge, MA: Ballinger.

D'Zurilla, T. J. (1988). Problem-solving therapy. In K. Dobson (Ed.), *Handbook of cognitive-behavioral therapies* (pp. 85–135). NY: Guilford.

D'Zurilla, T. J., & Goldfried, M. (1971). Problem-solving and behavior modification. *Journal of Abnormal Psychology, 78*, 107–126.

Ellis, A. (1962). *Reason and emotion in psychotherapy*. NY: Stuart.

Ellis, A., & Harper, R. A. (1975). *A new guide to rational living*. North Hollywood, CA: Wilshire Books.

Erdelyi, M. H. (1985). *Psychoanalysis: Freud's cognitive psychology.* NY: W. H. Freeman.

Fabris, N., Garcia, E., Hadden, J., & Mitchinson, N. A. (Eds.). (1983). *Immunoregulation.* NY: Plenum Press.

Farina, A. (1981). Are women nicer than men? Sex and the stigma of mental disorders. *Clinical Psychology Review, 1(2),* 223–244.

Folkman, S. & Lazarus, R. S. (1980). An analysis of coping in a middle-aged community sample. *Journal of Health and Social Behavior, 21,* 219–239.

Foulkes, D. (1985). *Dreaming: A cognitive-psychological analysis.* Hillsdale, NJ: Lawrence Erlbaum Associates.

Frank, J. D. (1971). Therapeutic factors in psychotherapy. *American Journal of Psychotherapy, 25(3),* 350–361.

Freudenberger, H. J., & Richelson, G. (1980). *Burn-out.* London: Arrow Books.

Friedman, M., & Rosenman, R. H. (1974). *Type A behavior and your heart.* NY: Knopf.

Gabor, D. (1983). *How to start a conversation and make friends.* NY: Simon & Schuster.

Gendlin, E. T. (1978). *Focusing.* NY: Everest House.

Glasglow, R. E., & Terborg, J. R. (1988). Occupational health promotion programs to reduce cardiovascular risk. *Journal of Consulting and Clinical Psychology, 56,* 365–373.

Goldfried, M. R. (1971). Systematic desensitization as training in self-control. *Journal of Consulting and Clinical Psychology, 37* 228–234.

Goldfried, M. R., & Davison, G. C. (1976). *Clinical behavior therapy.* NY: Holt, Rinehart, and Winston.

Goldstein, A. J., & Chambless, D. L. (1978). A re-analysis of agoraphobia. *Behavior Therapy, 9,* 47–59.

Goldstein, A. P., & Simonson, N. R. (1971). Social psychological approaches to psychotherapy research. In A. E. Bergin, & S. L. Garfield (Eds.), *Handbook of psychotherapy and behavior change: An empirical analysis* (pp. 154–195). NY: Wiley.

Greenberg, L. S., & Safran, J. D. (1987). *Emotion in psychotherapy.* NY: Guilford.

Guidano, V. F., & Liotti, G. A. (1983). *Cognitive processes and emotional disorders.* NY: Guilford.

Guidano, V. F., & Liotti, G. A. (1985). A constructivistic foundation for cognitive therapy. In M. J. Mahoney, & A. Freeman (Eds.), *Cognition and psychotherapy* (pp. 101–142). NY: Plenum Press.

Haaga, D. A. (1987). Treatment of the Type A behavior pattern. *Clinical Psychology Review, 7,* 557–574.

Hall, R. C. W., Popkin, M. D., De Vaul, R. A., Faillace, L. A., & Stickney, S. K. (1978). Physical illness presenting as psychiatric disease. *Archives of General Psychiatry, 35,* 1315–1320.

Haskell, W. L. (1984). Overview; Health benefit of exercise. In J. D. Matarazzo, S. M. Weiss, J. A. Herd, N. E. Miller, & S. M. Weiss (Eds.), *Behavioral health: A handbook of health enhancement and disease prevention* (pp. 409–432). NY: Wiley.

Haynes. R. B., Taylor, D. W., & Sackett, D. L. (Eds.). (1979). *Compliance in health care.* Baltimore, MD: Johns Hopkins University Press.

Heimberg, R. G., & Becker, R. E. (1981). Cognitive and behavioral models of assertive behavior: Review, analysis and integration. *Clinical Psychology Review, 1(3),* 353–374.

Henry, J. P., & Stephens, P. M. (1977). *Stress, health and the social environment: A sociobiologic approach to medicine.* NY: Springer.

Hirsch, J. (1973). Adipose cellularity in relation to human obesity. *Advances in Internal Medicine, 17,* 289–300.

Hodgson, R. J., & Rachman, S. (1976). The modification of compulsive behavior. In H. J. Eysenck (Ed.), *Case studies in behavior therapy* (pp. 17–41). London: Routhledge and Kegan Paul.

Holmes, T. H., & Rahe, R. H. (1967). The social re-adjustment rating scale. *Journal of Psychosomatic Research, II,* 213–218.

Hops, H. (1976). Behavioral treatment of marital problems. In W. E. Craighead, A. E. Kazdin, & M. J. Mahoney (Eds.), *Behavior modification* (pp. 431–446). Boston MA: Houghton Mifflin Company.

Horowitz, A. (1977). The pathways into psychiatric treatment: Some differences between men and women. *Journal of Health and Social Behavior, 18*, 169–178.

Hugdahl, K. (1981). Three three-systems model of fear and emotion: A critical examination. *Behavior Therapy and Research, 19*, 75–85.

Jacobson, E. (1929). *Progressive relaxation.* Chicago: University of Chicago Press.

Jacobson, N. S., & Margolin, G. (1979). *Martial therapy.* NY: Brunner Mazel.

James, W. (1890). *The principles of psychology,* (Vol. I). NY: Holt.

Jemmott, J. B. III, & Locke, S. E. (1984). Psychosocial factors, immunologic mediations and human susceptibility to infectious diseases. How much do we know? *Psychological Bulletin, 95*, 78–108.

Jones, E. E., & Nisbett, E. E. (1971). The actor and the observer: Divergent perceptions of the causes of behavior. In E. E. Jones, D. E. Kanouse, H. H. Kelley, S. Valins, & B. Weiner (Eds.), *Perceiving the causes of behavior* (pp. 79–94). Morristown, NJ: General Learning Press.

Kanfer, F. H., & Karoly, P. (1972). Self-control: A behavioristic excursion into the lion's den. *Behavior Therapy, 3*, 398–416.

Kanner, A., Coyne, J. C., Schaefer, C., & Lazarus, R. S. (1981). Comparison of two modes of stress measurement: Daily hassles and uplifts versus major life events. *Journal of Behavioral Medicine, 4(1)*, 1–39.

Kazdin, A. E., & Wilcoxon, L. A. (1976). Systematic desensitization and non-specific treatment effects: A methodological evaluation. *Psychological Bulletin, 83(5)*, 729–758.

Kelly, G. (1955). *The psychology of personal constructs.* NY: Norton.

Kelly, J. A. (1982). *Social skills training: A practitioner's guide for intervention.* NY: Springer.

Kinsey, A. C., Pomeroy, W. B., & Martin, C. E. (1948). *Sexual behavior in the human male.* Philadelphia, PA: W. B. Saunders and Company.

Kinsey, A. C., Pomeroy, W. B., & Martin, C. E. (1953). *Sexual behavior in the human female.* Philadelphia, PA: W. B. Saunders and Company.

Kirschenbaum, D. S. (1987). Self-regulatory failure: A review with clinical implications. *Clinical Psychology Review, 7*, 77–104.

Kolodny, R. C., Masters, W. H., & Johnson, V. E. (1979). *Textbook of sexual medicine.* Boston, MA: Little Brown and Company.

Krantz, S. (1987). A tip for relapse prevention in depression. *International Cognitive Therapy Newsletter, 3(2)*, 1–2.

Lader, M. (1975). The nature of clinical anxiety in modern society. In C. D. Spielberger, & I. G. Sarason (Eds.), *Stress and anxiety* (Vol. I, pp. 3–26). NY: Wiley.

Landfield, A. W. (1980). Personal construct psychology: A theory to be elaborated. In M. J. Mahoney (Ed), *Psychotherapy process: Current issues and future directions* (pp. 61–83). NY: Plenum Press.

Lang, P. J. (1968). Fear reduction and fear behavior: Problems in treating a construct. In J. M. Shlien (Ed.), *Research in psychotherapy* (Vol. 3, pp. 90–102). Washington DC: American Psychological Association.

Lang, P. J. (1977). Imagery in therapy: An information-processing analysis of fear. *Behavior Therapy, 8*, 862–886.

Langer, E. J. (1978). Re-thinking the role of thought in social interaction. In J. Harvey, W. J. Ickes, & R. F. Kidd (Eds.), New directions in attribution research (Vol. 2, pp. 35–58). Hillsdale, NJ: Lawrence Erlbaum Associates.

Langer, E. J., & Roth, J. (1975). Heads I win, tails, it's chance: The illusion of control as a function of the sequence of outcomes in a purely chance task. *Journal of Personality and Social Psychology, 32*, 951–955.

Lazarus, A. A. (1971). *Behavior therapy and beyond.* NY: McGraw-Hill.

Lazarus, A. A. (1984). *In the mind's eye.* NY: Guilford.

Lazarus, A. A., & Fay, P. (1975). *I can if I want to.* NY: Warner Books.

Lazarus, R. S. (1982). Thoughts on the relations between emotion and cognition. *American Psychologist, 37,* 1019–1024.

Lazarus, R. S. (1984a). Puzzles in the study of daily hassles. *Journal of Behavioral Medicine, 7(4),* 375–389.

Lazarus, R. S. (1984b). On the primacy of cognition. *American Psychologist, 39,* 124–129.

Lazarus, R. S. (1985). The trivialization of distress. In J. C. Rosen, & L. J. Solomon (Eds.), *Preventing health risk behavior in promoting coping with illness* (Vol. 8; Vermont Conference on the primary prevention of psychopathology (pp. 279–298). Hanover, NH: University Press of New England.

Lazarus, R. S., & Folkman, S. (1984). *Stress, appraisal and coping.* NY: Springer.

Leibel, R. L., & Hirsch, J. (1984). Diminished energy requirements in reduced-obese patients. *Metabolism, 33,* 328–342.

Leon, G. R., & Chamberlain, K. (1973). Emotional arousal, eating patterns and body image as differential factors associated with varying success in maintaining a weight loss. *Journal of Consulting and Clinical Psychology, 40,* 474–480.

Lewinsohn, P. M. (1975). The behavioral study and treatment of depression. In M. Hersen, R. M. Eisler, & P. M. Miller (Eds.), *Progress in behavior modification* (Vol. I, pp. 19–64). NY: Academic Press.

Lewinsohn, P. M., Hoberman, H., Teri, L., & Hautzinger, M. (1985). An integrative theory of depression. In S. Reiss, & R. Bootzin (Eds.), *Theoretical issues in behavior therapy* (pp. 331–359). NY: Academic Press.

Ley, F. (1975). What did your doctor tell you? *New Behavior, I,* 58–61.

Luborsky, L., Singer, B., & Luborsky, L. (1977). Comparative studies in psychotherapies. *Archives of General Psychiatry, 32,* 995–1008.

Luria, A. (1961). The role of speech in the regulation of normal and abnormal behavior (J. Tizard, trans.). NY: Liveright.

Mahoney, M. J. (1986). Paradoxical intention, symptom prescription and the principles of therapeutic change. *The Counseling Psychologist, 14(2),* 283–289.

Mahoney, M. J. (1988). The cognitive sciences and psychotherapy: Patterns in a developing relationship. In K. S. Dobson (Ed.), *Handbook of cognitive-behavioral therapies* (pp. 357–386). NY: Guilford.

Mahoney, M. J., & Gabriel, T. J. (1987). Psychotherapy and the cognitive sciences: An evolving alliance. *Journal of Cognitive Psychotherapy, An International Quarterly, I(I),* 40–59.

Mandler, G. (1984). *Mind and body: Psychology of emotion and stress.* NY: W.W. Norton.

Margolin, G. (1981). A behavioral-systems approach to the treatment of marital jealousy. *Clinical Psychology Review, I,* 469–487.

Marks, I. (1969). *Fears and phobias:* NY: Academic Press.

Marlatt, G. A., & Gordon, J. R. (Eds.). (1985). *Relapse prevention: Maintenance strategies in addictive behavior change.* NY: Guildford.

Masters, W. H., & Johnson, V. E. (1966). *Human sexual response.* Boston, MA: Little Brown and Company.

Masters, W. H., & Johnson, V. E. (1970). *Human sexual inadequacy.* Boston, MA: Little Brown and Company.

McGlynn, F. D., Mealiea, W. L., & Landau, D. L. (1981). The current status of systematic desensitization. *Clinical Psychology Review, I,* 147–179.

McKenzie, A., & Kay, W. (1986). *About time.* NY: McGraw-Hill.

McKeon, P. (1986). *Coping with depression and elation.* London: Sheldon Press.

McMorrow, M. J., & Foxx, R. M. (1983). Nicotine's role in smoking: An analysis of nictoine regulation. *Psychological Bulletin, 2,* 302–327.

Mechanic, D. (1962). The concept of illness behavior. *Journal of Chronic Diseases, 15,* 189–194.

Meichenbaum, D. (1977). *Cognitive behavior modification.* NY: Plenum Press.

Meichenbaum, D., & Turk, D. (1987). *Facilitating treatment adherence: A practitioner's guide.* NY: Plenum Press.

Meile, R. L., Johnson, D. R., & Peters, L. S. (1976). Marital role, education, and mental disorder among women: Test of an interaction hypothesis. *Journal of Health and Social Behavior, 17,* 295–301.

Miller, G. A. (1956). The magical number seven, plus or minus two: Some limits on our capacity for processing information. *Psychological Review, 63,* 81–97.

Miller, S. A. (Ed.). (1981). *Nutrition and behavior.* Hillsdale, NJ: Lawrence Erlbaum Associates.

Miransky, J., & Langer, E. J. (1977). Burglary non(prevention); An instance of relinquishing control. Mimeograph. Harvard University.

Monroe, S. M. (1982). Life events assessment: Current practices and emerging trends. *Clinical Psychology Review, 2,* 435–453.

Nathanson, D. (1975). Illness and the female role: A theoretical review. *Social Science and Medicine, 9,* 57–62.

Neimeyer, R. A. (1985). Personal constructs in clinical practice. In P. Kendall (Ed.), *Advances in cognitive behavioral research and therapy* (Vol. 4, pp. 275–339). NY: Academic Press.

Neisser, V. (1967). *Cognitive psychology.* NY: Appleton-Century-Crofts.

Nisbett, R. E., & Wilson, T. D. (1977). Telling more than we can know: Verbal reports on mental processes. *Psychological Review, 84,* 231–259.

Novaco, R. W. (1978). Anger and coping with stress. In J. Foreyt, & D. Rathjen (Eds.), *Cognitive behavior therapy: Research and application* (pp. 135–162). NY: Plenum Press.

Padesky, C. A., & Hammen, C. L. (1981). Sex differences in depressive symptom expression and help-seeking among students. *Sex Roles, 7,* 309–320.

Paine, W. S. (1984). *Job stress and burnout: Research, theory and intervention perspectives.* London: Sage Publications.

Paul, G. L. (1966). *Insight versus desensitization in psychotherapy.* Stanford, CA: Stanford University Press.

Pavlov, I. P. (1927). *Conditioned reflexes.* NY: Oxford University Press.

Pearlin, L. T., Lieberman, M. A., Menaghan, E. G., & Mullan, J. T. (1981). The stress process. *Journal of Health and Social Behavior, 22,* 337–356.

Perri, M. G., McAdoo, W. G., Spevak, P. A., & Newlin, D. G. (1984). Effects of a multicomponent maintenance program on long-term weight loss. *Journal of Consulting and Clinical Psychology, 52,* 480–481.

Phillips, D. L., & Segal, B. (1969). Sexual status and psychiatric symptoms. *American Sociological Review, 29,* 679–687.

Piaget, J. (1970). Piaget's theory. In P. A. Mussen (Ed.), *Carmichael's manual of child psychology:* (Vol. I, pp. 703–732). NY: Wiley.

Pomerleau, O. F. (1979). Behavioral medicine: The contribution of the experimental analysis of behavior to medical care. *American Psychologist, 34(8),* 654–663.

Pomerleau, O. F., Bass, F., & Crown, V. (1975). The role of behavior modification in preventive medicine. *New England Journal of Medicine, 292,* 1277–1282.

Pomerleau, O. F., & Pomerleau, C. S. (1984). Neuroregulators and the reinforcement of smoking: Towards a bio-behavioral explanation. *Neuroscience and Biobehavioral Reviews, 8,* 503–513.

Pressman, M. R. (1986). Sleep and sleep disorders. *Clinical Psychology Review, 6(1),* 1–10.

Quick, J. C., & Quick, J. D. (1984). *Organizational stress and preventive management.* London: McGraw-Hill.

Rachman, S. (1976). The modification of obessions: A new formulation. *Behavior Research and Therapy, 14,* 437–443.

Rachman, S. (1978a). *Fear and courage.* San Francisco: W. H. Freeman.

Rachman, S. (1978b). An anatomy of obessions. *Behavior Analysis and Modification, 2:4,* 253–278.

Rachman, S., & Hodgson, R. J. (1980). *Obsessions and compulsions.* (Century Psychology Series). Englewood-Cliffs, NJ: Prentice Hall.

Richardson, A. (1977). Verbalizer-visualizer: A cognitive style dimension. *Journal of Mental Imagery, 1,* 109–126.

Rinehart, L. (1972). *The diceman.* London: Granada Publishing Company.

Rodin, J. (1981). The current status of the internality-externality hypothesis of obesity: What went wrong? American Psychologist, *36,* 361–372.

Rogers, C. R. (1958). The characteristics of a helping relationship. *Personnel and Guidance Journal, 37,* 6–16.

Ross, L., Greene, D., & House, P. (1977). The 'false consensus effect': An egocentric bias in social perception and attribution processes. *Journal of Experimental and Social Psychology, 13,* 279–301.

Rossman, M. L. (1987). *Healing yourself: A step by step program for better health through imagery.* NY: Walker and Company.

Rotter, J. B. (1954). *Social learning and clinical psychology.* Englewood Cliffs, NJ: Prentice-Hall.

Salter, A. (1949). *Conditioned reflex therapy.* NY: Creative Age.

Schwartrz, R. M. (1982). Cognitive behavior modification: A conceptual review. *Clinical Psychology Review, 2,* 267–294.

Seligman, M. E. P. (1971). Phobias and preparedness. *Behavior Therapy, 2,* 307–321.

Seligman, M. E. P. (1975). *Helplessness.* San Francisco, CA: W. H. Freeman.

Seligman, M. E. P., & Hager, J. L. (Eds.). (1972). *Biological boundaries of learning.* NY: Appleton-Century-Crofts.

Shapiro, A. K. (1971). Placebo effects in medicine, psychotherapy and psychoanalysis. In A. E. Bergin, & S. L. Garfield (Eds.), *Handbook of psychotherapy and behavior change: An empirical analysis* (pp. 439–473). NY: Wiley.

Shiffman, S. (1982). Relapse following smoking cessation: A situational analysis. *Journal of Consulting and Clinical Psychology, 50,* 71–86.

Shiffman, S., & Willis, T. A. (Eds.). (1985). *Coping and substance abuse.* Orlando, FL: Academic Press.

Sime, W. E. (1984). Psychological benefits of exercise training in the healthy individual. In J. D. Matarazzo, S. M. Weiss, J. A. Herd, M. E. Miller, & S. M. Weiss (Eds.), *Behavioral health: A handbook of health enhancement and disease prevention* (pp. 488–507). NY: Wiley.

Simonton, O. C., Simonton, S., & Creighton, J. (1978). *Getting well again.* Los Angeles, CA: J. P. Tarcher.

Singer, J. L. (1974). *Image and daydream methods in psychotherapy and behavior modification.* NY: Academic Press.

Singer, J. L., & Antrobus, J. S. (1972). Daydreams, imaginal processes and personality: A normative study. In P. W. Sheehan (Ed.), *The function and nature of imagery* (pp. 175–202). NY: Academic Press.

Singer, J. L., & Pope, K. S. (Eds.). (1978). *The power of human imagination.* NY: Plenum Press.

Skinner, B. F. (1969). *Contingencies of reinforcement.* NY: Appleton-Century-Crofts.

Smith, M., & Glass, G. V. (1977). Meta-analysis of psychotherapy outcome studies. *American Psychologist, 32,* 752–760.

Stein, D. M., & Lambert, M. J. (1984). On the relationship between therapist experience and psychotherapy outcome. *Clinical Psychology Review, 4,* 127–142.

Stern, R., Lipsedge, M., & Marks, I. (1973). Obsessive ruminations: A controlled trial of a thought-stopping technique. *Behavior Research and Therapy, II,* 659–662.

Stuart, R. B. (1980a). Weight loss and beyond: Are they taking it off and keeping it off? In P. O. Davidson, & S. M. Davidson (Eds.), *Behavioral medicine: Changing health lifestyles* (pp. 151–194). NY: Brunner Mazel.

Stuart, R. B. (1980b). *Helping couples change.* NY: Guilford.

Stunkard, A. J. (1986). The control of obesity: Social and community perspectives. In K. D. Brownell, & J. P. Foreyt (Eds.), *The physiology, psychology and treatment of eating disorders* (pp. 213–228). NY: Basic Books.

Stunkard, A. J., Sorenson, T. I. A., Hanis, C., Teasdale, T. W., Chakraborty, R., Schull, W. J., & Schulsinger, F. (1986). An adoption study of obesity. *New England Journal of Medicine, 314,* 193–198.

Sullivan, G. (1977). *Work smart, not hard.* NY: Facts On File Publications.

Thompson, J. K., Jarvie, G. K., Lahey, B. B., & Cureton, K. J. (1982). Exercise and obesity: Etiology, physiology and intervention. *Psychological Bulletin, 91,* 58–79.

Thoresen, C. E., & Mahoney, M. J. (1974). *Behavioral self-control.* NY: Holt.

Tisdelle, D., & St. Lawrence, J. S. (1986). Interpersonal problem-solving competency: Review and critique of the literature. *Clinical Psychology Review, 6,* 337–356.

Tobias, A. L., & Gordon, J. B. (1980). Social consequences of obesity. *Journal of the American Dietetic Association, 76,* 328–342.

Tower, R. B., & Singer, J. (1981). The measurement of imagery: How can it be clinically useful? In P. Kendall, & S. Hollon (Eds.), *Assessment strategies for cognitive-behavioral interventions* (pp. 119–159). NY: Academic Press.

Trower, P., Bryant, B., & Argyle, M. (1978). *Social skills and mental health.* London: Methuen.

Tryon, G. S., & Tryon, W. W. (1982). Issues in the lives of dual-career couples. *Clinical Psychology Review, 2,* 49–65.

Verbrugge, L. M. (1976). Females and illness: Recent trends in sex differences in the United States. *Journal of Health and Social Behavior, 17,* 387–403.

Walker, C. E. (1975). *Learn to relax: Thirteen ways to reduce tension.* Englewood Cliffs, NJ: Prentice-Hall.

Warren, L. (1983). Male intolerance of depression: A review with implications for psychotherapy. *Clinical Psychology Review, 3*(2), 147–156.

Weekes, C. (1984). *Simple effective treatment for agoraphobia.* London: Angus and Robertson.

Wilkins, W. (1971). Desensitization: Social and cognitive factors underlying the effectiveness of Wolpe's procedure. *Psychological Bulletin, 76,* 311–317.

Wills, T. A., Weiss, R. L., & Patterson, G. R. (1974). A behavioral analysis of the determinants of marital satisfaction. *Journal of Counseling and Clinical Psychology, 42,* 802–811.

Wilson, G. T. (1985). Psychological prognostic factors in the treatment of obesity. In J. Hirsch, & T. B. Van Itallie (Eds.), *Recent advances in obesity research:* (Vol. 4, pp. 301–311). London: John Libbey and Company.

Wolpe, J. (1958). *Psychotherapy by reciprocal inhibition.* Stanford, CA: Stanford University Press.

Woolfolk, R. L., & Richardson, F. L. (1978). *Stress, sanity and survival.* NY: New American Library.

Wright, J., Perreault, M. D., & Mattieu, M. (1977). The treatment of sexual dysfunction: A review. *Archives of General Psychiatry, 34,* 881–890.

Yates, A. J. (1981). Behavior therapy: Past, present and future imperfect? *Clinical Psychology Review, 1,* 269–292.

Zajonc, R. B. (1980). Feeling and thinking: Preferences need no inferences. *American Psychologist, 35,* 151–175.

Zajonc, R. B. (1984). On the primacy of affect. *American Psychologist, 39,* 117–123.

Zimbardo, P. (1981). *Shyness.* London: Pan Books.

Author Index

Subject Index